INFAMY

INFAMY

THE SHOCKING STORY OF
THE JAPANESE AMERICAN INTERNMENT
IN WORLD WAR II

Richard Reeves

Henry Holt and Company
New York

Henry Holt and Company, LLC
Publishers since 1866
175 Fifth Avenue
New York, New York 10010
www.henryholt.com

Henry Holt® and 🅷® are registered trademarks of
Henry Holt and Company, LLC.

Library of Congress Cataloging-in-Publication Data

Reeves, Richard, 1936–
 Infamy : the shocking story of the Japanese American internment in World
War II / Richard Reeves.—First edition.
     pages cm
 Includes bibliographical references and index.
 ISBN 978-0-8050-9408-4 (hardcover)—ISBN 978-0-8050-9939-3 (electronic
book) 1. Japanese Americans—Evacuation and relocation, 1942–1945.
2. World War, 1939–1945—Japanese Americans. I. Title.
 D769.8.A6R43 2015
 940.53′1773—dc23

2014033329

Henry Holt books are available for special promotions and premiums.
For details contact: Director, Special Markets.

First Edition 2015

Designed by Meryl Sussman Levavi

Printed in the United States of America

1 3 5 7 9 10 8 6 4 2

This book is for
Lavinia Josephine Catherine O'Neill

CONTENTS

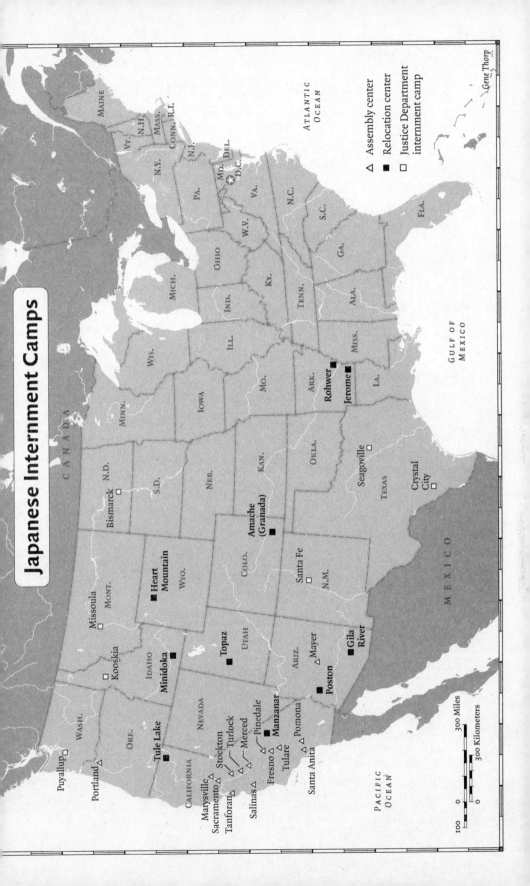

Japanese Internment Camps

△ Assembly center
■ Relocation center
□ Justice Department internment camp

CANADA

ATLANTIC OCEAN

Puyallup □
Portland △
Kooskia □
Missoula □
Bismarck □

WASH.
ORE.
IDAHO
MONT.
N.D.

Tule Lake ■
Minidoka ■
Heart Mountain ■
S.D.

Marysville △
Sacramento △
Tanforan △
Salinas △
Stockton △
Turlock △
Merced △
Pinedale △
Fresno △
Tulare △
Manzanar ■
Pomona △
Santa Anita △

NEVADA
CALIFORNIA
Topaz ■
UTAH

Mayer △
Poston ■
Gila River ■
ARIZ.

Amache (Granada) ■
COLO.
Santa Fe □
N.M.

WYO.
NEB.
KAN.
OKLA.

MINN.
IOWA
MO.
ARK.

Seagoville □
Crystal City □
TEXAS

Rohwer ■
Jerome ■
LA.

WIS.
ILL.
MICH.
IND.
OHIO
KY.
TENN.
MISS.
ALA.
GA.
FLA.

PA.
N.Y.
VT.
N.H.
MASS.
CONN. R.I.
N.J.
DEL.
MD.
D.C.
W.VA.
VA.
N.C.
S.C.

MEXICO

GULF OF MEXICO

PACIFIC OCEAN

100
300 Miles
0
300 Kilometers

Gene Thorp

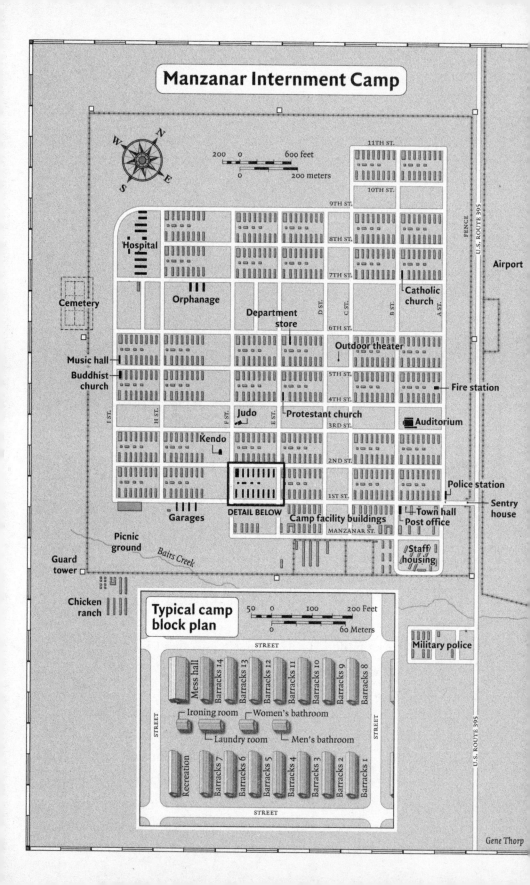

Manzanar Internment Camp

Gene Thorp

INTRODUCTION

People who live in Southern California sometimes head north from Los Angeles on U.S. Route 395, usually on the way to skiing on Mammoth Mountain on the eastern slopes of the Sierra Nevada mountain range. It's a long, boring six-hour drive through mostly uninhabited territory. About halfway there, in the desolate high desert framed by distant mountains, they would see a sign: MANZANAR WAR RELOCATION CENTER.

Few people stop there. Driving past, someone in a car might ask, "Isn't that where they put the Japanese?"

Yes it is. More than 120,000 American Japanese were forced from their homes and incarcerated in ten "relocation centers" and several prisons during World War II. Within months of the attack on Pearl Harbor, President Franklin Delano Roosevelt sent them to these "concentration camps" by executive order. Most of the evacuees and prisoners, more than 70 percent of them, were American citizens, born in the United States. Their first-generation immigrant parents, however, were forever aliens, prevented from gaining naturalized citizenship by the Immigration Act of 1924. Most of them, citizens and aliens alike, were fiercely patriotic. Guarded by soldiers in machine-gun towers, none of them were charged with any crime against the United States. In fact, there was not a single American of Japanese descent, alien or citizen, charged with espionage or sabotage during the war. These men, women, and children were locked up for the duration of the war because they looked like the enemy, the troops of Imperial Japan, a place most of them had never seen.

Living in California on and off for years, I've passed Manzanar many times, each time thinking I should stop, each time thinking I should write about what happened there and in the other camps in Arizona, Colorado, Wyoming, Utah, and Arkansas. I am from a part of the country, New York, where most of the people I know had only the vaguest notion that these events happened. I finally decided to write this book when I saw that my country, not for the first time, began turning on immigrants, blaming them for the American troubles of the day. Seventy years ago, it was American Japanese, most of them loyal to their new country; now it is Muslims and Hispanics. This story is not about Japanese Americans, it is about Americans, on both sides of the barbed wire surrounding the relocation centers, the Americans crammed into tar-paper barracks and the Americans with machine guns and searchlights in watchtowers.

The sweeping story of what happened to the American Japanese and the Caucasians who imprisoned them is not a series of isolated events, but a look into a dark side of the "American way." The story goes back at least to the treatment of Native Americans, to the persecution of British loyalists after the American Revolution, to the enslavement of Africans in the

New World, to the treatment of American Germans during World War I, to Jewish quotas and "Irish Need Not Apply," to the excesses of official bodies such as the House Un-American Activities Committee. And, at least to me, it seems there is always the possibility of similar persecutions happening again if fear and hysteria overwhelm what Abraham Lincoln called "the better angels of our nature."

The dangers of history repeating itself seem greater given that this story is often forgotten, or treated as a footnote in the larger, mostly heroic description of World War II found in American history textbooks. Even at the time, the American Japanese concentration camps were underreported or misrepresented. Although there were periodic national stories about the roundup and incarceration of the American Japanese, much of that coverage treated the evacuation as something like a vacation trip to the country. The camps were generally portrayed as resorts; "pioneer communities" was the euphemism of the day. Americans, their sons shipping off to Europe and the Pacific, had a lot on their minds in those days—and California was still far away from most of America.

The United States government and military had no reason to publicize the evacuation and incarceration. President Franklin D. Roosevelt, who within ten weeks of the Imperial Japanese attack on Pearl Harbor had signed Executive Order 9066 authorizing the detention of the American Japanese, did not want the incarceration debated as a political issue. The evacuees themselves were, for decades, reluctant to tell their stories even to, especially to, their own families. The truth was simply too painful.

Then, partly because of the black civil rights and anti–Vietnam War protest movements in the 1960s and 1970s, young Japanese Americans began questioning their parents and grandparents about what happened to them in the 1940s. Soon enough, books and memoirs by American Japanese held in camps began to appear; many of them were striking works of literature, many privately published, many never published, and, significantly, a large number of them were books for children and young adults. Japanese American organizations were energized by the questions asked by the new generations; oral history projects were created, letters became public, small museums were opened, and activists lobbied for official apologies, financial redress, and the designation of some of the camp sites, like Manzanar, as national historical monuments. Government records of the evacuation began to be discovered or declassified. Soon academic tracts and legal texts were written focusing on the constitutionality (or unconstitutionality) of what happened during the war.

The men of history who had demanded and overseen the relocation camps tried in later years to explain themselves in books and hearings. They had striking injustices to explain. The Supreme Court had delayed or ignored challenges to the mass incarceration, deciding instead to protect President Roosevelt by waiting to hear all related cases until after the 1944 presidential election, and in the end the justices approved the concentration camps. Assistant Secretary of War John J. McCloy said in a memo, "We can cover the legal situation . . . in spite of the Constitution. Why the Constitution is just a scrap of paper to me." The governor of Wyoming, Nels Smith, shouted at Milton Eisenhower, then director of the War Relocation Authority, "If you bring Japanese into my state, I promise you they will be hanging from every tree." The governor of Idaho, Chase Clark, added, "The Japs live like rats, breed like rats and act like rats."

Two army officers of the Western Defense Command, Lieutenant General John DeWitt and Colonel Karl Bendetsen, both bigots, the former a fool, the latter a brilliant pathological liar, drove the process, grossly exaggerating the dangers posed by West Coast Japanese. The theory advocated before the House

Committee on Naval Affairs by General DeWitt (and many others) was simply, "A Jap is a Jap! There is no way to determine their loyalty."

While DeWitt was recognized by peers as weak and ignorant, Bendetsen could have been a calculating character in a bad spy novel. He stated in his 1944 entry in *Who's Who in America* that he had "conceived the method, formulated the details, and directed the evacuation of 120,000 persons of Japanese ancestry from military areas." When the Japanese evacuation was being investigated by congressional committees in the 1970s, he was asked about his involvement, and he replied, "Of course, I wasn't in high-level meetings. I was just a Major."

The villains of this story include California attorney general Earl Warren, who rode the anti-Japanese tide to the governorship of California; Secretary of State Cordell Hull; Secretary of War Henry Stimson; Assistant Secretary of War John McCloy; Roger Baldwin, the hypocritical founder of the American Civil Liberties Union; Supreme Court justices Tom Clark and William O. Douglas; as well as William Randolph Hearst, Walter Lippmann, Edward R. Murrow, and hundreds of other raving journalists.

There were heroes, too, though lesser known, including Secretary of the Interior Harold Ickes, assistant attorneys general Edward Ennis and James Rowe, and San Francisco civil liberties lawyers Ernest Besig and Wayne Collins. There were also many ordinary folks, everyday heroes, like the fire chief Bob Fletcher in Florin, California, "The Strawberry Capital of the World," who took real risks to protect the property of his American Japanese former neighbors, while other white men were taking over their land or burning down their houses and vandalizing the depositories filled with the possessions of the incarcerated—usually churches and Buddhist temples.

The heart of the book is formed by the stories of the evacuated families who were caught between those heroes and villains. This is an American story of enduring themes: racism and greed, injustice and denial—and then soul-searching, an apology, and the most American of coping mechanisms, moving on. Through it all, the desert heat and windstorms and bitter cold, the breakdowns and suicides, the overwhelming majority of the Japanese aliens and Japanese Americans remained loyal to the United States. Even as their country's government humiliated first-generation immigrants, or Issei, in front of their Nisei children, young people strove to resume some semblance of normal American life in the camps. They were organized into Cub packs and Boy Scout troops and baseball leagues in the camps; high school yearbooks from the camps have a jitterbugging Judy Garland–Mickey Rooney look, with photos cropped to hide the soldiers with bayonets at the doors. Many graduates of those camp schools were among the thirty thousand Nisei who served in the army, some serving in the all-Nisei 442nd Regimental Combat Team in Europe, which fought across Italy and France and became, per capita, the most decorated unit in army history. The 442nd won fourteen Congressional Medals of Honor, including one to Sergeant Daniel Inouye, who would one day become a U.S. senator. Six thousand more served secretly as combat interpreters and translators in the Pacific war against Imperial Japan, heroically saving tens of thousands of American lives.

At the same time, many young American Japanese refused to fight for the country that imprisoned their families. Some stayed in the camps to care for their elderly parents; others felt betrayed and came to hate America.

Despite their forced evacuation, almost all of the former camp students went on to productive lives around the country, even if many college graduates became gardeners. In the 1960s, *Time* magazine called Japanese Americans and other Asian immigrants "the Model Minority." In 1976, on the thirty-fourth anniversary of Roosevelt's signing of Executive Order 9066—the legal basis for the detention—President Gerald Ford, who served as a lieutenant commander in the navy during the Pacific war, said:

> We now know what we should have known then—not only was that evacuation wrong, but Japanese-Americans were and are loyal Americans. On the battlefield and at home, Japanese-Americans—names like Hamada, Mitsu-mori, Marimoto, Noguchi, Yamasaki, Kido, Munemori and Miyamura—have been and continue to be written in our history for the sacrifices and the contributions they have made to the well-being and security of this, our common Nation.

I was only five years old when all this began, but for some reason I remember vividly a patriotic song, sung in 1942 by Frank Sinatra, who grew up a couple of miles from my family home, called "The House I Live In." The song ends, "All races and religions / That's America to me." That popular song was made into a short film that was played in most every theater in the country. Maybe I saw it. But while it was playing, 120,000 American Japanese were incarcerated in camps on barren desert land and swamps from California to Arkansas.

The story of the "Japanese Internment," as it is usually called, is a tale of the best and worst of America. I learned, I think, that what pushes America forward and expands our liberty is not the old Anglo-Saxon Protestant values of the Founders, but the almost blind faith of each wave of immigrants—including the ones we put behind barbed wire: The Germans. The Irish. The Italians. The Jews. The Chinese. The Japanese. The Latinos. The South Asians. The African Americans. We are not only a nation of immigrants. We are a nation made by immigrants, foreigners who were needed for their labor and skills and faith—but were often hated because they were not like us until they were us.

•   •   •

A final note: Scholars continue to debate the language used to tell the stories of Japanese American citizens and Japanese aliens during World War II. Among others, Japanese American writers Lane Ryo Hirabayashi and Robert Asahina told me that the most common complaints involve the use of the terms *internment* and *concentration camps*.

In legal terminology, *internment* applies only to government regulation of aliens, not citizens, and more than two-thirds of the American Japanese rounded up in 1942 were citizens of the United States. However, the word *internment* was commonly used to describe the detention of both citizens and aliens during the war.

The term *concentration camp* was commonly used in government offices during those years to describe the ten officially named relocation centers around the country. Among those who called them concentration camps was the president of the United States, Franklin D. Roosevelt. Understanding that the meaning of the term *concentration camp* changed forever because of the death camps of Nazi-occupied Europe, I have used those words interchangeably, as Americans did in the early 1940s, along with the officially sanctioned terms *evacuation* and *relocation centers*.

There can also be some confusion about the use of the word *Japanese*. Obviously, it has more than one meaning when one is writing about World War II. It describes the citizens and soldiers of the Empire of Japan, the enemy. In the United States, it was also used to identify both American-born citizens and their alien parents and grandparents who were born in Japan and not allowed to apply for American citizenship because of their race.

I have used the words *American Japanese* and the Japanese word *Nikkei* to identify both citizens and aliens living in the United States at the beginning of the war. The word *Issei* describes aliens, the first generation of people born in Japan who had immigrated to the United States. The word *Nisei* describes the second generation, men and women born in the United States, citizens. Finally, the word *Kibei* describes men and women born in the United States who were sent back to be educated in Japan before returning to America.

RICHARD REEVES
Los Angeles, California
October 2014

INFAMY

PEARL HARBOR

DECEMBER 7, 1941

On that terrible Sunday, December 7, 1941, eighteen-year-old Daniel Inouye heard of the Pearl Harbor attack on the radio, stepped outside his Honolulu house, and saw three planes as they flew over, gray planes with red circles on their wings. "I knew they were Japanese," he remembered. Inouye later became a United States senator representing Hawaii, but at the time he had just been accepted as a premedical student at the University of Hawaii. "I felt that the world I had known, and had dreams about and planned for, had come to a shattering end." Already trained in first aid, the teenager bicycled to the harbor to help medical personnel. More than twenty-four hundred sailors, soldiers, and civilians were killed in the attack. He helped doctors there for five days before returning home.

Soon after hearing of the attack, Saburo Kido ran to his office in San Francisco at the *New World Sun*, a Japanese-language newspaper. Kido was the president of the twenty-five-year-old

Japanese American Citizens League, a strongly pro-American organization, and he was also an attorney and a columnist for the paper; when he arrived every phone was ringing, mostly calls from eastern newspapers looking for details and quotes. He handled as many as he could, then sent a telegram to President Franklin D. Roosevelt, stating, "In this solemn hour we pledge our fullest cooperation to you Mr. President, and to our country. . . . Now that Japan has instituted this attack upon our land, we are ready and prepared to extend every effort to repel this invasion together with our fellow Americans."

The largest Japanese-language newspaper in the United States, *Rafu Shimpo*, which published many of its articles in English, said in an editorial in its next edition, "We have lived long enough in America to appreciate liberty and justice. We cannot tolerate the attempt of a few to dominate the world. . . . Japan started this war and it is now up to the United States to end the war by crushing the Japanese Empire and her ruthless, barbaric leaders. In order to live, we must be ready to die for our country." The editorial went on to say, "Fellow Americans, give us a chance to do our share to make this world a better place to live in."

Despite the patriotic words streaming from the community, soon after the attack hundreds of *Nikkei*, or American Japanese, were being arrested across the country. In Nebraska, Mike Masaoka, the field secretary of JACL, was speaking to fifty or so members of the small local Japanese community in the basement of the North Platte Episcopal Church when two men burst through the back doors shouting, "Where's Masaoka?" They were Federal Bureau of Investigation agents. Outside the church, the FBI men put handcuffs on Masaoka and took him to the city jail.

When Kido learned that Masaoka, who lived in Salt Lake City, Utah, was in jail, he telephoned Senator Elbert Thomas of Utah, who then called around Washington to have Masaoka released and put on a train to San Francisco. On the train, a Cheyenne, Wyoming, police officer took one look at Masaoka and arrested him then and there. Senator Thomas intervened again, this time getting permission for two soldiers to travel with Masaoka to San Francisco.

Masaoka was among more than twelve hundred American Japanese community leaders identified from "Suspect Enemy Aliens" lists secretly compiled by the FBI with the help of the Census Bureau. Merchants, priests, teachers, newspapermen, and heads of various civic organizations were arrested without charges within forty-eight hours of the attack on Pearl Harbor. More than a thousand of them were from California, Oregon, Washington, and Hawaii. Thirteen of them were women.

Less than twenty-four hours after the attack, President Franklin D. Roosevelt asked a joint session of Congress for a Declaration of War against Japan, stating, "Yesterday, December 7, 1941, a date that will live in infamy, the United States of America was suddenly and deliberately attacked by naval and air forces of the Empire of Japan." A few hours later, after Germany and Italy declared war on the United States, FBI director J. Edgar Hoover informed the White House that 620 Germans and 98 Italians were also taken into custody. The Germans arrested included leaders of such organizations as the uniformed and openly pro-Hitler German-American Bund, which had a membership of more than forty thousand in the Northeast and Midwest.

The Italian number might have been a bit larger, but the FBI decided not to incarcerate a San Francisco alien named Giuseppe Paolo DiMaggio, a fisherman from Sicily, who lived in the United States for forty years without applying for citizenship. The bureau, however, did stop him from going near Fisherman's Wharf, where he and his wife owned a boat and a restaurant. In memos and phone calls, government officials worried about the publicity that would come if they put Joe DiMaggio's parents in jail during the year that "Joltin' Joe" of the New York Yankees had been named the American League's Most Valuable Player after hitting in fifty-six straight games.

The same was true for the mayor of New York and the mayor of San Francisco: the parents of Fiorello La Guardia and Angelo Rossi were Italian aliens who had never applied for American citizenship. President Roosevelt had already told his attorney general, Francis Biddle, to take it easy on Italians and Italian Americans. "They're just a bunch of opera singers." Ironically, the FBI in New York did arrest one of the more famous opera singers, Ezio Pinza, an Italian citizen who was first basso of the Metropolitan Opera. Like the DiMaggios, he had lived in the United States for more than twenty years without seeking to become naturalized. Two FBI agents entered his home in Bronxville without warning. After searching the house for hours, one of the agents spotted a framed page of writing in Italian on the wall of his study.

"What is this?"

"It's a letter written by Verdi."

"Who?" asked the agent.

The other agent said, "In the name of the President of the United States, you are under arrest."

That was front page news in the *New York Times*, under the headline, "Ezio Pinza Seized as Enemy Alien; FBI Takes Singer to Ellis Island." The singer was one of the 126 Japanese, German, and Italian men held there. He suffered some kind of breakdown, barely speaking, until he was released three months later, thanks to a team of high-priced lawyers and the backing of New York mayor La Guardia. Pinza believed he was arrested because of an untruthful report from a Met rival saying he was a friend of Italian dictator Benito Mussolini. Like other imprisoned aliens, Pinza was never charged, but later wrote that interrogators accused him of secretly sending messages to Mussolini—a man he had never met—by changing the tempo of his voice during radio broadcasts from the Metropolitan Opera.

There were, however, important differences in dealing with immigrants to the United States from Europe and immigrants from Asia. Europeans, including Pinza and the DiMaggios, could have become naturalized U.S. citizens. U.S. residents born in Japan could not become citizens and could not own land in the United States under the Immigration Act of 1924, a special provision of the Johnson-Reed Act of 1924. The prohibitions on land ownership were popularized by distinguished Californians such as Dr. Edward Alsworth Ross, a famous professor of sociology at Stanford, who wrote of the Japanese as early as 1900:

1. They are unassimilable.
2. They work for low wages and thereby undermine the existing work standards of American workmen.
3. Their standards of living are much lower than American workmen.
4. They lack a proper political feeling for American democratic institutions.

The denial of citizenship to Japanese immigrants had begun with the case of Takao Ozawa, a graduate of Berkeley High School and a junior at the University of California, Berkeley, which reached the Supreme Court in November of 1922. The justices ruled that he was not a "free white person" and was therefore ineligible for citizenship. "The decision provoked wild resentment in Japan," wrote Carey McWilliams in his 1944 book *Prejudice*. "In commenting upon the decision, the *Osaka Mainichi* said that 'Americans are as spiteful as snakes and vipers—we do not hesitate to call that government a studied deceiver.'"

Those American laws were part of a buildup of tension between the United States and Imperial Japan and between

Caucasian and American Japanese merchants and farmers living on the West Coast. Within hours of Pearl Harbor, the government moved against American Japanese. When Yoshiko Uchida, a Christian, came home from church that Sunday, she opened the door to her house in Berkeley and was shocked to see a white man sitting in the living room. He was an FBI agent and he had already searched the house, leaving it a mess. He wanted to know where her father, a prosperous San Francisco–based executive of Mitsui Export, a Japanese-owned shipping line, was "hiding."

"I'll be back," the man said.

Her father, Dwight Takashi Uchida, returned an hour later, took one look at the house, and called the police, saying, "There's been a burglary here!" The police arrived in minutes—with three men from the FBI. They took Uchida away, saying, "It'll only be a short while." One agent stayed to answer the family's phone, saying they were not available. Friends who came to the door for Sunday visits were turned away.

It was not until five days later that a friend called and told the family that Uchida was being held in jail with about one hundred other men at the Presidio, army headquarters in San Francisco. They received a postcard from him the next day, asking for shirts and shaving gear.

He told his wife he was going to be taken to a federal prison in Missoula, Montana. Other prisons, used by the Justice Department to hold aliens, were also far from California, in Bismarck, North Dakota; Kooskia, Idaho; Santa Fe, New Mexico; and Crystal City and Seagoville, Texas. In his next letter home from Missoula, Uchida told his wife that their bank accounts were frozen and she should go to the bank and try to get enough money on which to live, perhaps $100 a month. Then he added: "Don't forget to lubricate the car. And be sure to prune the roses in January. Brush Laddie every day and give him a pat for me. Don't forget to send a monthly check to Grandma and take my Christmas offering to church."

To the north, in Washington State, Mitsuno Matsuda, the wife of a strawberry farmer on Vashon Island, in Puget Sound, twenty minutes from Seattle by ferry, received a call from Hisaye Yamamoto, her friend on Bainbridge, another island in the sound. "The FBI came to our house and searched everything. It was awful, just awful. They even ran their hands through our rice and sugar bowls, looking for guns and radios or anything with Japanese writing," said Yamamoto. "Vashon must be next."

That evening Mitsuno and Heisuke Matsuda and their two children, teenagers, Yoneichi and Mary, began to destroy anything that they thought might look too Japanese to a policeman or an FBI agent. "This is it," Mary remembered her father saying as he walked to the dining room stove with his favorite phonograph record. "This one is 'Sakura,' Yoshiko-san's voice is so clear."

He broke the record in two and threw it into the fire. For an hour, the family burned their family photographs and books. Mary began throwing her dolls, in little kimonos, into the stove. The FBI came two weeks later. The two agents took away Yoneichi's .22 caliber rifle and the family's radio. They found one book.

"What is this book?" an agent asked.

"This is my parents' New Testament in Japanese," said Mary. "We are Methodists."

In Petaluma, California, Jahachi Najima packed his suitcase after he heard that his friends, other prominent Japanese, had been arrested. His daughter, Irene, was at home when the FBI came, along with local police, in a long black limousine.

"Where's your father?" one asked.

He was working on the ranch, his ranch. Irene went out to get him and when he came back to the house the FBI men immediately put him in handcuffs.

"Would you permit me to change my clothes?" he asked.

They took off the handcuffs and let him put on a business suit. When Irene asked where they were going, she got no answer. Irene and her mother spent days making phone calls and visiting jails to find Najima. They finally found him at the Presidio. After a few more days they were able to visit him. As they left he said, "This is war. We may never see each other again."

Another "dangerous" person picked up after December 7, Edward Oshita, owner of a small factory making miso, left his house assuring his wife, Grace, "Don't worry. Don't worry. This is America." In Hood River Valley, Oregon, home to 130 American Japanese farming families, FBI agents arrived in town at 3:00 a.m. on December 8. They ransacked homes and took away a dozen community leaders, including Tomeshichi Akiyama, president of the local Japanese Society. His son George was in the United States Army, one of 3,188 Nisei serving in the armed forces the day before Pearl Harbor was attacked.

Barry Saiki, a senior at the University of California in Berkeley, watched as the FBI took away his father in Stockton. "Wait," the old man said, handing his son an envelope. "You may need these."

Inside was a small stack of U.S. war bonds.

• • •

The FBI roundup of first-generation American Japanese aliens, the Issei, was not unexpected and its lists were not particularly sophisticated documents. Hysteria about spies and saboteurs had been building on the West Coast and in Washington, D.C., for years. On August 1, 1941, the *Washington Post* had published a "Confidential report on Japanese activities in California."

The paper said, among other things, that Japanese consulates were forcing Issei and Nisei farmers to move near oil wells, instructing them to be prepared to attack them if war came; that 90 percent of Japanese fishermen were actually Japanese naval officers and seamen; and that cooks, butlers, and laundrymen were expected to "cripple vital utilities, bridges, and tunnels."

There were stacks of reports like that in government offices, going back decades before Congress passed the Immigration Act of 1924, which excluded all Asian immigration by reinstating a 1790 naturalization law that reserved citizenship for "free white persons of good character." During the 1924 debate, Ulysses S. Webb, California's attorney general, testified before Congress, saying of Asians, particularly Chinese and Japanese: "They are different in color; different in ideals; different in race; different in ambitions; different in their theory of political economy and government. They speak a different language; they worship another God. They have not in common with the Caucasian a single trait." Ten years after that, as political and economic relations between the United States and Imperial Japan were deteriorating, a secret State Department investigation concluded that if war broke out between the countries, "The entire [American Japanese] population on the West Coast will rise and commit sabotage." In October of 1940, Secretary of the Navy Frank Knox presented President Roosevelt with a fifteen-point program for what should be done if war with Japan came. The twelfth recommendation was: "Prepare plans for concentration camps."

The reports reaching the president and his principal aides were totally and ridiculously false, but some of the same stories were circulating in newspapers and on radio. One set of stories in California journals said that Japanese and Japanese Americans were moving to surround ports and U.S. naval bases and Army Air Corps installations, along with defense plants.

What was true and was reported on the front page of the *Los Angeles Times* under the headline "Japanese Put Under F.B.I. Inquiry Here," on November 13, 1941, was that Justice Department officials and FBI agents had been interviewing leaders of Japanese and Japanese American organizations since at least early October. They had taken truckloads of business records to look for donations to charities and other organizations back in Japan. Local officials in West Coast states had been doing the same thing for years. In Hood River Valley, Oregon, for instance, in 1937 Sheriff John Sheldrake deputized and paid white residents to spy on the valley's Japanese families.

After the *Times* article appeared, the Los Angeles office of *Time* magazine reported, in a confidential and calm memo back to New York, "Southern California's Japanese colony is on edge over the prospect of wholesale firings in the event of . . . war." The memo went on to state that "most work as agricultural laborers or fishermen. In Los Angeles proper they are principally employed as gardeners or servants. They have all lived here for a long time . . . and the great majority are loyal." But reasoned words in memos did little to stall the inflation of the number of names on the "suspicious persons" lists compiled by the FBI and other law enforcement agencies.

The FBI arrest lists were bolstered by names collected by Lieutenant Commander Kenneth Ringle of the Office of Naval Intelligence, who spoke Japanese and had obtained the membership rolls of the small American offshoots of the Black Dragon Society, a Japan-based group that was formed in 1901 to spy on Russia, Korea, and Manchuria before the Russo-Japanese War. He had also built his own informant network with the cooperation of the pro-American JACL. Most of the FBI names, the businessmen, clergymen, doctors, and editors, even martial arts instructors, were no more than what could have been, and often were, the patrons and donors at a Chamber of Commerce dinner. They simply disappeared on December 7 and the following days.

The FBI, with the approval of the Justice Department back in Washington, had made up so-called A, B, C lists. Those categorized "A" for unspecified reasons were immediately arrested and incarcerated. Fishermen who owned boats and radios, prosperous farmers and small merchants considered to have some influence in Japanese communities were on the "B" list. The "C" list was more random, including anyone who had made a donation to a Japanese organization or charity or a few who were denounced by neighbors and friends, both Caucasian and *Nikkei*.

The Reverend Fuji Usui of San Diego was on an "A" list. His daughter, Mitsuo, went to St. Mary's Church in San Diego that Sunday morning, and while she was gone the FBI had searched the house, leaving it a mess. When she arrived home she found her mother crying in a corner, hysterical. "They took Papa!" her mother shouted. "They chained him and numbered him like an animal."

Another "A" list Issei, Yutaka Akimoto, was an officer in two Japanese civic organizations in Stockton. Police and FBI agents came through the door of his house with leveled submachine guns. His twenty-one-year-old son, George, a college student, watched as the government men searched the house. Among the things they took was his mother's Japanese knitting manual—knit one, purl two—thinking it might be a codebook. The next time the family heard from Akimoto, he was in a Justice Department camp in Bismarck, North Dakota.

The knock on the door of Sally Kirita in San Diego came in the night. The local sheriff and FBI agents took her father away without a word. It would be two and a half years before his family saw him again.

Nearby, the agents came for Margaret Ishino's father. A junior at San Diego High School, Margaret watched as they searched the house. Her mother was in bed, having just given birth to Margaret's brother, Thomas. An agent ripped the blankets and sheet off the bed to see if anything was hidden there. Her father, knowing friends had already been arrested, had packed a suitcase; the FBI took that as a sign he was a spy preparing to flee.

Those community leaders, Issei, were shipped to twenty-six Justice Department facilities, prisons, around the country. More often than not, their families had no idea where their husbands and fathers were being held or even whether they were alive. West Coast *Nikkei*—aliens and citizens—were stripped of civic leadership. Thousands of women and children were without means of support; their situation was made worse when Japanese aliens and Japanese Americans learned that their bank accounts had been frozen the day after Pearl Harbor.

• • •

Lieutenant Commander Ringle, whose intelligence reports had circulated in Washington, was possibly the American who knew the most about Japanese living in the country. Long before Pearl Harbor, the navy had assigned Ringle to check the security of naval bases in the three states bordering the Pacific Coast. Ringle, who had been attached to the United States embassy in Tokyo for three years, had a network of friends and local informants in Tokyo and in the Japanese communities of California, Oregon, and Washington. Those people, the American Japanese, helped him uncover a spy ring in 1941 organized by an Imperial Japanese naval officer named Itaru Tachibana, whose agents included Toraichi Kono, the valet of actor Charlie Chaplin. Tachibana was arrested and deported. Ringle also managed a secret April 1941 break-in at the Japanese consulate in Los Angeles, which involved bringing in a professional safecracker from

San Quentin State Prison. What Ringle learned from papers in the consulate was that the Japanese reporting to Tokyo did not trust either Issei or Nisei, describing them as "cultural traitors," and expected them to side with the United States in any war. The same distrust of American Japanese was expressed in four thousand so-called MAGIC cables between Tokyo and Japanese embassies and consulates in the United States, messages that were intercepted and decoded by the U.S. Army's Signal Intelligence Service. On January 30, 1941, for instance, a cable on intelligence warned against using Japanese Americans or aliens. Instead, Japanese consulates in the United States were urged to recruit "communists, labor union members, Negroes, and anti-Semites."

Ringle first served on the West Coast for a year in 1936 and 1937—in that year a magazine published by the University of California speculated that American Japanese might be "slaughtered on the spot" if war came. Ringle was then sent back to Japan. He was brought back to California in July of 1940. He felt he understood the American Japanese, and he liked them, but he was hardly sentimental about Japan or about the Japanese in America, including his friends and informants—most of whom saw themselves as patriotic Americans and willingly reported to him about the "disloyal" minority in their community. As the roundups began after Pearl Harbor, Ringle wrote to his superiors in Washington.

> The entire "Japanese Problem" has been magnified out of its true proportion, largely because of the physical characteristics of the people. It should be handled on the basis of the *individual*, regardless of citizenship, and *not* on a racial basis. . . . It is submitted that the *Nisei* could be accorded a place in the national war effort without risk or danger, that such a step would go farther than anything

else towards cementing their loyalty to the United
States. . . . The opinion outlined in this paragraph is considered most urgent.

There were obvious danger points, Ringle said, but he estimated
that at least three-quarters of the Nisei were actively loyal and the
great majority of Issei were very old, very tired, and tended to be
passively loyal. He also pointed out that one group, the *Kibei*,
whose Issei parents sent them back to Japan for education, had to
be interned and their loyalties questioned and tested. "These people, the *Kibei*, are essentially and inherently Japanese and may
have been deliberately sent to the United States as agents. In spite
of their legal [American] citizenship, they should be looked at as
enemy aliens and many of them placed in custodial detention."

Ringle was, however, appalled at the idea of mass evacuation
and incarceration; he later noted with some grim satisfaction
that, after "careful investigations on both the West Coast and
Hawaii, there was never a shred of evidence found of sabotage,
subversive acts, spying, or Fifth Column activity on the part of
the *Nisei* or long-time local residents." The phrase "Fifth
Column" was first used in the Spanish Civil War by a Nationalist general, Emilio Mola Vidal, as four columns of troops were
fighting their way to Madrid to overthrow the elected Republican government. Mola Vidal stated he expected support from
secret Nationalists in the Spanish military and government
offices—a secret "Fifth Column" that would provide information to the Nationalist forces and rise up as combatants if needed.

In the end, Ringle concluded that perhaps thirty-five hundred Japanese or Japanese Americans in the United States posed
potential security risks.

That information was pretty much ignored by the navy,
because naval authorities considered homeland intelligence an
army matter, and so it never got to army intelligence. It did,

however, get to President Roosevelt, who had a personal spy service—financed by a secret White House fund managed by Secretary of War Henry Stimson—which included some government officials, businessmen, and journalists who reported to him and to him only. One of FDR's private spies was a Chicago businessman named Curtis B. Munson, who was dispatched to the West Coast by John Franklin Carter, a secret FDR spy who was a syndicated newspaper columnist under the name "Jay Franklin."

Munson, who conferred with Ringle and with the FBI, wrote to Carter and the president as early as November 7, 1941, saying "99 percent of the most intelligent views on the Japanese were crystallized by Lt. Commander K.D. Ringle." Summarizing all of the reports, Carter wrote to FDR:

> There will be no armed uprising of Japanese. . . . The essence of what Munson has to report is that, to date, he has found no evidence which would indicate that there is a danger of widespread anti-American activities among this population group. He feels that the Japanese are in more danger from the whites than the other way around. . . . There will undoubtedly be some sabotage financed by Japan and executed largely by imported agents or agents already imported. There will be the odd case of fanatical sabotage by some Japanese "crackpot." . . . The Japanese are hampered as saboteurs because of their easily recognized physical appearance. It will be hard for them to get near anything to blow up *if it is guarded*. . . . The dangerous part of their espionage is that they would be very effective as far as movement of supplies, movement of troops, and movement of ships out of harbor mouths and over railroads is concerned. . . . Japan will commit some sabotage largely depending on imported Japanese as they are afraid of and do not trust the *Nisei*.

A week later Munson added in his report to the president: "The *Nisei* are universally estimated from 90 to 98 percent loyal to the United States if the Japanese-educated *Kibei* are excluded. The *Nisei* are pathetically eager to show this loyalty. They are not Japanese in culture. They are foreigners to Japan."

Added Carter in 'a cover note: "For the most part the local Japanese are loyal to the United States or, at worst, hope that by remaining quiet they can avoid concentration camps or irresponsible mobs. We do not believe that they would be at least any more disloyal than any other racial group in the United States with whom we went to war."

Carter, who worked in the National Press Building, near the White House, passed more Munson and Ringle opinions to Roosevelt on December 16. The president responded to only one point, that unguarded bridges and other infrastructure might be vulnerable to sabotage. The president asked for more information on that problem.

• • •

For about two weeks after Pearl Harbor, newspapers and public officials in California called for calm and tolerance. West Coast newspapers were printing stories about Japanese Americans and their alien parents pledging loyalty to the United States. Editorials and radio broadcasts often mirrored this one in the *San Francisco Chronicle* on December 9: "The roundup of Japanese citizens in various parts of the country . . . is not a call for volunteer spy hunters to go into action. . . . Neither is it a reason to lift an eyebrow at a Japanese whether American-born or not. . . . There is no excuse to wound the sensibilities of any persons in America by showing suspicion or prejudice."

Southeast of Los Angeles, the *Brawley News* editorialized: "Americans should remain calm and considerate. In this community we have many Japanese neighbors and citizens whose loyalty to their adopted country remains steadfast during the time of crisis."

"In California we have many citizens of Japanese parentage," wrote the *San Francisco News*. "A large proportion of them are native-born Americans. They must not be made to suffer for the sins of a government for whom they have no sympathy or allegiance." Three days later, the *News* went further, saying, "To subject these people to illegal search and seizure, then arrest them without warrant to confinement without trial, is to violate the principles of Democracy as set forth in our Constitution."

Politicians, most notably Governor Culbert Olson and State Attorney General Earl Warren, also called for calm and restraint—at first. Governor Olson, a self-professed pacifist who was chairman of a high-minded group, the Northern California Committee for Fair Play for Citizens and Aliens of Japanese Ancestry, said: "Californians have kept their heads. . . . The American tradition of fair play has been observed. All the organs of public influence and information—press, pulpit, school welfare agencies, radio, and cinema—have discouraged mob violence and have pleaded for tolerance and justice for all law-abiding residents of whatever race."

There were some early signs of hope for peace and tolerance among West Coast schools, as well. In some schools, white students hugged their Japanese friends as they arrived on that charged Monday after the attacks. In Seattle, the principal of Washington Middle School, Arthur Sears, called all the students together for a morning assembly on December 8. "We are all Americans and we here at Washington want no part of race hatred," he said. "We are all under the same roof." After he spoke, students were assigned to write to their teachers about what he had said. A sixth grader named Betty wrote to Ellen Evanson, her teacher, "Mr. Sears told us that even if we have a different color face, it's alright because we're American Citizens. . . . When we were saluting the flag I was proud to salute the flag. Some people were crying because they were proud of their country." Another sixth grader named Emiko wrote to Miss Evanson: "Because of this situation, we [may be] asked to leave this dear city of Seattle and its surroundings . . . if the school I will attend next would have a teacher like you I will be only too glad. When I am on my way my memories will flow back to the time I was attending this school and the assemblies that were held in the hall. Wherever I go I will be a loyal American."

Soon enough, however, fear and prejudice, politics and greed, began to spread quickly among white Californians. Politicians, military commanders, and the press began responding to or whipping up hysteria, passing on and publishing rumors of imminent Japanese bombing and invasion of California. The Los Angeles Police Department closed down the stores and shops on East First Street, the main thoroughfare of Little Tokyo, a community of more than thirty thousand Japanese and Japanese Americans, part of a colony that operated one thousand fruit and vegetable stands in the city, doing business of $25 million a year. Japanese florists had annual revenues of more than $4 million. Suddenly, carloads of people from other areas of the city descended on the streets of Little Tokyo and attacked the Japanese stores and stands. The vigilante "patriots" overturned carts and tables and threw tomatoes and potatoes at anyone with an Asian face.

Nisei schoolchildren were sometimes mocked. Some teachers refused to allow Japanese Americans to participate in each morning's Pledge of Allegiance to the American flag. Kay Uno of Los Angeles, a third grader, was walking to school the morning of December 8 when she heard someone call, "There goes that little Jap!"

"I'm looking around," she said later. "Who's a Jap? Who's a Jap? Then it dawned on me, I'm the Jap."

In Seattle that same Monday morning, Sumie Barta, a secretarial student, told this story:

> I was at the bus stop going for a brush-up course at Knapp's Business College. The driver did not greet me with the usual, "Hi, Sumi! How's tricks!" I heard someone from the back of the bus yell, "Get that damn Jap girl off the bus, Curly." He said, "Are you Japanese," and I said I am an American Japanese. "You got any proof of that?" he sneers. . . . "I was born in King County." Then Curly ordered me off the bus, saying, "You are still a damn Jap." I could not continue my classes. I was suddenly afraid to be alone on the highway.

The hatred continued to spread. The president of the University of Arizona, Alfred Atkinson, prevented the school's libraries from lending books to students with Japanese names, saying, "We are at war and *these people* are our enemies."

Forcing Barta off the bus and blocking American Japanese at libraries were harbingers of what was to come. Within days, there was a brisk business in buttons sold to American Japanese and other Asians saying: "I am an American!" and "I am Chinese!" Most Americans, even on the West Coast, could not tell the difference. *Life* magazine, one of the country's most influential journals, ran a section on how to identify the difference between a "Jap" and a "Chinese." A popular cartoonist, Milton Caniff, creator of the comic strip *Terry and the Pirates*, published around the country a six-panel strip called "How to Spot a Jap." The copy included:

> A Chinese man or woman "C" is about the size of the average American. The Jap is shorter and looks as if his

legs are joined directly to his chest. . . . "C" usually has evenly set chompers—Jap has buck teeth. . . . The Chinese strides. The Jap shuffles. . . . The Chinese and other Asiatics have fairly normal feet. . . . The Japs will usually have a fairly wide space between the first and second toes. Jap can't pronounce our liquid "L" . . . hisses on any "S" sound.

● ● ●

Whatever goodwill there had been toward Issei and Nisei after Pearl Harbor was soon gone as news arrived daily of seemingly invincible and brutal Japanese armies running wild though the Philippines, Burma, Hong Kong, Malaya, and the Dutch East Indies. Tolerance of any kind was replaced by fear and by the greed of white merchants and farmers who wanted to eliminate competition from California's six thousand Japanese-operated farms, which totaled at least 250,000 acres and were worth more than $75 million. More than 40 percent of California's produce was from American Japanese farms that often stood on land white farmers ignored as too poor for cultivation.

In the cities, many white businessmen coveted the stores, businesses, and fishing boats of Japanese competitors. The leader of one agricultural organization, Austin Anson, managing secretary of the Grower-Shipper Vegetable Association of the Salinas Valley, told the *Saturday Evening Post*:

> We're charged with wanting to get rid of the Japanese for selfish reasons. We might as well be honest. We do. It's a question of whether the white man lives on the Pacific Coast or the brown man. . . . They undersell the white man in the markets. They can do this because they raise their own labor. They work their women and children while the white farmer has to pay wages for his help.

Soon after Pearl Harbor, Caucasian shopkeepers joined the farmers in outspoken hatred, with signs saying THIS RESTAURANT POISONS BOTH RATS AND JAPS and OPEN HUNTING SEASON FOR JAPS. A barbershop put up this one: JAPS SHAVED: NOT RESPONSIBLE FOR ACCIDENTS. Then there was Burma Shave, a shaving cream company that advertised with rhyming signs placed in sequence along highways. The company replaced the advertisement, "A shave / That's real / No cuts to heal / A soothing / Velvet after-feel / Burma-Shave" with this new one, "Slap / The Jap / With / Iron / Scrap / Burma-Shave."

The California hysteria was also beginning to reach across the country. The editorial cartoonist of PM, New York City's most liberal newspaper, drew a cartoon showing multitudes of bucktoothed, squint-eyed Japanese lined up across the entire West Coast to be given packs of dynamite at a stand called "Honorable Fifth Column." The caption was "Waiting for the Signal from Home." The artist's name was Theodor Seuss Geisel, later to become famous writing children's books under the name Dr. Seuss.

• • •

Assistant Attorney General Thomas C. Clark, who happened to be in California in December of 1941, working on a federal antitrust case, began collecting newspapers with headlines such as "Los Angeles Bombed" and "L.A. Raided," and reports of mass suicides among the Japanese in California. Most of those rumors were not true, but there were a number of individual suicides up and down the state after Pearl Harbor. Dr. Honda Rikita, a physician in Gardena who had served as medical officer in the Japanese army as a young man, was picked up on December 7, one of the "dangerous" leaders. Imprisoned in solitary confinement, he was interrogated for a week by the FBI before he killed himself by slashing his wrists. Some Issei and Tokyo radio claimed he was beaten to death during questioning. He did leave a series of suicide notes, one reading: "A doctor's vocation is to save lives. In order to save lives it is a doctor's highest honor to sacrifice himself. I have dedicated myself to Japanese-American friendship."

Bombing stories, many of them coming from U.S. Army bases in California, were never confirmed. The civilian reports that the Justice Department's Clark saw were even more imaginative. One reported seeing Japanese admirals in northern California wearing flamboyant uniforms and cocked hats with feathers. That one turned out to be a meeting of a local Masonic lodge. Clark, whose knowledge of evacuation issues was negligible—he once asked an assistant what "Nisei" meant—was the first Justice Department official to publicly support military control of all coastal operations, military and civilian. He began traveling from city to city and town to town along the coast, making speeches on the way, saying: "When you hire a doctor, you usually do what he says, or you get another doctor. We have our Army people and they tell us to do this and we must try to do this with as little disruption as possible."

The army source Clark trusted and talked to every day was Lieutenant General John DeWitt, the sixty-one-year-old commander of the Western Command and the Fourth Army, five divisions of soldiers and marines, one hundred thousand half-trained and ill-equipped men scattered at bases from Puget Sound in Washington to San Diego, California. DeWitt, like many of the leaders of the peacetime military, was ill equipped himself, a military bureaucrat, an organizer of the Civilian Conservation Corps during the Great Depression of the 1930s, whose career had been mainly in the Quartermaster Corps.

Now headquartered at the Presidio in San Francisco, DeWitt was an officer with a reputation for changing his mind, often echoing the last person he had talked to on the telephone. He was also noted for covering his career flanks. He had refused to talk to either Ringle or Munson, probably because he believed neither the navy nor political Washington had any business evaluating army performance. One point that stuck in DeWitt's mind and often appeared in his conversations was that after Pearl Harbor both the army and navy commanders of Hawaii—General Walter Short and Admiral Husband Kimmel—were being charged with dereliction of duty for not having contingency plans in case of attack from Japan. Ironically, as part of his staff duties in the 1920s, DeWitt was responsible for a contingency plan for the aftermath of a Japanese attack on Pearl Harbor. The plan was forgotten or ignored, but its essential elements were total military control of the islands and internment of Japanese workers throughout Hawaii.

DeWitt's headquarters was reporting enemy sightings day after day, stating that Japanese air force planes and submarines were engaged in constant reconnoitering all along the Pacific Coast—and wilder tales of bombardment from the sea, arson around Seattle, and illegal radio transmissions up and down the coastline. Almost all of that was untrue.

The second-ranked soldier in the West was Major General Joseph Stilwell, commander of Fort Ord in California, later to become famous as "Vinegar Joe" Stilwell in China and India. He kept a pocket diary during those early days. Some of his notations beginning on December 8 included:

> Dec. 8—Saw DeWitt Sunday night "air raid" at San Francisco. . . . Fourth Army kind of jittery. Much depressed.
>
> Dec. 9— . . . Fleet of thirty-four [Japanese] ships between San Francisco and Los Angeles. Later—not authentic. (Sinking feeling is growing.) More threats of raids and landings . . .

> Dec. 11—[Phone call from Fourth Army] "The main Japanese fleet is 164 miles off San Francisco." I believed it, like a damn fool. . . . Of course, the attack never materialized. The [Fourth Army] passed the buck on this report. They had it from a "usually reliable source," but they should never have put it out without check.

> Dec. 13—Not content with the above blah, [Fourth] Army pulled another at ten-thirty today. "Reliable information that attack on Los Angeles is imminent. A general alarm being considered. . . ." What jackass would send a general alarm [which would have called for the evacuation of Los Angeles] under the circumstances. The [Fourth] Army G-2 [Intelligence] is just another amateur, just like all the rest of the staff. Rule: the higher the headquarters, the more important is *calm*.

Stilwell knew, of course, who the "jackass" was: his immediate superior, General DeWitt.

On December 21, Stilwell was ordered out of California. He was called to Washington to work on planning for an Allied invasion of North Africa toward the end of the coming year. He was more than glad to leave. His diary was filled with what he called:

> The wild, farcical and fantastic stuff that G-2 Fourth Army pushes out! The latest is a two-pound bundle of crap. An investigation of a PhD, at California Tech, a distinguished research man in weather, who runs a service for orange growers. He voluntarily discontinued his broadcast when the war broke out, but [Fourth Army] had him investigated by FBI. . . . Report from Army that secret airfield had been reported about 20 miles north of Palomar (in San Diego County), the planes being concealed under alfalfa. . . . Where is our Navy? Five Mexican destroyers coming up

from Panama to patrol Baja California. (The day has come
we lean on Mexican Navy!)

Then something did happen. On December 23, a Japanese
submarine torpedoed and sank a Union Oil tanker, the company's largest, the USS *Montebello*, in sight of the beaches of the
town of Cambria, halfway between Los Angeles and San Francisco. No one was killed or wounded and four lifeboats brought
the thirty-six-man crew safely to shore. This time, because of
rising fear and hysteria across the state, the navy and Coast Guard
denied there was an attack. The news that two other smaller
freighters were torpedoed off the California coast that same
week, the *Abbaroka* and the *Emidio*, was also censored by the
Coast Guard. Before and after the three real incidents, there were
dozens if not hundreds of rumored stories, including one that
Japanese farmers were cutting or burning arrows into their fields
to guide Japanese planes to American bases and factories.

The rumors won the day. By Christmas of 1941, soldiers, FBI
agents, police, and local authorities were conducting raids on
homes across California, Oregon, and Washington, arresting
people whose names had never appeared on the sloppiest government lists. Sometimes breaking down doors, the agents and
police were confiscating ordinary radios and binoculars along
with guns and anything with Japanese characters on it. After
raids on Japanese farms in the Palos Verdes section of Los
Angeles, city law enforcement officials proudly showed the
results of the raid to local newspapers: a length of water pipe
called a possible cannon part; wires for hanging clothes identified as a possible shortwave radio antenna; and insecticides,
which were called poison gas. "Our goose was cooked," wrote
Thomas Sisata, after seeing such photos in the *Los Angeles
Times* and after his fiancée was fired from a housekeeper's job

on the day after Pearl Harbor. "I really began to believe," he wrote in a college paper, "that the average intelligence of people in the United States was that of a high grade moron."

The FBI officials and local police reported that they had confiscated guns in the hundreds from Japanese residents of California. What they did not report was that most of those arms were collected at Japanese-owned or -operated sporting goods stores, of which there were more than a hundred in a state noted for its hunting. The count of confiscated items for the three West Coast states came to 2,592 guns, 199,000 rounds of ammunition, 1,652 sticks of dynamite, 1,458 radios, and 2,015 cameras. The Justice Department secretly advised the president, "We have not, however, uncovered through these searches any dangerous persons. We have not found a single machine gun nor have we found any gun in any circumstances indicating it was to be used in a manner helpful to our enemies."

• • •

When the war began there were only a few thousand Japanese and Japanese Americans, mostly farmers, living east of the Rocky Mountains. In Hershey, Nebraska, Ben and Fred Kuroki, who had been at the North Platte church meeting where Mike Masaoka was arrested, told their father that night that they wanted to join the army. "This is your country," said their father, Shosuke Kuroki. "Fight for it." So the next morning the brothers got in the farm truck for the 150-mile drive to Grand Island, the nearest army recruitment station. They filled out the papers but then never heard back. Two weeks later, Ben Kuroki heard on the radio that the Army Air Corps was looking for men and had opened a station in North Platte. This time they were accepted. When they asked why the Air Corps would accept them, the sergeant in charge of the office said, "I get $2 for every enlistee. Welcome to the United States Army Air Corps." A photo of the Nisei brothers taking their oath to serve the United States made the front page of the state's largest newspaper, the *Omaha World-Herald*.

But it wasn't all quite that easy for the two farm boys. Even on the train ride to Fort Leavenworth, Kansas, a couple of other enlistees began hassling them. "What are those two lousy Japs doing here?" one said. "I thought this was the American Army." Fred was assigned to digging ditches and Ben, who had learned to fly in a little Piper Cub, spent his first twenty-one days in the army peeling potatoes—and pretending not to hear the "Jap" jokes and threats of white soldiers and airmen. "We were the two loneliest men in the United States Army," Ben recalled.

Finally, the Air Corps separated the brothers, sending Ben to clerical school at Fort Logan, Colorado. Then it was on to Barksdale Field near Shreveport, Louisiana, and more KP, peeling potatoes again. He was depressed and lonely, and his misery got worse when he learned that his brother had been dropped by the Air Corps and assigned to an infantry unit. After a month of pleading, begging really, with officers, he was assigned to a combat unit, the 409th Squadron of the Ninety-Third Bomb Group. It took three months in the Ninety-Third, but more and more of the white guys were nodding when they passed by and a few began talking with him. Still, many of them were soon on their way overseas and Ben was still begging officers to send him with those groups. Then it happened, and the boy from Nebraska was on the *Queen Elizabeth* with nineteen thousand other soldiers passing the Statue of Liberty on their way to England. Soon enough about eighteen thousand of them, including Kuroki, were pale and vomiting for five rough days.

At the same time, back in Washington, D.C., there was confusion, contradiction, and debate about what to do about young Japanese Americans already in the military or trying to join. Corporal Akiji Yoshimura, an army medic at Crissy Field in San Francisco, was taken to jail by two FBI agents for interrogation.

"Will you fight against Japan if you are called upon to do so?" asked one agent.

"Of course, I would. Anytime, anywhere," said Yoshimura.

"You sonofabitch," said the interrogator. "I expect you to say that you will shoot down the Emperor and tear down the Jap flag and stomp it into the ground."

Yoshimura, like many of the more than three thousand Japanese Americans serving in the military, draftees and men who had enlisted before Pearl Harbor, was discharged from the army. Later he volunteered for the Military Intelligence Service, a secret unit of Japanese-speaking Nisei training to serve as interpreters in the Pacific Theater, winning a battlefield commission as a lieutenant.

In Nebraska, the Kuroki boys were accepted for enlistment after Pearl Harbor, but, in California, Nisei were routinely being turned away. Most of the Nisei in military service before Pearl Harbor were summarily discharged by March of 1942, especially those in California. "We don't want any Japs in our Army, you guys are no damn good. So get out of here," an army recruiting officer in San Jose told one Nisei, Yasuko Morimoto.

But at the same time, there were others still in uniform in many states and young reservists were being called to active duty in Hawaii. The new Military Intelligence Service was based at the Presidio, close to DeWitt's headquarters. Sixty-five Nisei and *Kibei* were secretly studying military Japanese before being sent to army units in the Pacific. After Pearl Harbor, General DeWitt demanded that the military move the MIS, and so the handful of teachers and the sixty-five trainees were sent to Camp Savage in Minnesota.

• • •

On December 12, a small newspaper published north of Los Angeles, the *San Luis Obispo Independent*, was the first on the West Coast to call for the evacuation of *all* Japanese, citizens or not, from Pacific coastal areas. The *New York Times* reported a rumor that the Japanese had a secret air base in Baja California, the Mexican state south of San Diego. Its source was Earl Warren, California's attorney general. The paper quoted General DeWitt as saying that anyone who disbelieved these reports was "inane, idiotic, and foolish." On December 15, after a visit to Hawaii, Secretary of the Navy Frank Knox, a former publisher of the *Chicago Daily News* and the Republican nominee for vice president of the United States in 1936, held a press conference in Washington. Knox portrayed the tens of thousands of Japanese and Japanese Americans living on the islands as a gigantic spy nest and claimed that "the most effective 'Fifth Column' work of the war was done there."

Untrue, every word. If Knox had a reason to say that, it was to shift blame for the devastation at Pearl Harbor from the navy, which had been unprepared for sneak attack, even though, for weeks, there had been military intelligence predicting some sort of assault. Dorothy Thompson, a nationally syndicated columnist, writing the day after Knox's performance, said: "There is a monstrous fifth column in the United States—just as there is fifth column in Hawaii, which contributed to the disaster at Pearl Harbor. Have those people been found? And are they still operating?" They were certainly in plain view; *Nikkei* were 37 percent of Hawaii's population. Except for General DeWitt, few officials even thought about interning Hawaiians because there was no doubt the local economy would crash if Japanese were taken away from the islands' huge fruit and sugar plantations. And, of course, the Hawaiian Fifth Column would never be found because it did not exist.

There were certainly many Japanese in Hawaii and California who sympathized with the rise and ambitions of the Old Country, but there was no evidence of sabotage or spying in either place. Instead, there were cadres of nervous military men and panicking politicians reacting to rumors and sensational news reports. There were also thousands of Californians who would benefit economically if the state's Japanese were forced out of their farms and businesses.

California's Governor Olson put forward a plan in mid-December to restrict all Japanese and Japanese Americans to their homes. It amounted to house arrest, but Olson argued that it would prevent violence and riots by angry white Americans. The plan was rejected by the California State Council of Defense, which countered that because Japanese farmers owned or worked so many of California's farms, there might be a food shortage if they stopped working. At the same time, General DeWitt was sending secret plans to his superiors in Washington. His first proposal, cabled to Washington on December 19, called for the relocation of all males, enemy aliens and citizens alike, over fourteen years old, including Germans and Italians, to camps east of the Rockies where they would be held "under restraint." It was the first of dozens of often contradictory plans put forward by DeWitt. The "restraint" proposal, whatever that word meant, was turned down by Major General Allen Gullion, the army's provost marshal general—because it did not go far enough. Gullion, formerly the army's chief legal officer, wanted Japanese of all ages, noncitizens and citizens, brought under military control. Germans and Italians were essentially exempt from the treatment forced on *Nikkei*. The reason was simple enough: officials in the Justice Department estimated that Italian Americans and German Americans in California had more than fifty million relatives in other parts of the country—a third of the nation—and without their help the United States had little chance of winning the war.

• • •

It seemed the worst of times, from the Pacific to the Atlantic. The confusion and fear touched every American, including the First Lady in Washington. In December, Eleanor Roosevelt wrote to her daughter Anna, who lived in Seattle: "Dearest, the news of the war has just come and I've put in a call for you and Johnny as you may want to send the children East. . . . I must go dear and talk to Father. Much, much love, Mother."

Despite her own fears, though, Mrs. Roosevelt traveled to California to publicly meet with prominent Nisei women in Los Angeles on Decemeber 11, and she then wrote in her nationally syndicated column My Day: "This is, perhaps, the greatest test this country has ever met. . . . Our citizens come from all the nations of the world . . . If we can not meet the challenge of fairness to our citizens of every nationality, of really believing in the Bill of Rights and making it a reality for all loyal American citizens, regardless of race, creed, or color, if we cannot keep in check anti-Semitism, anti-racial feelings, as well as anti-religous feelings, then we shall have removed the one real hope for the future on which all humanity must now rely."

2

BY ORDER OF THE PRESIDENT

SIGNING OF EXECUTIVE ORDER 9066: FEBRUARY 19, 1942

On the next to last day of 1941, December 30, Saburo Kido, the San Francisco attorney who was the president of the Japanese American Citizens League, had a visitor, his friend Fred Nomura, an insurance agent. "Sab," Nomura said, "I hear they're going to put all the Japanese in concentration camps. Do you know anything about that?"

"Who says so?" asked Kido.

"The chief of police in Oakland told me. He told me everybody—Issei, Nisei, even the little kids are going to be interned."

"He's crazy. They can't do that to us. We're American citizens."

The first public call for all American Japanese, aliens and citizens, men, women, and children, to be moved into "concentration camps" was on January 14, 1942, in the *Placerville Times*, the newspaper in a small town forty miles east of Sacramento. Two weeks later, on January 29, California's attorney general, Warren, who had been an important voice for moderation, essentially switched sides, issuing a press release that read, "I have come to the conclusion that the Japanese situation as it exists in this state today, may well be the Achilles Heel of the entire civil defense effort. Unless something is done it may bring about a repetition of Pearl Harbor."

Governor Olson, a Democrat who expected that Warren, a Republican and a member of the whites-only Native Sons of the Golden West, would be his opponent in the election in November of 1942, did the same thing, testifying before a congressional hearing a week later, saying: "Because of the extreme difficulty in distinguishing between loyal Japanese-Americans, and there are many who are loyal to this country, and those other Japanese whose loyalty is to the Mikado, I believe in the wholesale evacuation of the Japanese people from coastal California." Then the governor gave a statewide radio address, saying, "It is known that there are Japanese residents of California who have sought to aid the Japanese enemy by way of communicating information or have shown indications of preparation for Fifth Column activities."

In Los Angeles, Mayor Fletcher Bowron, after dismissing all city employees of Japanese lineage, declared, "Right here in our own city are those who may spring to action at an appointed time in accordance with a prearranged plan wherein each of our little Japanese friends will know his part in the event of any possible attempted invasion or air raid. . . . We cannot run the risk of another Pearl Harbor episode in Southern California." He later added, "There isn't a shadow of a doubt but that Lincoln, the mild-mannered man whose memory we regard with almost saint-like reverence, would make short work of rounding up the

Japanese and putting them where they could do no harm." He continued by calling the Japanese Americans "the people born on American soil who have secret loyalty to the Japanese Emperor."

California's officeholders were soon joined by politicians from all over the country, particularly southerners in Congress. "This is a race war," said Representative John Rankin of Mississippi. "I say it is of vital importance that we get rid of every Japanese, whether in Hawaii or the mainland. . . . Damn them! Let's get rid of them now."

One congressman, Jed Johnson of Oklahoma, was demanding the sterilization of all American Japanese. Talk like that, and some secret experiments as well, were part of American life then. Even the president, Franklin Roosevelt, was comfortable with the casual racial myths and theories, including eugenics, that had emerged in the United States in the 1920s—and were cited by Hitler when he came to power. By any modern standards, Roosevelt and millions of people who voted for him were racists and, often, anti-Semites. The president, in conversations with friends, speculated that the reason Japanese were "devious and treacherous" was the shape of their skulls—less developed skulls, "two thousand years behind Caucasians," in the words of eminent anthropologist Ales Hrdlicka, director of the Smithsonian Institution and a friend of the president. "Could that be dealt with surgically?" Roosevelt asked in conversation with Hrdlicka in 1942. In August of 1944, at a cabinet meeting, Roosevelt talked of sterilizing fifty thousand German leaders and officers. A few days after that, the president told his secretary of the Treasury, Henry Morgenthau, "You either have to castrate the German people or you have got to treat them in such a manner so they can't go on reproducing people who want to continue the way they have in the past."

● ● ●

In California, the bigger city papers, following or leading their readers, were soon hardening their positions on the American Japanese. Both the *Los Angeles Times* and *San Francisco Examiner* published a column by a Hearst writer, Henry McLemore, that began:

> Speaking strictly as an American, I think Americans are nuts. . . . The only Japanese apprehended have been the ones the FBI actually had something on. The rest of them, so help me, are free as birds. . . . I know this is the melting pot of the world and all men are created equal and there must be no such thing as race or creed hatred, but do these things go when a country is fighting for its life? . . . I am for immediate removal of every Japanese on the West Coast to a point deep in the interior. I don't mean a nice part of the interior either. . . . Personally, I hate the Japanese. And that goes for all of them. . . . Let 'em be pinched, hurt, hungry and dead up against it.

The Examiner's rival the *San Francisco Chronicle* went the other way for three days, editorializing: "It is not necessary to imitate Hitler by herding whole populations, the guilty and the innocent together into even humane concentration camps." But on its front page, the paper printed these headlines beginning on December 10, 1941, and continuing through January: "Crime and Poverty Go Hand in Hand with Asiatic Labor," "Brown Men Are Made Citizens Illegally," and "Japanese a Menace to American Women."

Stories like that were standard newspaper fare going back to the turn of the century. The *Chronicle* had focused on the Japanese, editorializing: "The Chinese are faithful laborers and do not buy land. The Japanese are unfaithful laborers and do buy land." The *Los Angeles Times* added: "Japanese males are taught by their elders to look upon American girls with a view to sex relations. The proposed assimilation of the two races is unthinkable. It is morally indefensible and biologically impossible." The paper went on to defend "American womanhood," which it considered "far too sacred to be subjected to such degeneracy. An American who would not die fighting rather than yield to this infamy does not deserve the name."

The *Times* mirrored the San Francisco papers with front-page headlines for the same period reading: "Jap Boat Flashes Message Ashore," "Enemy Planes Sighted over California Coast," "Caps on Japanese Tomato Plants Point to Airfields."

California's capital newspaper, the *Sacramento Bee*, had focused hatred on a small Japanese settlement called Florin, nine miles south of the capital city. The paper's publisher, V. S. McClatchy, founder of the Japanese Exclusion League of California, who died in 1938, had as a boy delivered papers by bicycle to that little enclave, and written: "As soon as a Jap can produce a lease, he is entitled to a wife. He sends a copy of the lease back home, gets a picture bride and they increase like rats. Florin is producing 85 American-born Japs a year."

And as early as February of 1940, William Randolph Hearst, the owner of the *Los Angeles Examiner* and its sister paper the *Examiner* in San Francisco, wrote a page one editorial in both papers inviting cabinet members and military men to travel west: "Come see the myriads of little Japs peacefully raising fruits and flowers and vegetables on California sunshine and saying hopefully and wistfully, 'Someday I come with Japanese Army and take all this. Yes, sir, thank you.'" He continued, "Then see the fleets of peaceful little Japanese fishing boats, plying up and down the California coast, catching fish and taking photographs."

Following the attack on Pearl Harbor, the fear and the exaggeration ran up and down the coast into the new year. On February 21, 1942, the *Chronicle* went so far as to claim that the Japanese in Hawaii were at the ready before the attacks, accusing them of deliberately blocking traffic with their cars and trucks to trap navy and army officers and men from reaching their ships and stations during the bombings. The piece went on to say that "among all the Japanese who knew the plot there was not one, no matter where born, who came forward to warn the United States." That was not true, but the editorial ended by saying, "This is a fight for survival. . . . We have to be tough, even if civil rights do take a beating for a time."

Two days after that, the *Bee* editorialized: "The necessity for action has been growing for the past ten weeks as the possibility of a Japanese attack on the coast has loomed ever larger. . . . Californians never can feel secure until all enemy aliens and Fifth Column citizens, too—are put in place and surrounded with conditions which will make it utterly impossible for them to serve superiors in any totalitarian capital whose deadly purpose is to destroy the United States of America."

The papers were joined by hundreds of California organizations, among them Lions and Elks clubs, the Supreme Pyramid of the Sciots, the California Townsend Clubs, and the Magnolia Study Club of Anaheim. Radio also joined in. A prominent Mutual Broadcasting Company commentator, John B. Hughes—"News and Views from John B. Hughes"—was telling the nation, west and east, day after day, that 99 percent of Japanese, alien and citizen, were "primarily loyal to Japan. . . . The Japanese are a far greater menace in our midst than any other axis patriots. They will die joyously for the honor of Japan." One of the most famous of graduates of Washington State University, Edward R. Murrow of CBS News, said in a January 1942 speech in Pullman, Washington, "I think it's probable that, if Seattle ever does get bombed, you will be able to look up and see some University of Washington sweaters on the boys doing the bombing." To the south, in Hollywood, the fear was pervasive enough that film studios joined together to ship reels of their negatives to underground vaults in the Midwest.

There were few men in press or politics willing to stand up for the rights of the Japanese living on the West Coast. The *Santa Ana Register* in Orange County, with a daily circulation of about fifteen thousand, was probably the most conservative daily in the state. The paper was owned by R. C. Hoiles, an early libertarian whose columns and editorials argued for limited government, free markets, property rights, and individual liberty—and against public schools, collective bargaining, social-welfare laws, and taxes. As early as February 5, 1942, Hoiles wrote: "The recommendation of the grand jury to have all alien enemies removed from Orange County calls for a difficult undertaking. Every bit of wealth that these workers are prevented from creating, which we so badly need during the war, will have to be created by the labor of some other worker." He went on to urge restraint: "It would seem that we should not become too skeptical of the loyalty of those people who were born in a foreign country and have lived in the country as good citizens for many years. It is very hard to believe that they are dangerous."

A small number of national columnists and commentators in other cities also resisted the California hysteria, among them Ernie Pyle of Scripps Howard and Chester Rowell, whose columns appeared in the *San Francisco Chronicle*.

• • •

In Washington, D.C., meanwhile, the struggle for the mind of President Roosevelt continued. But he was a man with a lot on his mind. It was possible that he had already decided in favor of the idea of evacuation of the West Coast Japanese and intended to leave the details to others. He was absorbed with the logistics and politics of a two-front war—against the Nazis and Fascists across the Atlantic and Imperial Japan across the Pacific. The great oceans that had protected and isolated America for centuries had become the paths to World War II.

Attorney General Francis Biddle was against mass evacuation, in private, as were most of his young assistants at the Justice Department. Biddle was a Philadelphia lawyer of distinguished American lineage—his family traced its American heritage to 1671 and his great-great-grandfather Edmund Jennings Randolph was attorney general under President George Washington. And Biddle believed that the evacuation was unconstitutional if it included American citizens. The attorney general thought the real domestic danger was German and Italian aliens on the East Coast, where German submarines were in action torpedoing dozens of American supply ships headed for Europe. He was against evacuating the Japanese and Japanese Americans in the West, but he had been in office only five months and, as a man of the establishment, he deferred not only to the president but to most senior officials, particularly Secretary of War Henry Stimson.

Although Biddle did not make his own opposition public at first, the principal official dissent in the capital was coming from his department. Assistant Attorneys General Edward Ennis and James Rowe, and J. Edgar Hoover, the director of the FBI, were against talk of evacuation. "I must say," said Ennis, director of the Justice Department's Enemy Alien Control Unit, "it looked to me as if the army was itching to do something. They couldn't fight the Japanese in California, so they found someone else to fight, and that was the Americans of Japanese ancestry." Rowe sent a memo to the president's secretary, Grace Tully, asking her to tell the boss that California politicians were likely to call for "one of the great mass exoduses of history." Hoover, whose agents were doing double duty, was rounding up aliens on their "danger lists" and insisting that they could handle any disloyalty cases on the West Coast or Hawaii without military help.

In memos to Biddle dated February 2 and February 3, Hoover wrote, "The necessity for mass evacuation is based primarily upon public and political pressure rather than on factual data. Public hysteria and in some instances, the comments of the press and radio announcers, have resulted in a tremendous amount of pressure being brought to bear on Governor Olson and Earl Warren, Attorney General of the State, and on the military authorities." The army's deputy chief of staff General Mark Clark, who had served in Hawaii, was one of the few military men willing to say that he thought evacuation of the 160,000 Japanese and Japanese Americans on the islands was not necessary. He also said the chances of a Japanese attack on the West Coast was "nil."

The FBI director and General Clark were backed up the next day, February 4, by cablegrams from Honolulu's police chief William Gabrielson and Lieutenant General Delos Emmons, the army commander in Hawaii, stating that there were no acts of sabotage preceding or during the attack on Pearl Harbor.

• • •

General DeWitt, however, more often than not pressed the idea that mass evacuation was necessary and critical. He phoned Assistant Secretary of War John J. McCloy on February 3 and insisted that a way be found to get around constitutional guarantees of liberties for American citizens. "Out here," said DeWitt, "a Jap is a Jap to these people now. . . . You can't tell one Jap from another. They all look the same."

McCloy, a New York lawyer before entering the administration, was well known for having proved that German agents were responsible for the "Black Tom" munitions depot explosion, which killed seven people during World War I. He replied to DeWitt that something could be worked out, adding, "You are putting a Wall Street lawyer in a helluva box, but if it is a question of the safety of the country and the Constitution . . . why the Constitution is just a scrap of paper to me."

On February 14, DeWitt followed up his conversations with McCloy in a long memo to Secretary of War Stimson, writing:

> In the war in which we are now engaged, racial affinities are not severed by migration. The Japanese race is an enemy race and while many second and third generation Japanese born on United States soil, possessed of American citizenship, have become "Americanized," the racial strains are undiluted. To conclude otherwise is to expect that children born of white parents on Japanese soil sever all racial affinity and become loyal Japanese and, if necessary, die for Japan against the nation of their parents. That Japan is allied with Germany and Italy in this struggle is no ground for assuming that any Japanese, barred from assimilation by convention as he is, though born and raised in the United States will not turn against this nation when the final test of loyalty comes.

DeWitt told Stimson that he believed that every one of the more than 112,000 American Japanese living along the Pacific Coast were "potential enemies of Japanese extraction" and that "there are indications that they were organized and ready for concerted operation at a favorable opportunity. The very fact that no sabotage has taken place to date is a disturbing and confirming indication that such action will be taken." He then laid out what he thought was likely to happen: sabotage, naval attacks, and air raids "assisted by enemy agents signaling from the coastline."

The official story being spread on the West Coast by politicians and the press—and by California agricultural interests eager to take over Japanese fields and crops—was that the Japanese had deliberately moved onto farms close to military bases, airports, defense factories, power stations, and power lines. That fantasy was "verified" by California officials, particularly Attorney General Warren, who, with the help of the state's county sheriffs, prepared maps of the distribution of California Japanese, including entries as vague as "Jap across the street from boat works [in Sausalito]." What the maps did not show was that Japanese farmers and workers had usually been there for decades, even generations, before the bases and other facilities were built.

The press was also buying any story the military was selling. The *New York Times* reported on February 18 an example of "threats to national security" that was almost comical: "On the farm of Isaburo Saki, 48 years old, agents found binoculars, flashlights, a radio, and what appeared to be a homemade blackjack."

The official phrase "military necessity" was the argument being fueled in Washington by daily reports from DeWitt's headquarters. The general was reporting on every wild rumor bouncing around the state. After the *Montebello* incident, he told Washington that substantially every ship leaving a West Coast port was attacked by enemy submarines. Part of his paper war was an effort to discredit naval and FBI intelligence, who were stating that the West Coast Japanese were not a real threat. One of DeWitt's memos reported that Japanese submarines were being signaled to by "enemy agents on shore"—even as navy intelligence was reporting that the Japanese navy had only one submarine between Hawaii and California. DeWitt, who was sixty-two years old, was no different than many of the mediocre officers who managed to survive in a smaller army after World War I. General Gullion, sixty-one, also favored mass evacuation as soon as war was declared and had already suggested that camps be built to hold all Japanese, citizens and aliens, men, women, and children. Secretary of War Stimson immediately rejected the idea. After being blocked by Stimson and snubbed by Attorney General Biddle, Gullion called DeWitt as early as December 22, 1941, and urged him to do the job. He wanted DeWitt to recommend the evacuation and incarceration. But as memos and calls went back and forth between Washington and San Francisco, DeWitt sometimes seemed to be changing his mind, something he did regularly. Twice before December 26, DeWitt sent Gullion reports arguing against mass evacuation, saying, "If we go ahead and arrest the 93,000 Japanese, native born and foreign born, we are going to have an awful job on our hands and are very liable to alienate the loyal Japanese from disloyal. . . . I'm very doubtful that it would be common sense procedure to try and intern or to intern 117,000 Japanese in this theater." He went on to say that the evacuation would not be sensible: "An American citizen, after all, is an American citizen. And while they all may not be loyal, I think we can weed the disloyal out of the loyal and lock them up if necessary."

Gullion, the army's top legal officer, was learning what others already knew: men who worked with DeWitt saw him as indecisive, often influenced by the last person with whom he talked. One day he would tell California congressmen he favored evacuation of all Japanese, the next he would be arguing that mass evacuation would be a logistical nightmare. Those who knew the general, his chief deputy General Stilwell among them, thought his real concern was evading the fate of Pearl Harbor commanders Admiral Husband Kimmel and General Walter Short, whose military careers were essentially ended because they were totally unprepared for the sneak attack.

In fact, General DeWitt, the army's man on the West Coast, tried to avoid confronting the politicians of California, Oregon, and Washington. Those politicians were giving in to public hysteria and to their states' racists, including farmers and fishermen determined to eliminate Japanese competition.

Despite what he had been telling Gullion about logistics, DeWitt was still using his "A Jap's a Jap" line, talking of segregation of all Japanese of "undiluted racial strain." Then, day after day, he changed, twisting his arguments again and again—often depending on his audience of the moment. At times, he characterized evacuation warnings and preparations as "damned nonsense"—and then he suggested that the War Department issue a proclamation declaring the states of Idaho, Montana, Nevada, and Utah as military zones. That grand plan was quickly killed in Washington and Provost General Gullion soon realized that DeWitt was too weak or ignorant to be trusted.

The provost general's next move was to send one of his young assistants, a thirty-three-year-old captain named Karl Bendetson, to San Francisco by plane to be an "adviser" to General DeWitt. Bendetson was a talented and ambitious Stanford Law School graduate from Aberdeen, Washington, a small town 110 miles southwest of Seattle, whose army reserve unit was called up early in 1941. He was then assigned to Gullion's staff in Washington, D.C. The thinking of the young captain and General DeWitt was not dissimilar. In one phone call between them, DeWitt, speaking of the Japanese Americans offering to cooperate in the war effort, said, "Those are the fellows I suspect the most." Bendetson agreed, saying, "Definitely. The ones who are giving you lip service are the ones always to suspect."

Bendetson quickly became DeWitt's confidant and deputy chief of staff. He had also, on February 4, 1942, changed the spelling of his name from "Bendetson" to "Bendetsen" to make it seem less Jewish. "Bendetsen" was, in fact, a serial liar from a prominent Orthodox Jewish family that had emigrated from Lithuania in 1869, settling first in Elmira, New York, then moving west to the Seattle area. But in 1929 he denied all that, claiming to be a Christian to get into a Stanford fraternity, Theta Delta Chi, which barred Jews from membership. As the years went by, he created a new biography under the name Bendetsen, saying that he was from a Danish logging family and that a fictional great-grandfather had come from Denmark to America in 1670.

Bendetsen signed the first official document with his new name that same day, February 4, in a memorandum to McCloy titled, "Alien Enemies on the West Coast." In the memo, he endorsed the idea that there was an American Japanese Fifth Column: "A substantial majority of the *Nisei* bear allegiance to Japan, are well controlled and disciplined by the enemy, and at the proper time will engage in organized sabotage, particularly should a raid along the Pacific Coast be attempted by the Japanese. . . . This will require an evacuation and internment problem of some considerable proportions."

In Washington, the young lawyer had quickly earned Gullion's trust by creating a craftily worded legal strategy to evacuate the Japanese and Japanese Americans from the West Coast: the military would have authority to remove any American from new "Military Zones" and the power to allow any of them to return to the zones. "Race," "ethnicity," or "ancestry" were never mentioned in regard to the zones. The plan was described by Stetson Conn, the chief historian of the Department of the Army: "Bendetsen recommended the designation of military areas from which all persons who did not have permission to enter or remain would be excluded as a matter of military necessity. In his opinion, this plan was clearly legal and he recommended that it be executed in three steps: first, the issuance of an executive order by the President authorizing the Secretary of War to designate military areas; second, the designation of 'Military Zones' in the Western United States on the recommendation of the Western commander, General DeWitt; and third, the immediate evacuation from areas so designated of all persons to whom it was not proposed to issue licenses to re-enter or remain."

The proposed licenses were not authorized, but they did not have to be. Only one group of "persons," Japanese and Japanese Americans, would be denied permission to enter or remain in the zones.

The first military zone designated by General DeWitt was all of the West Coast from California to Washington State and a corner of Arizona within two hundred miles of the coast. The idea could then be presented to President Roosevelt as a way to authorize the relocation of the West Coast Japanese and Japanese Americans, with an executive document that did not mention race—and then not allow any of them to return.

Bendetsen, the chief strategist for both Gullion and DeWitt, the reservist from a one-man law office, was promoted again and again. He had been promoted from captain to major and then lieutenant colonel on February 4, 1942, and then, ten days later, to full colonel on February 14, 1942. Along with McCloy, he tweaked and polished their ideas into an executive order. McCloy, who favored evacuation, said he thought it was barely constitutional. But he was willing to go along and told Bendetsen and DeWitt, "We can cover the legal situation."

Bendetsen had already explained more of his thinking in a memo to Gullion, calling mass evacuation "undoubtedly the safest course to follow, that is to say as you cannot distinguish or penetrate Oriental thinking and as you cannot tell which ones are loyal and which ones are not and it is, therefore, the easiest course (aside from the mechanical problem involved) to remove them all from the West Coast and place them in the 'Zone of the Interior' in uninhabited areas where they can do no harm under guard."

Deeming them all to be potential traitors, Bendetsen wanted all American Japanese removed from western states. Back in his family's hometown in Aberdeen, Washington, there was only one Japanese American family, the Saitos. Natsu Saito, a forty-two-year-old widow and mother, owned the Oriental Art Store, a novelty shop down the street from Bendetsen's law office. Fluent in both Japanese and English, Mrs. Saito had been arrested within forty-eight hours of the attack on Pearl Harbor. To the extent that there were any charges against her, it was that her shop catered to Japanese seamen in town who came by while their ships were loaded with timber, and that her oldest son, Lincoln, was a student at a Presbyterian seminary in Japan. That was more than enough for the FBI. Agents ransacked her store before she was taken away from her three younger children. They had no idea where she was for more than three weeks. Learning that their mother was being held in a detention center in Seattle, the teenage children, Morse, Perry, and Dahlia, drove the 112 miles to the big city on Christmas day. They were turned away, told there were no visiting hours on the holiday. They returned home and tried to run their mother's shop, but many of the customers who came knocked goods off shelves and then spit in their faces. After several hearings, Mrs. Saito was released on probation, and she and the three children were ordered to take a bus to Olympia, Washington—paying their own way—to board a train to the Tule Lake camp on a barren lava field in northern California, five miles from the Oregon border.

When Bendetsen said he wanted to remove "anyone" of Japanese ancestry, he meant what he said: old people in hospitals were scheduled for evacuation and were kept under military guard until they died or were able to travel. Grace Watanabe of Los Angeles, along with her mother, were loaded aboard a troop train to an unknown destination. She was forced to leave her father, a Methodist minister suffering from cancer, in a hospital. Two soldiers guarded the door of his hospital room. He was one of more than one thousand Japanese too sick to travel—each one guarded by soldiers, as if they could escape.

Japanese infants were included in the evacuation and so were children adopted by Caucasian parents. And orphans, too. Federal agents visited West Coast orphanages looking for children with Japanese features. A Catholic priest in charge of an orphanage, Father Hugh Lavery of the Maryknoll Center in Los Angeles, said that Bendetsen "showed himself to be a little Hitler. I mentioned that we had an orphanage with children of Japanese ancestry, and that some of these children were half Japanese, others one-fourth or less. I asked which children we should send. . . . Bendetsen said, 'I am determined that if they have one drop of Japanese blood in them, they must go to camp.'"

The new colonel did not make any distinction between the forces of Imperial Japan and American Japanese. He wrote: "The Army's job is to kill Japanese not to save Japanese. . . . If the Army is to devote its facilities to resettlement and social welfare work among Japanese aliens, it will be that much more difficult for it to get on to its primary task, that of winning the war."

• • •

As Attorney General Biddle's opposition to mass evacuation became public, he became a principal target not only of the army but of the West Coast press. In the *San Francisco Examiner* and other newspapers around the country, the Hearst columnist Henry McLemore wrote on February 5: "Mr. Biddle could not even win the post of third assistant dog catcher in charge of liver-spotted Airedales. That's the way they feel about Mr. 'Blueblood' Biddle out here. . . . It would be a shame wouldn't it, and an affront to civil liberties, to move the Japanese from in and about defense centers without proper warning. It might even upset their plans of sabotage."

In Washington, the embattled attorney general lunched with the president on February 7, saying, according to his notes, that "there was no reason for mass evacuation and I thought the army should be directed to prepare a detailed plan for evacuation in case of an emergency caused by an air raid or attempted landing on the West Coast." He then wrote a letter to Secretary of War Stimson the next day repeating his position. Stimson shared some of the concerns of the attorney general about the forced evacuation of American citizens being unconstitutional. "We cannot discriminate among our citizens on the basis of racial origin," he told members of his staff and a few officers on February 4. But the aides, particularly McCloy and Gullion, were pressing him every day, arguing that there was indeed a possibility that the Japanese could invade the West Coast.

In his diary that night, the secretary of war wrote, "The second generation Japanese can only be evacuated either as part of a total evacuation, giving access only to the areas only by permits, or by frankly trying to put them out on the ground that their racial characteristics are such that we cannot understand or trust even the citizen Japanese. The latter is the fact but I am afraid it will make a tremendous hole in our constitutional system to apply it."

Meanwhile, important figures from Washington were traveling across the country to meet with General DeWitt and Attorney General Warren. Among the visitors to California in those frenzied February days was Walter Lippmann, the most respected newspaper columnist in the nation's capital. He arrived on February 8 and had dinner with Warren and Percy Heckendorf, the district attorney of Santa Barbara County, who later said the columnist wrote almost word for word what Warren told him. This is what Lippmann wrote for publication in his column Today and

Tomorrow in the *Washington Post*, the *New York Herald Tribune*, and 250 other newspapers on February 13, 1942:

> The Pacific Coast is in imminent danger of a combined attack from within and without. . . . It is a fact . . . [that] there has been no important sabotage on the Pacific Coast. From what we know about Hawaii and about the fifth column in Europe, this is not, as some would like to think, a sign there is nothing to be feared. It is a sign that the blow is well organized and that it is held back until it can be struck with maximum effect.

Lippmann went on to say, "There is the assumption that if the rights of a citizen are abridged anywhere they have been abridged everywhere." He concluded: "Nobody's constitutional rights include the right to reside and do business on a battlefield."

Enraged by the column, Biddle sent a memo to the president, saying that Lippmann and other commentators were "Armchair Strategists and Junior G-Men. . . . It comes close to yelling 'FIRE!' in the theater."

The attorney general was too late. The column had tremendous impact in Washington and the rest of the country. Others followed, notably columnist Damon Runyon in New York and Westbrook Pegler, a Hearst columnist, who wrote that if the great Lippmann expected sabotage and infiltration, it must be true, writing, "Do you get what he says? This is a high grade fellow, with a heavy sense of responsibility. . . . We are so damned dumb and considerate of the minute political feelings and influence of people. . . . The Germans round them all up and keep them in pens."

Lippmann was essentially writing to an audience of one: Franklin D. Roosevelt. What happened next was predictable. On the day after the Lippmann column, all members of Congress from California, Oregon, and Washington signed on to a letter to the president saying, "We recommend the immediate evacuation of all persons of Japanese lineage and all others, aliens and citizens alike, whose presence shall be deemed dangerous or inimical to the defense of the United States from all strategic areas."

• • •

Secretary Stimson asked for a meeting with the president but was told there were many more pressing concerns than the "West Coast problem." The president and the secretary spoke by telephone instead. Stimson was an elder statesman, a seventy-four-year-old Republican, who had served as secretary of state in Republican administrations. He was personally close to the president and he was an old-fashioned "president's man," loyal to the chief, even if he was not comfortable with what was happening. During their telephone call, Stimson asked whether Roosevelt was prepared to remove both citizens and aliens from the West Coast. The president, certainly influenced by the news that day that Japanese troops were invading Singapore and other Asian targets, told the secretary of war to make the decision himself on how to handle Japanese citizens at home. "But . . . " the president added, "be as reasonable as you can."

Stimson called in his deputy McCloy, who was also a Republican, and told him what the president had said. McCloy interpreted that to mean Roosevelt was giving them, in McCloy's words, "carte blanche" to deal with the West Coast problem. McCloy then called Bendetsen and DeWitt, saying, "We talked to the President, and the President, in substance, says go ahead and do anything you think necessary. . . . If it involves citizens, we will take care of them too. He says there will probably be repercussions, but it has to be dictated by military necessity."

The secretary of war and his aggressive deputy understood that the president wanted to stay as far from the operation as possible, and that the military side—Stimson, Gullion, DeWitt, and Bendetsen—would be in charge of the evacuation. Beyond the Bendetsen-DeWitt declaration that all of the West Coast was a "War Zone," no real preparations had been made for such a complicated operation. In the beginning, even though American Japanese were prohibited from traveling more than five miles from their homes and were subject to an 8:00 p.m. to 6:00 a.m. curfew, DeWitt also announced that Japanese and Japanese Americans were free to move "voluntarily" from the new West Coast "War Zone" to states and places east of the zone. But move where? Few of the West Coast Japanese, a clannish bunch, had family or knew anyone in other parts of the country. And they were afraid, expecting open hostility across the country. One of the army's arguments for what Roosevelt himself had called "concentration camps" was to protect the Japanese from their fellow Americans. Lippmann and McCloy were among those who would later maintain that their primary concern was to protect the American Japanese from the potential vigilante violence of their white neighbors.

On February 17, Roosevelt officially told Stimson and McCloy to draft an executive order authorizing evacuation—without informing Biddle. The matter, if not the manner, was settled. Roosevelt had made it as clear as he could: he did not want to hear any more of this. Stimson began working on an executive order that declared the evacuation "a matter of Military Necessity." The final draft of the executive order did not mention the words "Japanese," "Japanese American," or "citizen." Internal memos referred to American citizens of Japanese descent as "non-aliens."

That evening, Colonel Bendetsen and Assistant Attorney General Clark, who had flown into Washington the night before, went to Biddle's home to meet with the attorney general, McCloy, and Gullion. After two of Biddle's assistants, Ennis and Rowe, laid out the legal case against incarceration, Gullion pulled out the draft order approved by both War and Justice. Biddle's assistants were stunned. Ennis was near tears. The attorney general himself said nothing, although he had sent a memo to the president that same day, saying: "A great many West Coast people distrust the Japanese, various special interests would welcome their removal from good farm land and the elimination of their competition. . . . My last advice from the War Department is that there is no evidence of imminent attack and from the FBI that there is no evidence of planned sabotage."

There was no answer from Roosevelt. The next day, Biddle said he and the Justice Department would have nothing to do with any evacuation. Gullion was beside himself, telling General Mark Clark that he had called Biddle and said, " 'Well listen Mr. Biddle, do you mean to tell me that if the Army, the men on the ground, determine it is a military necessity to move citizens, Jap citizens, that you won't help me?' He didn't give a direct answer, he said the Department of Justice would be through if we interfered with citizens and the right of *habeas corpus*, etc."

Biddle also received a call from California congressman Leland Ford, who had originally opposed evacuation and attacked Southern advocates of the idea as racists. Now, switching sides, Ford told his staff:

I phoned the Attorney General's office and told them to stop fucking around. I gave them twenty-four hours' notice that unless they would issue a mass evacuation notice I would drag the whole matter out on the floor of the House and of the Senate and give the bastards everything we could with both barrels. I told them they had given us the runaround long enough . . . and that if they would not take immediate action, we would clean the god damned office out in one sweep. I cussed at the Attorney General and his staff . . . and he knew damn well I meant business.

So the military was going to have its way on evacuation. All Japanese, citizens and aliens, were going to be removed from the Pacific Coast.

• • •

On February 19, without comment, the president of the United States signed Executive Order 9066, which read, in part:

Authorizing the Secretary of War to Prescribe Military Areas

I hereby further authorize and direct the Secretary of War and the said Military Commanders to take such other steps as he or the appropriate Military Commander may deem advisable to enforce compliance with the restrictions applicable to each Military area herein above authorized to be designated, including the use of Federal troops and other Federal Agencies, with authority to accept assistance of state and local agencies.

In California, the district attorney of Santa Barbara County, Percy Heckendorf, who had been at dinner with Warren and Lippmann, congratulated the California attorney general, saying, "I have no doubt that the presidential order stems back to the article written by Lippmann following the talk with you."

The day after the president signed Executive Order 9066, Secretary of War Stimson authorized General DeWitt to carry out the intent of the order. Within two weeks, DeWitt designated the western halves of California, Oregon, and Washington as

well as southern Arizona as Military Area No. 1 of the Western
Defense Command. At the same time, California attorney general Warren called a conference of the state's district attorneys
and sheriffs. Warren used, almost word for word, the line DeWitt
and he had been feeding in private to the War Department and
the press: the fact that there had been no sabotage was proof there
would be. Warren told them that he considered "fifth column
activities" to be "a tremendous problem in California." He considered it to be "significant" that California hadn't had any such
activities nor any sabotage reported, and went on to say that "it
looks very much to me as though it is a studied effort not to have
any until the zero hour arrives. . . . That is the history of Pearl
Harbor. I can't help believing that the same thing is planned for
California." Warren concluded that "every alien Japanese should
be considered in the light of a potential fifth columnist."

Then, testifying before congressional committees, Warren,
this time in public, repeated the argument that he and DeWitt
had been making in private meetings: "The only reason we
haven't had disaster in California is because it has been timed
for a different date. . . . For us to believe to the contrary is just
not realistic." He compared the situation in his state with that
of countries occupied by German troops in Europe.

Warren continued his argument, saying, "It is certainly evi-
dent that the Japanese population of California is, as a whole,
ideally situated, with reference to points of strategic importance,
to carry into execution a tremendous program of sabotage on a
mass scale." He went on to warn, "I believe that we are just being
lulled into a sense of security. Our day of reckoning is bound to
come. . . . We are approaching an invisible deadline."

Warren then produced a list of what he called danger
points around the state, which included "Japs adjacent to" and
"Japs in vicinity of": Livermore Field, a gravel runway used as
an emergency landing site by the navy; Southern Pacific and

Western Pacific Railroads; Oakland Airport; Holt Caterpillar Tractor Company; and all dams supplying water to San Diego and vicinity.

The chairman of one of the congressional committees, Representative John Tolan, who was from California, interrupted to say, "When that came up in our committee hearings there was not a single case of sabotage reported on the Pacific Coast. The sabotage would come coincident with [an] attack, would it not?"

"Exactly," Warren answered.

3

ONLY WHAT THEY COULD CARRY

PUBLIC PROCLAMATION NUMBER I: MARCH 2, 1942

I n late January, before the president's order, Secretary of the
Navy Frank Knox announced that all Japanese, men and
women, citizens and aliens, would be removed from Terminal Island off San Pedro Harbor at the southern tip of Los Angeles. The island was owned by the U.S. Navy, which had a base and
an airstrip there, Reeves Field. The navy also supervised two
shipyards on the island. Many Issei leaders, fishermen with their
own boats and radios, aliens on FBI lists, had been taken away
within twenty-four hours after Pearl Harbor. They were scattered
in twenty-seven Justice Department jails, prisons, and new camps
around the country. Their families did not know where they were
being held—or if they were alive. After the fishing community
leaders were arrested, the one-mile-by-five-mile island had
become a place mostly inhabited by women—who worked in
island canneries—their children, and old people. They were told
they would have weeks to prepare for the evacuation.

Rumors and hysteria kept building along the coast. One story, a true one among dozens of rumors, frightened many Californians: the shelling of an oil storage depot near Santa Barbara by a submarine. There had been other submarine attacks off the coast, but news of real incidents had been censored; this one, on February 23, was witnessed by hundreds of local people watching the submarine from the beach, as if it were part of a fireworks show. Fifteen shells were fired, hitting one oil tank. The target, the Bankline oil refinery in Goleta, estimated the damage at $500, but newspaper headlines compared it to the attack on Pearl Harbor. The puny shelling of the American mainland was the first since the British attacked Washington, D.C., in the War of 1812. "The Battle of Los Angeles," as newspapers called it, was fought the next night, February 24, with army antiaircraft guns blasting hundreds of rounds into the sky for almost an hour. Five people died, two of heart attacks and three in automobile accidents, as Angelenos fled for their lives. The guns failed to bring down the "enemy," a U.S. Navy weather balloon. The *Los Angeles Times* headlined: "LA Area Raided; Jap Planes Peril Santa Monica, El Segundo, Long Beach."

Continuing bad war news from the Pacific Theater heightened the demands to remove American Japanese from the coast. On February 25, the Terminal Islanders were told they had to leave in less than forty-eight hours. They would be allowed to take away only what they could carry.

At dawn on February 26, 1942, a joint federal-local operation was launched on the island with armored cars and jeeps crawling through the narrow streets, machine guns aimed at the small houses rented to workers by the canneries. Not far behind the army vehicles were empty trucks driven by civilians, junk dealers, secondhand furniture and appliance dealers, offering to buy items at humiliating prices. "You won't have any need for them where you're going," was the call of the scavengers. Islanders called them "the vultures" or "the Jews." Some of the unwelcome visitors pretended to be FBI agents, warning residents that they would be forcibly evacuated within hours. Then an hour later, other white men, accomplices, would come attempting to buy whatever families had left.

More than a hundred fishing boats were left bobbing at anchor in the harbor, many with "For Sale" signs on their cabins. Left unsold, many of the boats were requisitioned by the Coast Guard or the navy to be refitted as patrol boats, used mainly along the Panama Canal. Acres of expensive nets covered the beaches. Ko Wakatsuki, who lived in Santa Monica, was the owner of two boats, the large one, the *Nereid*, was worth about $25,000. He disappeared. His family never knew where he was until they read in a Santa Monica paper that he was charged with carrying oil to Japanese submarines. The Coast Guard had arrested him when they saw oil drums on deck. The drums were filled with fish heads and other chum used for bait. He ended up in jail in Bismarck, North Dakota. As she was packing to leave, his wife, Riku, was harassed by scavengers wanting to buy her best dishes, worth about $200. One by one, she took the dishes out of their velvet jackets and smashed them at the men's feet.

As the islanders were frantically packing, the island's physician, Dr. Fred Fujikawa, a graduate of Berkeley and Creighton University Medical School, stayed up for two nights, dismantling his X-ray machine and other equipment. Mrs. Misako Shigekawa, owner of the island's only pharmacy and a graduate of the University of Southern California School of Pharmacy, locked up the place, leaving the medicines and equipment there. She never saw them again. The doctor's wife, Kiyo, had two houseguests, friends from Sacramento, who could not get off the island because the only bridge to the mainland was blocked by soldiers who had also shut down the island's ferry. Dr. Fujikawa went to the Terminal Island immigration office to ask if they could go home.

He was pushed into a room, had his fingerprints taken, and then was photographed holding a number across his chest. The *Los Angeles Times* headline the next day read: "Japs Evicted on Terminal Island—FBI Police and Deputy Sheriffs Round Up 336 of estimated 800 Aliens in Harbor Area."

• • •

The Terminal Island evacuation was the first large roundup of American Japanese since the days immediately after Pearl Harbor. When Executive Order 9066 was signed, federal agents, under Justice Department orders, began new rounds of "search and seizure" arrests of alien fishermen, boat owners, and community leaders up and down the West Coast—almost always without charges. Almost all of those jailed were immigrants from Japan, but some, particularly in the San Francisco area, were Italian aliens. Most of the Japanese were detained or arrested and their boats were seized. Almost all the Italians were simply ordered not to go to sea. Younger Italian Americans, American citizens, were allowed to fish only in areas designated by the government. In Santa Cruz, twelve Italians and twenty Japanese were taken into custody on February 9—the Italians were quickly released—and similar roundups were done in San Diego and Monterey. The Italians called it *la mole notte*, "the sad night." The *Santa Cruz Sentinel*, which had been calling for restraint and pleading the case of the Italians and a few Germans working in Monterey Bay and San Francisco, ran a banner front-page headline that declared, "Fishermen with 23 Sons in Army and Navy Are Bound to Wharf While Boats Lie Idle and Sea Food Is Needed." On the editorial page it said, "With its problem of separating fifth columnists from peaceful and worthy residents of foreign birth, the Department of Justice has had no time to work out formulae which will safeguard the nation and at the same time allow such men as Santa Cruz's fishermen to earn a living for their families and add to the country's food supply."

In fact, very few Italians and Italian Americans were affected by curfews or relocation. The State Department summarized its dealings with Bendetsen in a memo on February 22, 1942: "It now appears to the Army that these persons are not as danger- ous as was at first thought. . . . In this connection, Bendetsen mentioned the DiMaggio family." Still, General DeWitt wanted Joe DiMaggio's alien parents evacuated. "No exceptions," he said. As late as May 20, 1942, he was insisting that Germans and Italians should be evacuated.

That was too much for McCloy, who responded, "I want to explain to you personally that in approving this program, both the President and the Secretary of War did so with the expecta- tion that the exclusions would not reach such numbers. . . . We want, if at all possible, to avoid the necessity of establishing addi- tional relocation settlements." Unmentioned was the fact that if Americans of German and Italian ancestry were incarcerated, camps would have to be built for millions of people.

In the end, the DiMaggios, who had never applied for Amer- ican citizenship, were not jailed, but they were not allowed to use their fishing boat or go to the small restaurant they owned on Fisherman's Wharf. By the end of the waterfront sweeps, 787 California fishermen were banned from coastal areas. One of the fishermen prevented from going to sea was Stefano Ghio, the father of three of the Santa Cruz men in the military. One of the sons, Victor Ghio, told the *Sentinel*, the local newspaper:

> Here I was in the Navy. I had another brother in the Navy and another brother in the Army, and they do this to my father? It was a bunch of B.S., a lot of B.S. I talked to my superiors about it, but hell, there was nothing they could do. They told me to do my duty and that was it. It's too

bad, that's all. My dad and some of the rest lost some good fishing seasons, I'll tell you that.

One Italian American sailor stationed in San Francisco went to the Presidio and confronted General DeWitt. "He wouldn't listen to any reason whatsoever, to nothing," said Chief Boatswain Mario Stagnaro. "Everybody to him was an enemy that wasn't an American citizen." Stagnaro described their meeting: he said to DeWitt, "These are the greatest people in the world," and DeWitt replied, "Well! Why didn't they become citizens?" Stagnaro said, "General, they never had the opportunity; never had an opportunity to learn; they raised big families, and they stayed at home." But DeWitt was not persuaded, and Stagnaro later concluded, "He was a damn fool, a complete nut, in my opinion."

Fool or not, General DeWitt was now the most powerful man on the West Coast.

* * *

It was clear that mass evacuation was coming—and soon. John McCloy of the War Department traveled to San Francisco and asked Japanese American Citizens League leaders to support the government and help with evacuations: "We know that the great majority of citizens and aliens are loyal and being appreciative of that, we are most anxious to see that you don't suffer any more than necessary the loss of property values. We want to have conditions just as humane and comfortable as is possible. . . . Above all, we want to give you protection."

In Monterey, an Issei and a World War I veteran named Hideo Murata went to see Sheriff Alex Bordges, an old friend, and asked whether this was really going to happen, that Japanese were going to be put in concentration camps. He showed the sheriff an "Honorary Citizen" certificate awarded him by the Monterey County board of supervisors, which read, "Monterey County presents this testimonial of heartfelt gratitude, of honor and respect for your loyal and splendid service to the country in the Great War. Our flag was assaulted and you gallantly took up its defense."

"It's not a joke; it's happening," said Bordges.

Murata went to a hotel in Pismo Beach, paid for a room, and shot himself in the head. In his left hand, he clutched the testimonial from the county.

He was not the first or the last Japanese American suicide. And there were other ominous stories. Another World War I vet who was rejected when he tried to enlist, Joseph Kurihara, angrily declared, "I am going to become 100 percent Japanese." He began forming a unit of the anti-American "Black Dragons."

• • •

On February 28, the *New York Times* headlined, "Japanese Moving Day Looms: West Coast Opinion Hardens in Favor of Removal of Aliens and Citizens Alike."

"Investigations by Earl Warren, State Attorney General," wrote Lawrence Davies, "showed instances in which an airfield was surrounded entirely by Japanese-occupied land. An air base was located next to arid waste tracts on which 'not even a jack-rabbit could grow' but on which Japanese began farming."

After quoting Warren several times, Davies wrote, "All of these developments changed the mood of the public and made Japanese in some sections of the Coast, particularly California, fearful for their safety."

The article ended in puzzlement: "Federal officials take the position that although the Army can order American-born Japanese out of military areas they cannot tell them where to go, because such orders or even advice would deprive them of their rights as American citizens."

Indeed. With West Coast Japanese living under travel restrictions and curfews, DeWitt and Bendetsen continued working on various evacuation plans. On March 2, General DeWitt issued Public Proclamation Number 1, declaring parts of California, Oregon, Washington, and Arizona as Military Area No. 1. Other parts of those states were declared Military Area No. 2.

On March 11, the general announced the formation of the Western Defense Command and Fourth Army Wartime Civil Control Administration (WCCA), to be headed by Colonel Bendetsen. Back in Washington a week later, President Roosevelt established the War Relocation Authority (WRA). The WCCA was given a mandate to find "assembly centers" to temporarily hold the more than one hundred thousand Japanese on the West Coast and southern Arizona for months, while the WRA was to build permanent concentration camps east of the Sierra Nevada in California and the Cascades in Oregon and Washington. The army announced that the first evacuees would be Japanese, aliens and citizens—and later Germans and Italians. The second part never happened. Suspect German and Italian agents were in Justice Department prisons and camps, but despite DeWitt's pleadings there was never any serious discussion of mass evacuation.

On March 18, the president called Milton Eisenhower, a forty-three-year-old assistant to Secretary of Agriculture Claude Wickard, to the White House and said, "Milton, your war job, starting immediately, is to set up a War Relocation Administration to move the Japanese-Americans off the West Coast . . . . And Milton, the greatest possible speed is imperative." Once again, the army got what it wanted, evacuation, which was, in fact, already under way. The War Department, however, was only willing to handle the logistics of the relocation of the *Nikkei* in seventeen temporary assembly centers and then to move them on to the ten relocation camps being built east of the Sierra Mountains. The job of actually running camps was passed to civilians under Eisenhower, the youngest brother of Dwight Eisenhower, an army brigadier general largely unknown outside the service but, importantly, a favorite of army chief of staff George Marshall.

On March 27, DeWitt rescinded the order allowing Japanese Americans to "voluntarily" move to other parts of the country. The raids on Terminal Island and smaller Japanese enclaves had effectively ended a widely publicized army program called "Voluntary Evacuation," which allowed aliens and citizens alike the option to relocate east of the Sierra and Cascade mountain ranges. The program was backed by the Japanese American Citizens League, which told members, "You are not being accused of any crime. You are being removed only to protect you and because there might be one of you who would be dangerous to the United States. It is your contribution to the war effort. You should be glad to make the sacrifice to prove your loyalty." That statement largely defined the wartime position of the JACL, the largest Japanese American organization in the United States, and it would produce almost as many adversaries as supporters by the end of the war.

In fact, very few American Japanese had tried to go east. One who did, Mariko Kikuchi, borrowed $55 from her brother Charles, a graduate student at Berkeley, to pay for a train ticket to Chicago, where she did not know a single person. She was lucky. Most of the *Nikkei* who tried were more often than not turned back by hostile Caucasians, often armed men. Restaurants, stores, and gas stations refused to give them food, water, and fuel. Some of the Japanese "volunteers" were badly beaten. Fewer than 9,000 American Japanese made it past the Sierras. Most of them ended up being trapped in a second "War Zone" that General DeWitt created without prior notification in the eastern areas of the Pacific Coast states, lands east of the Sierras and the Cascades. Like the Japanese residents in Military Area No. 1, those east of the mountains were immediately restricted from traveling more than five miles from where they were and were placed under the same 8:00 p.m. to 6:00 a.m. curfew. Of the "volunteers," only

4,000 or so found places to live outside the two war zones, with 1,963 going to Colorado, 1,519 to Utah, and the rest to other states.

In California's largest cities, Los Angeles, San Francisco, Oakland, and San Diego, posters appeared on March 24, 1942, announcing where and when Japanese aliens and Japanese Americans were expected to arrive to be carried away by buses and trains to assembly centers. They were allowed, in the usual wording, to bring "only what you can carry," usually two suitcases. There was almost no resistance on designated street corners of the cities as the evacuees lined up on the orders of soldiers with bayonets attached to their rifles. In West Oakland, a boy named Ron Dellums was pushed away by soldiers when he ran after a truck on Wood Street taking away his best friend, a boy named Rolland. "Don't take my friend. Don't take my friend!" Dellums yelled. Up the road, in Berkeley, a white woman approached the line of American Japanese assembling at a church and asked, "Do you have any Chinese members of this church? My Japanese servant has had to leave, and I thought maybe you could find a Chinese for me. I just don't know what I'm going to do."

Bendetsen's WCCA was responsible for getting the Japanese to assembly centers where they would be held under guard, until ten relocation centers were erected on distant and isolated sites from California to Arkansas. These camps were located on unused government property and Indian reservations, in deserts, swamps, and other terrible places where few people had ever lived or ever would. Seventeen assembly centers were set up along the West Coast, basically taking over large public spaces such as racetracks, fairgrounds, livestock auction grounds, and one abandoned Civilian Conservation Corps camp.

Inside the "War Zones," villages, towns, and city neighborhoods were turned into subzones, where, each few days after March 24, all Japanese and those with some Japanese ancestry were ordered to bus stops and train stations. Surrounded by armed soldiers, the evacuees were loaded onto buses, trucks, and trains and taken to the assembly centers. They were unloaded at California centers in or near Fresno, Independence, Marysville, Merced, Pinedale, Pomona, Sacramento, Salinas, the Santa Anita racetrack in Los Angeles, Stockton, Tanforan racetrack near San Francisco, Tulare, and Turlock. Arizona residents were taken to Mayer. Oregonians were taken to the Pacific International Stock Exposition grounds in Portland. Washingtonians were divided between Puyallup and Manzanar, California, the only site to serve as both an assembly center and, later, a relocation camp.

That said, the army or the WCCA—aided by the polite compliance of Japanese families—did a remarkably efficient job of the logistics of moving more than one hundred thousand people to the assembly centers and then on to far and barren relocation sites in six months. Among those who praised the logistics of the moves to the camps was Carey McWilliams, a liberal, even radical, author and California's commissioner of Housing and Immigration.

The "assembling" of Japanese and Japanese Americans continued through the spring and summer. The evacuation of downtown Los Angeles, where thirty thousand people of Japanese ancestry once lived, was completed on May 8. The *Los Angeles Times* reported on the closing of the last Japanese restaurant in the center of the city under the headline, "Japs Enjoy Their Last Meals in Café Before Internment—Beginning at 8 a.m. Today 2,200 Alien Residents of Colony Will Depart for Santa Anita Center."

The article began, "Today is the beginning of the end for the little Nipponese settlement just east of City Hall. . . . With their departure, Little Tokyo will become a ghost community." The stores became ghost stores, closed and dusty, often with signs in the windows, like the one at an empty grocery in Little Tokyo, which said, MANY THANKS FOR YOUR PATRONAGE. HOPE TO SERVE YOU IN THE NEAR FUTURE. GOD BE WITH YOU UNTIL WE MEET AGAIN. MR. AND MRS. KISERI.

In San Francisco, American Japanese found notes with very different messages slipped under their doors, like this one to the Tamaki family: "This is a warning. Get out. We don't want you in our beautiful country. Go where your ancestors came from. Once a Jap, always one. Get out."

On that same day, in Seattle, Yoshi and Theresa Takayoshi, who had been given a surprise going-away party by Caucasian neighbors, sold their popular ice cream shop. For weeks, they had bought a classified advertisement in local newspapers: "Ice creamery, library lunches, residential spot, sacrifice, evacuee." The shop had machines and inventory insured for $18,000. Dozens of people answered the ad, offering $100 or $200 for the whole thing. The Takayoshis finally settled with a Caucasian buyer for $1,000. They sold their 1940 Oldsmobile for $25.

Theresa, whose father was Japanese and her mother Irish-American, was from New York. She had two sons and they did not find much more kindness after arriving at the Puyallup Assembly Center. The younger one, Thomas, was diagnosed with mumps when his throat began swelling. For six weeks, the growth swelled, turning red. Finally, Theresa's cousin, a registered nurse, came around and then persuaded a physician to come to their stall and he quickly found that the boy had a swollen lymph gland. Then when her older son began vomiting—it was ptomaine poisoning, common in the camps—the same doctor ordered him taken to a hospital in Tacoma. An army car, with a security guard, took mother and son there. Nurses met her with a wheelchair for the boy, but when she began to follow him, the nurse in charge told her, "You can't come in. You're supposed to be in the prison camp."

One of the saddest of many sad stories was told by Hiroshi Kashiwagi of Sacramento. His forty-year-old mother had dental problems, particularly a painful impacted tooth. Because of curfews it was difficult for her to see a dentist. When she did find a dentist, he told her there would be no dental care where she was going. He then proceeded to pull out all her teeth one by one.

* * *

On March 24, uniformed soldiers appeared along the coast, tacking "Civilian Exclusion Order No. 1" on the trees, telephone poles, and walls of Bainbridge Island off Seattle in Puget Sound. The posters read:

NOTICE

HEADQUARTERS: WESTERN DEFENSE COMMAND
AND FOURTH ARMY

1. Pursuant to the provisions of Public Proclamations Nos. 1 and 2 . . . dated March 2, 1942, and March 16, 1942, respectively, it is hereby ordered that all persons of Japanese ancestry, including aliens and non-aliens, be excluded from that portion of Military Area No. 1, described as "Bainbridge Island," in the State of Washington, on or before 12 o'clock noon, P.W.T., of the 30th day of March, 1942.

2. Such exclusion will be accomplished in the following manner:

(a) Such persons may, with permission, on or prior to March 29, 1942, proceed to any approved place of their choosing beyond the limits of Military Area No. 1. . . . On March 30, 1942, all such persons who have not removed themselves from Bainbridge Island in accordance with Paragraph I hereof, shall, in accordance with instructions of the Commanding General, Northwestern Sector, report to the Civil Control Office referred to above on Bainbridge Island for evacuation in such manner and to such place or places shall then be prescribed.

J.L. DeWITT
Lieutenant General, U.S.A.

Booklets dropped on doorsteps listed what the evacuees must carry: "Blankets and linens for each member of the family; Toilet articles for each member of the family; Clothing for each member of the family; Sufficient knives, forks, spoons, plates, bowls, and cups for each member of the family. . . . All items carried will be securely packaged, tied and plainly marked in accordance with instructions received at the Civil Control Office."

There were soldiers and chaos on the island, as there had been when Terminal Island had been cleared by the navy. The scavengers were on Bainbridge, too. Bill Hosokawa, who had just graduated from the University of Washington in Seattle, described their trucks rolling through his neighborhood with drivers shouting, "Hey, you Japs! You're going to get kicked out of here tomorrow. I'll give you ten bucks for that refrigerator. I'll give you fifteen bucks for your piano. I'll give you two bucks and fifty cents for that washing machine." Hiroshi Kamiya was forced to sell his family's pickup truck, with a new battery and four new tires—the brand-new tires alone cost $125—for just $25.

"You trying to sell them?" a man said to Mary Takeuchi, pointing to the gold-ringed china, the family's most treasured possession. He offered $17.50 for the set. Weeping uncontrollably Mrs. Takeuchi, like Mrs. Wakatsuki on Terminal Island, took the plates down one at a time and smashed them at the feet of the man.

So the 271 Japanese and Japanese Americans of Bainbridge Island, 91 aliens and 180 American citizens, mostly farmers and their families who produced three million pounds of strawberries a year, wearing their best clothes, marched to the ferry *Kehloken*, which would take them to Seattle and beyond. They had no idea where beyond was.

The *Seattle Times* reported rather romantically on the departure of the Islanders, editorializing, "If anything ever illustrated the repute of these United States as a melting pot of diverse races, it was the evacuation of Japanese residents, American and foreign-born, from the pleasant countryside of Bainbridge Island. . . . The Japanese departed their homes cheerfully, knowing full well, most of them, that the measures were designed to help preserve the precious, kindly camaraderie among divergent races which is one of this country's great contributions to humanity."

Thirteen of the marchers that day were seniors at Bainbridge High School, who had not been allowed to attend their senior ball the night before because of the 8:00 p.m. curfew for all American Japanese. Many of the white residents of the island lined the ferry road, some of them crying and calling out to friends in the march. Some of the spectators were holding the dogs and cats of the evacuees, who were not allowed to carry pets. Many of the dogs had stopped eating when they were taken from their owners and died within a week or two.

The islanders traveled for more than two days in old railroad cars with curtains drawn to Manzanar, a barren, wind-whipped ghost town 230 miles northeast of Los Angeles in the eastern foothills of the Sierras, on the road between tiny places called Independence and Lone Pine. It was the first camp to open and would be the first camp under the stewardship of the new federal agency the War Relocation Authority.

There was no music and no crowd of white residents waving and crying when the families of Bainbridge arrived at Manzanar. There were construction workers, some of them Japanese volunteers, banging together 504 tar-paper barracks, each barrack divided into six units of sixteen by twenty feet. The camp was surrounded by barbed-wire fences and guard towers with machine guns pointed in toward thirty-six blocks of barracks.

One of the evacuees, Paul Ohtaki, had been a correspondent for the *Bainbridge Island Review*, which had strongly opposed the evacuation, and he filed an upbeat report of that thousand-mile trip from Seattle.

> CAMP MANZANAR, Calif. Wednesday, April 1— Bainbridge Island's evacuated Japanese residents, well and cheerful, arrived here at 12:30 o'clock this afternoon.
>
> The last stage of the trip—which began in Seattle Monday morning—was accomplished by a fleet of busses that met the train at Mojave early this morning. Islanders were greeted by warm sunshine. They found the Owen Valley region to be level land, with high mountains nearby.
>
> Everyone enjoyed the trip, but missed their Island friends. On the train there was group singing, card playing, and "chatting" with the soldiers who accompanied the evacuees. Islanders were treated "swell" by the Army. . . . From private to commanding officer, they extended help and kindness to the Japanese. Some soldiers wept as they guarded the move.

Life magazine took the same tone in six pages of coverage published on April 6. The popular magazine emphasized the beauty of Mount Whitney towering over the horizon fifteen miles away, reporting that other "volunteer" evacuees drove the 240 miles from Los Angeles to Manzanar in a four-mile-long motorcade of their own cars with army jeeps between each ten vehicles. One unnamed evacuee was quoted saying, "We're coming here without bitterness or rancor, wanting to show our loyalty in deeds and words." Then the magazine did add, "Yet Manzanar, for all its hopes and assets, was no idyllic country club. Manzanar was a concentration camp, designed eventually to detain at least 10,000 potential enemies of the United States."

Most first impressions of Manzanar were a great deal more negative than Ohtaki's. Jeanne Wakatsuki said after her first night in Block 16, "We woke early, shivering and coated with dust that had blown up through the knotholes in the floor and through the slits under the door."

Another early arrival, named Yuri Tateishi, had more personal troubles. As she and her children were leaving for Manzanar from the Santa Anita Assembly Center, her one-year-old broke out in measles—epidemics were common in the centers—and was taken from her and kept in a Los Angeles hospital for three weeks. "When we got to Manzanar," she said,

> we went to the mess hall, and I remember the first meal we were given on those tin plates and cups. Canned wieners and canned spinach. . . . It was dark and there were trenches here and there. You'd fall in and get up until you finally got to the barracks. The floors were boarded, but they were about a quarter to a half-inch apart, and the next morning you could see the ground below. What hurt most were those hay mattresses. We were used to a regular home atmosphere. . . . It was depressing, a primitive feeling.

When they woke, on straw-filled bags called mattresses, still wearing street clothes, they discovered that the one faucet for the barracks was frozen solid. It wasn't until noon, as the desert warmed up, that water began to trickle from the faucet.

The place, Manzanar, had a history, primitive and modern. The original inhabitants of Owens Valley were several Native American tribes, particularly Paiutes, who were used as labor and then driven away in the mid-1860s by white settlers, miners, and then farmers attracted by fertile land and the plentiful waters of Lake Owens and the Owens River. It was by all accounts a beautiful place at the base of the snowcapped Sierra Nevada mountain range, often compared to Switzerland. Early in the twentieth century, the city of Los Angeles, desperate for water and expansion, began secretly buying up farms and ranches along the river, which was fed by the snowmelt of the mountains. By 1905, river water was being taken by aqueduct to Los Angeles, particularly for irrigation of the San Fernando Valley. By 1913, city officials wanted more water and built an aqueduct more than two hundred miles long from the valley to the city. Over time, Los Angeles was taking all the water from the river and the lake. By 1929, the valley was a desert wasteland plagued by dust storms from the dry remnants of the ancient lake bed, and the town of Manzanar was abandoned. Like many of the relocation sites, no one lived there after the Japanese left in 1945 and 1946.

· · ·

On May 8, the evacuation notices went up on Vashon Island, just south of Bainbridge. The Matsudas, who farmed two acres of strawberries, turned their farm and house over to a Filipino worker, Mack Garcia. Knowing Garcia could not handle the business side of the farm, they worked out an arrangement with a local sheriff's deputy, B. H. Hopkins, to keep the books and pay the mortgage and buy necessary supplies in return for half the profits. Mary and Yoneichi Matsuda were American citizens, born in Washington, but their tags marked "Family 19788" said "Non-Alien."

When the Vashon ferry reached Seattle, an angry group of white men in coveralls were waiting with shotguns. "Get outta here, you goddamned Japs," one shouted. "I oughta blast your heads off." He spat on Mary Matsuda.

As the evacuation notices went up throughout the western states, there continued to be widespread and growing fear among the American Japanese. It was not only that their lives were being smashed. The Issei, whose average age was fifty-nine, thought there was a chance the government was planning to execute them all. The Nisei, all of them citizens and most of them young—their average age was nineteen—were thoroughly American in their hopes and dreams, only to see their lives ripped up like pieces of paper. Often, the designated evacuees had just a day to put their affairs in order, to sell or rent their houses and farms and cars—usually at a fraction of their real value. Worse than that, thousands of families would lose their homes or farms to foreclosures by banks because their bank accounts were frozen by government order. Many lost their land and the work of a lifetime to plain and open thievery by local officials and residents because California's escheat laws allowed the state and banks to take over "abandoned properties." The furniture of the evacuees and, in fact, almost everything they owned was packed into churches, warehouses, and abandoned buildings, easy targets for thieves and vandals.

The Kobayashi family of Klamath Falls, Oregon, sold their house and barn, their land and crops, tractors and horses for $75. American Japanese in Los Angeles faced vultures who were grabbing up the businesses of Little Tokyo. Frank Emi had given up his pharmacy studies at the University of California in Berkeley to take over the family's prosperous food market at Eleventh and Alvarado Streets in Los Angeles, after his father was badly injured in an automobile accident. A serious young man at twenty-nine, already married and a father himself, he had spent $25,000, all the family had or could borrow, for modern refrigeration cabinets and shelving. Emi had built the place into a small modern supermarket before he was informed he would be evacuated. He had to sell the market and everything in it for $1,500.

Some families took creative measures to protect their property. The Najimas of Petaluma, California, whose father, Jahachi, was already in a Justice Department camp in Montana, got their evacuation notice in May. The two teenage boys in the family, who had pooled their money to buy a good 35 mm camera, were determined not to give it up to the government—or to scavengers and vandals. "They wrapped it up real tightly," said their sister, Irene. "We had an outhouse, and they wrapped up the camera and put it on a big fish hook. Then they lowered it down the outhouse toilet."

Others were overwhelmed with despair about their losses. John Kimoto decided he would burn down his house on the day he was evacuated. "I went to the storage shed to get the gasoline tank and pour the gasoline on my house, but my wife . . . said don't do it, maybe somebody can use this house; we are civilized people, we are not savages."

A few white neighbors promised to look after homes and farms—some kept the promises, some did not. In Sacramento, a state agricultural inspector named Bob Fletcher agreed to take over the maintenance of three Japanese farms with ninety acres of vineyards. He paid the mortgages and taxes in exchange for 50 percent of the profits. When the war ended, the Nitto, Okamoto, and Tsukamoto families returned; their land and their profits were waiting for them. The same kind of thing happened in Fresno, where a prosperous local farmer, a retired major league baseball player named Hubert "Dutch" Leonard, who had won 139 games as a pitcher in the American League between 1913 and 1925, agreed to manage a Japanese farm and turned over $20,000 in profits after the war. But such stories were rare.

• • •

Young people often had the hardest time understanding what was happening to them and their families. "As I passed my high school," remembered Sally Tsuneishi as her train to nowhere pulled out of Los Angeles, "I saw the American flag waving in the wind, and my emotions were in a turmoil. I thought of the prize-winning essay that I had written for my high school English class. It was entitled 'Why I Am Proud to Be an American.' As tears streamed down my face, an awful realization dawned on me: I am a loyal American, yet I have the face of an enemy."

In San Jose, an eleven-year-old boy named Norman Mineta, who was proudly wearing his Cub Scout uniform, had his baseball bat taken away from him by a soldier at his assembly point. Kids were allowed to bring gloves and balls—but no bats. "What did I do to scare the government?" he asked his father.

Another eleven-year-old, Ben Tateishi from San Diego, recalled his walk to an assembly point. "I remember seeing our neighbors peeking out of their curtains. They were friends we used to go to school with, and yet they were not coming out. . . . They were afraid of being called 'Jap lovers.' I felt like an outcast walking down that street. We had a strong feeling of shame."

When they were called to report at assembly points, young couples faced difficult decisions. Few of the American Japanese knew where they were going to be shipped to and, obviously, no one knew when and whether they would be able to return to their old lives. Even apparently benevolent policies designed to keep families together were actually tearing the lives and dreams of both families and individuals to shreds. Young lovers had to make decisions whether to marry; should they go wherever their parents were sent or should they stay together as a new family? And how do you get married when you have forty-eight hours of "freedom" left and are restricted to an area within five miles of your home and need a government license with a three-day waiting period? Arthur and Estelle Ishigo, an aspiring actor and his art student wife, were a mixed-race couple. He was a Nisei, she was Caucasian. They had married in Mexico because interracial marriages were illegal in California. Would she be forced to evacuate? The answer was no, but like several other Caucasian spouses, she chose to go with her husband.

There are a few stories of young people caught in the whirl-winds of local laws and local law enforcement. To begin with, Japanese American students were not allowed to leave their college campuses for Christmas vacations at home with their families. Love, marriage, and normal life were suspended.

Yoshimi Matsura was about to enter California Polytechnic Institute and planned to marry his American Japanese girlfriend in 1942. Forget that. "We decided to get married because we didn't know where her family would be sent," he said. But they needed to get a license from the city hall in Fresno, thirty miles way. They finally found a way to get to Visalia in Tulare County, got a license, and came back three days later to be married. "The government paid for our honeymoon," he said, "in a tar-papered barrack in Gila River, Arizona, with partitions between 'apartments' that did not reach the ceiling. Everyone in each barrack heard every sound."

Hideo Hoshide and his girlfriend walked and talked for hours about what to do. She lived in Seattle and he lived in Tacoma, in eastern Washington, which was then outside General DeWitt's Military Area No. 1. Finally he took her home to Seattle. He sat sadly watching her house for a half hour, a silent good-bye. Suddenly she appeared at the door with a suitcase and ran toward his car. He was stunned.

"I'm going with you," she said. Only thirty years later did she tell her husband that her father had said, "You belong in Tacoma with him."

• • •

The *San Diego Union* had run fourteen editorials in two months calling for the removal of Japanese residents. More than 1,500 internees from San Diego were sent to Santa Anita, one of the most luxurious racetracks in the country. It was immediately called "San Japanita." The internees from San Diego were among the more than 18,500 Southern Californians housed at the famous track. Many of them swore that they were in the stall used by Seabiscuit, the great racehorse of his day. One of the soldiers assigned to the center, Private Leonard Abrams, described what he saw that first day. "We were . . . issued full belts of live ammunition. . . .We formed part of a cordon of troops leading into the grounds, busses kept on arriving and many people walked along . . . many weeping or simply dazed or bewildered."

Richard "Babe" Karasawa, who was fourteen at the time and whose father was being held as a "dangerous person" in Santa Fe, New Mexico, also described the misery pervading the assembly center. The stables were filthy, so much so that Babe Karasawa's mother had tears in her eyes, saying, "We're not going in there." Still, they were lucky in that their neighbors let them borrow their buckets and brooms. In the end, though, as much as they tried to clean the dried horse crud in the crevices of the asphalt, they couldn't get rid of the stench. "There was manure in there with straw stuck on the side where the walls were spray-painted," he reported. "We just kept pouring water on the asphalt and scrubbing it with the broom until we got the asphalt clean and my mother said we could move in."

The conditions were almost unbearable for the evacuees; Karasawa went on to report: "The horse urine was so strong you could never get rid of that smell. So when I'd visit my friend, I couldn't stay there long because of the horse urine. I don't know how they could stand it . . . and I'm from a farm family, I was around horses all the time you know."

Santa Anita was "home" to thousands of strangers trying to re-create a normal life, with only one laundry shack at the beginning. "I never dreamed I would see my children behind barbed wire," said Toshio Kimura. "This is a terrible place. . . . We are not cattle but three times a day, in the morning, noon, and evening, to hear the gong, gong, gong of the bells. Then and there you will see men, women, and children come out of the stables. . . . My heart aches."

Dr. Fred Fujikawa, the Terminal Island physician, volunteered to work at Santa Anita. He remembered how they were forced to make the best of limited staffing and resources: "A long shed that is used for saddling horses was converted into a hospital. I was one of six MDs and two medical students caring for 18,000 people. . . . We treated these people as best we could." They managed to inoculate every person for typhoid, diphtheria, tetanus, and smallpox, but sadly, "Hundreds and hundreds had severe reactions . . . high fever, chills, sore arms and severe diarrhea. . . . Toilet facilities were inadequate with people fainting and releasing their watery stool while waiting their turn in line."

Ironically, Santa Anita may have been the best of the assembly centers. Mary Tsukamoto, who lived outside Sacramento, was sent to the Pinedale center near Fresno. She wrote back to friends: "I saw how terrible it looked, the dust, no trees—just barracks and a bunch of people . . . peeking out from behind the fence." From the Merced center, a woman wrote: "It's not very sanitary here and has caused a great deal of constipation. The toilets are in one big row of seats, that is, one straight board with holes cut a foot apart with no partitions at all. . . . The younger girls couldn't go to them at first until they couldn't stand it anymore."

After three days on a sealed train, Mary Matsuda was shocked when she saw barbed wire and towers at the Pinedale center. She remembered one of her first nights there, when she awoke at 4:00 a.m. and had to use the bathroom. She wrote later, "Once outside, a huge bright light flashed on me. . . . The search light at the nearby watchtower was focused on me. In the darkness the searchlight had grabbed my privacy and exposed it to the camp guards." She fled back to the barracks, but "the light followed me and waited at the doorway as I hid, pressing my body against the inside wall of my family's living space. Finally the searchlight resumed its automatic circuit. Shaking in the darkness I realized that at seventeen, I am a prisoner of war in my own country."

Back at Santa Anita, a five-year-old boy, George Takei, who later became a famous actor, was fond of the searchlights. He thought they were there to help him find his way to the latrine and back—rather than to prevent him from escaping.

The nights and days were an endless series of humiliations for the evacuees. From day one, incarceration began breaking up Japanese families, humiliating fathers and mothers in front of their children—if the fathers were there. At least two thousand heads of families, Issei men, were in prisons, some of them thousands of miles away from their wives and children. Many of the children found freedom and license they never knew before. Chiyo Kusumoto talked about herself and her friend Fusa Tsumagari, saying, "We were pretty sheltered. We didn't go out on dates. So when we got to Santa Anita it was just like a dream—having so many people and going to the grandstands where there were records—and boys and dancing."

Nice enough, but they never got to go to a senior prom or graduation. The 1942 valedictorian of the University of California at Berkeley, Harvey Itano, was in the Sacramento Assembly Center on his graduation day. "Harvey cannot be with us today," said university president Robert Gordon Sproul. "His country has called him elsewhere."

Behind barbed wire.

• • •

As the Bainbridge Island evacuation had dramatized, the Japanese and Japanese Americans on the West Coast were extraordinarily cooperative prisoners. They peaceably gathered at bus stations, parking lots, and crowded street corners, carrying a suitcase or two, a duffel bag, or possessions wrapped in a table-cloth. Their largest civic organization, the JACL, promoted total cooperation with authorities and actively worked with the military and all government personnel to facilitate the opera-tions that took people from their homes. One Washington State strawberry farmer, Mutsuo Hashiguchi, wrote an open letter to his local newspaper saying, "Dear lifetime buddies, pals, and friends, with the greatest of regrets, we leave you for the duration, knowing deep in our hearts that when we return, we will be welcomed back as neighbors. . . . We accept the military order with good grace. We write this letter to thank the community for its past favors shown to us, the spirit of sportsmanship showered upon us, and the wholesome compan-ionship afforded us."

In Berkeley, Yoshiko Uchida wrote on April 21, 1942, that she felt numb as she read the front-page story in the *Oakland Tri-bune* under the headline "Japs Given Evacuation Orders Here." The article reported, "Moving swiftly, without any advance notice, The Western Defense Command today ordered Berkeley's estimated 1,319 Japanese, aliens and citizens alike, to be evacu-ated to the Tanforan Assembly Center by noon, May 1. Evacu-ees will report at the Civil Control Station being set up in Pilgrim Hall of the First Congregational Church between the hours of 8:00 A.M. and 5:00 P.M. next Saturday and Sunday."

The Berkeley posters were Exclusion Order Number 19, uprooting families from their homes and sending them to the racetrack in San Bruno. The Uchidas had just nine days to move—Yoshiko's father, a prosperous businessman, was already in detention somewhere—and were helped by two neighboring families, one Swiss and the other Norwegian. "We had grown up with the two blond Norwegian girls," wrote Uchida. "Their ages nearly matched my sister's and mine. We had played anything from 'house' to 'cops and robbers' with them and had spent many hot summer afternoons happily sipping their father's home-made root beer."

The Uchidas were now "Family 13453"—with numbered tags hanging from their coats. Despite destroyed lives and uncertain futures, few of the victims of the racist hysteria and panic challenged the government. Only a few Nisei protested the government's authority to lock up their families. William Kochiyama angrily described his entrance to Tanforan: "At the entrance stood two lines of troops with rifles and bayonets pointed at the evacuees as they walked through guards to the prison compound. I screamed every obscenity I knew at the armed guards daring them to shoot me."

After families entered, they were in another world, a closed, fearful place. The official story was that the government was protecting the Japanese from violence by whites, but of course the first thing Japanese Americans noticed about the centers and, later, the camps was that the machine guns on towers were pointed in, not out. The Uchidas were assigned Barrack 16, apartment 40, at Tanforan. Yoshiko Uchida described her first sight of their new "home."

> When we reached stall number 40, we pushed open the narrow door and looked uneasily into the vacant darkness. The stall was about ten by twenty feet and empty except for three folded Army cots lying on the floor. Dust, dirt, and wood shavings covered the linoleum that had been laid over manure-covered boards, the smell of horses hung in the air, and the whitened corpses of many insects still clung to the hastily white-washed walls.
>
> High on either side of the entrance were two small windows which were our only source of daylight. The stall was divided into two sections by Dutch doors worn down by teeth marks, and each stall in the stable was separated

from the adjoining one only by rough partitions that stopped a foot short of the sloping roof. . . . Once we got inside the gloomy cavernous mess hall, I saw hundreds of people eating at wooden picnic tables, while those who had already eaten were shuffling aimlessly over the wet cement floor. When I reached the serving table and held out my plate, a cook reached into a dishpan full of canned sausages and dropped two onto my plate with his fingers. Another man gave me a boiled potato and a piece of butterless bread.

There was a daily struggle to make the assembly centers something close to livable. Charles Kikuchi wrote to a friend, "The whole family pitched in to build our new home at Tanforan. We raided the clubhouse and tore off the linoleum from the bar and put it on our floor so now it looks rather homelike. . . . We have only been here three days, but already it seems like weeks."

The facilities were awful at the assembly centers, but for most of the residents, particularly younger ones, a life of ordinary American things went on as if there were nothing unusual about living surrounded by fences, towers, and guns. There were boys playing baseball every day, jitterbug parties every week in most of the camps, where some of the boys wore zoot suits with big-shouldered jackets and tapered pants. One of the girls' social clubs at Tanforan ordered red jackets embroidered with the name "Tan-forettes."

But, as Kikuchi wrote in his diary, family lives were inevitably beginning to change.

Mom is gradually taking things into her own hands. . . . For 28 years she had been restricted in Vallejo, raising children and doing housework. . . . Now she finds herself here with a lot of Japanese, and it has given her a great deal of pleasure to make all these new social contacts. Pop on the

other hand rarely leaves the house and still retains his contempt for the majority of the Japanese residents. His attitude is intensified when he sees that Mom is gradually
moving away from him. I have a suspicion she rather enjoys
the whole thing. She dyed her hair today, and Pop made
some comment that she shouldn't try to act so young.

In fact, Kikuchi was more comfortable with the camp
guards. "Sort of feel sorry for the soldiers," he wrote in his
diary. "They are not supposed to talk to us, but they do. Most
are nice kids . . . but they have nothing to do. . . . One of the
soldiers suggested we get up a volleyball team and we can play
each other over the fence, but the administration would not
think of such a thing." He went on. "What a funny world. They
feel sorry for us in our present situation and we feel sorry for
them because things are so monotonous for them right now."

• • •

For all the army's efficiency in moving around large numbers of
people, army officers had no experience in re-creating civilian
life. Crews built barracks and prison camps—there was a common architecture—but little was done about setting up schools,
stores, or other civilian institutions. It was the evacuees themselves who began transforming the racetracks and livestock
pavilions into something like poor and overcrowded American
small towns with schools, churches, newspapers, and ordinary hospitals staffed by evacuee doctors and nurses. And there
were bars. Alcohol was prohibited in the assembly centers and
later the relocation camps, but small stills were everywhere,
making sake, the Japanese rice wine, and stronger stuff made
from raisins, potatoes, and sweet potatoes.

Men and children gathered scrap wood to build furniture for
their stables and to build playgrounds for young children. Within

weeks, even days, boys and men built baseball diamonds and organized more than eighty leagues at Santa Anita alone. There were Parent-Teacher Associations, garden clubs, Boy Scout and Girl Scout troops, and an American Legion post for the Issei who had served in World War I. Women made curtains for privacy in the latrines and shower rooms. At the Fresno Assembly Center, the evacuees formed a chorus to recite the Gettysburg Address to celebrate the Fourth of July. There were American flags everywhere in the centers and camps—and soon there were a few of the little red-white-and-blue window pennants showing a son was serving in the military. A couple already had a gold star in the center, indicating a son or husband had been killed in action. Evacuees also created newspapers in all the centers and camps. In April, the *Santa Anita Pacemaker* included these headlines: "Golf Driving Range Now Ready for Use," "Model Airplane Meet Results," "Henry Ogawa Upsets Tanaka in Sumo Bout."

Nisei students from Stanford, Berkeley, UCLA, and other colleges and universities organized elementary and high school classes in the grandstands or pavilions at the racetracks and fairgrounds. "We would have seminar classes. Of course, that was very difficult," said one young volunteer teacher. "Most of us were looking out beyond the trees and we could see cars whizzing by and wishing we were out there too."

"At the first high school assembly," said another volunteer, Toyo Kawakami, "after the morning program was finished, as the students stood to return . . . they began to sing, 'God Bless America.' These young people believed in the land of their birth. We teachers could only gaze at each other, some of us with tears."

• • •

Charles Kikuchi, who had always had trouble getting along with his father, had been put in an orphanage at age eight, the only Japanese boy in the place. He rejoined his family when they were interned at Tanforan, and it was the first and only time he lived among many other Japanese and Japanese Americans. By then, he was twenty-six years old and in his diary, on May 7, 1942, he provided a fairly detailed profile of his fellow detainees at Tanforan and their fracturing families.

> There are all different types of Japanese in company seven. The young *Nisei* are quite Americanized and have nice personalities. They smile easily and are not inhibited in their actions. They have taken things in stride and their sole concern is to meet the other sex, have dances so they can jitterbug, get a job to make money for "Cokes." Many are using the evacuation to break away from the strict control of parental rule.
>
> Other *Nisei* think more in terms of the future. . . . They want to continue their education in some sort of "career," to study and be successful. The background which they come from is very noticeable: their parents were better educated and had businesses. I asked a girl what her father expected to do after the war and she said that he and his wife would probably be forced to leave this country, but she expects to get married and stay here.

Kikuchi felt the same way, writing, "I just can't help identifying myself with America; I feel so much a part of it and I won't be rejected."

Another time, Kikuchi commented on how American Japanese "can't throw off the environmental effects of the American way of life which is ingrained in them." He went on to say with some hope: "The injustices of evacuation will someday come to light. It is a blot upon our national life—like the Negro problem, the way labor gets kicked around, the unequal distribution of wealth, the sad plight of the farmers, the slums of our large cities, and a multiple of things."

● ● ●

At the centers many kids ran wild for the first time in their lives. At Santa Anita, meals were served in shifts for three thousand people at a time, military-style at long tables seating at least thirty-two people. Instead of sitting with their parents, family-style, young Japanese Americans would go to far ends of the mess halls to sit and eat with their friends. Yoshiko Uchida, earning $16 a month at the Tanforan Assembly Center, a standard salary for evacuee teachers, noticed that when her second-grade girls at the makeshift school played house, they had their dolls lining up at a little mess hall.

Parents were being publicly shamed, unable to control their own children. Among the things they worried about were promiscuity, rape, and even prostitution. Charles Kikuchi, the grad student at Berkeley, wrote the diary he faithfully kept about a "bull session" with friends.

> J.Y. said that a lot of the bachelors sent an unsigned letter to the Administration asking for licensed prostitution here because they "were going nuts."
>
> J. thought the only solution was to put a few professional women here on a P&T (Professional and Technical) rating by the Administration to protect the young girls. . . . He claimed that promiscuity was growing after only three months here and the young fellows especially were developing a "what the hell" attitude. B. made some exaggerated claim that 300 unmarried girls were pregnant at Santa Anita. S. said a father over where he lived gives his daughter a loud cross-examination every time she goes out because he is so suspicious. He said that a lot of *Issei* parents don't let their daughters out at all because of all the rumors that they have heard about young girls being raped.

J. said the reason the most of the *Nisei* would not get married was because they still clung to the idea that we would be out of the camps in a year. "The Japanese in this country we're through," he said, "regardless of who wins the war."

• • •

When they were home in San Diego, many young Japanese had been befriended and mentored by an extraordinary woman named Clara Breed, the children's librarian at the city library's main branch. Dozens of young Nisei came to the building to study and read after school. Miss Breed, appalled at the mass roundups, went to the trains and buses leaving town and gave "her" children small gifts and, more important, her address, postcards, envelopes, and stamps. Their letters, collected in a 2006 book by Joanne Oppenheim, provide a unique view of the evacuation, the assembly centers, and camp life. Katherine Tasaki, a ten-year-old from San Diego, was one of dozens of children from that city who corresponded throughout the war with Clara Breed. In her first card from Santa Anita, Katherine was as cheerful as she was young: "I am having a good time. Lots of my relatives live here, we can see Mt. Wilson from here. The grandstand was made into a cafeteria. There is a playground for children."

There was indeed a playground, but the center was still in very rough shape. Latrines and laundry buildings were unfinished and, as Margaret Ishino wrote to Miss Breed, she was in charge of her two-and-half-month-old sister and the only place the baby could sleep was in a horse trough. The Ishinos did what almost everyone with any family money did: purchase mail-order supplies from the catalogs Sears Roebuck and Montgomery Ward. For the baby, they ordered a buggy.

Seventeen-year-old Louise Ogawa, who had been a junior at San Diego High, was one of Miss Breed's most faithful correspondents, one of many who would send her small amounts of money they earned as waitresses or doing other camp chores—they were paid $12 a month and professionals, such as doctors and teachers, were paid $16 or $19—and she would do shopping for them back in San Diego. One of Louise's first notes was dated January 6, 1942:

> Dear Miss Breed,
>
> I received the sweater and my brother's shorts. Thank you very much for going through so much trouble for me. . . . I was very glad to hear you liked the flowers. I wish I could have sent 10 dozen Am. beauty roses (red ones) to show my appreciation for everything you have done for me. In my last letter I said the fence was torn down—well, it is up again. This time a few feet further out. We have been told that the reason for the fence building was so the cattle won't come near our homes. In other words, cattle is going to be grazed outside the fence. But as yet, we have not seen any. Yes, I think the fence tends to weaken the morale of the people.

On April 23, Louise wrote:

> I just received two intensely interesting books which you so kindly sent. . . . The first thing I did after receiving the books was to run to my parents. . . . Then I ran to Margaret Ishino and showed them to her. I was so happy. . . .
>
> This is my third week at Santa Anita. It is a beautiful place. I visited Seabiscuit's statue and have gone around the racetrack several times. . . . "I am sleeping where Seabiscuit used to sleep" is a common saying here. . . . I heard we are going to have a library soon. It was the best news I've heard. . . .

> Every day there is a line blocks and blocks long. I often
> wait an hour or two at the mess hall. . . . Father, brother,
> sister and I went every day to the scrap wood pile to find
> wood to make our furniture. . . . Bitter feelings do not enter
> my head. . . . If I am helping the government by staying
> here, I am glad. I want so much to be some help for my Govt.

Miss Breed, who kept all of the letters she received, wrote an article on the incarceration for *Library Journal*, a national magazine, and, after visiting the Santa Anita Assembly Center, quoted a small girl she had overheard talking to her mother: "I am tired of Japan, Mother. Let's go back to America."

• • •

Masuo Yasui, a merchant, a member of the local Rotary Club, and an influential leader of the Japanese community in Hood River, Oregon, was arrested after Pearl Harbor and imprisoned in an army jail in Fort Missoula, Montana. Because his son Minoru was an attorney and a lieutenant in the army reserve, Minoru was allowed to sit in at his father's internment hearing in Fort Missoula. The evidence against the older man included the fact that he had vacationed in Japan in 1925 and was later awarded a medal by the Japanese government for fostering Japanese American friendship.

The military prosecutor in Missoula suddenly held up childish drawings of the Panama Canal. "Didn't you," the officer asked, "have these maps and drawings so you could direct the blowing up of the locks of the canal?"

"This is just the schoolwork of my children," said Masuo. The children's names were on the drawings.

"No," said the questioner. "We think you've cleverly disguised your nefarious intent and are using your children merely as a cover."

"No. No. No."

"Prove that you didn't intend to blow up the Panama Canal."

The Yasui children, almost laughingly, were no threat to the canal, but security of the path from the Atlantic to the Pacific was a legitimate obsession of American officials. Military security was only one of the reasons the United States, with the enthusiastic cooperation of Latin American countries, decided to take on the costs of rounding up at gunpoint more than two thousand Latin Americans of Japanese descent. In fact, the forced removal—kidnapping really—and imprisonment of Japanese immigrants and their descendants stretched across the Americas, from Latin America to Canada.

The U.S. Department of State, working with the Justice Department, concluded agreements with ten Central and South American countries to arrest residents of Japanese ancestry, most of whom were then turned over to American military authorities and flown by U.S. Army Air Corps planes to camps or prisons in the United States. The Latin American Japanese were held in American prisons to be used in bartering for the repatriation of American citizens held in Japan and in areas occupied by Imperial Japanese troops. A State Department internal memo on that project stated: "Nations of Central America and the Caribbean islands have in general been willing to send us subversive aliens without placing any limitation on our disposition of them. In other words, we could repatriate them, we could intern them, or we could hold them in escrow for bargaining purposes [with the government of Japan]."

The Army Air Corps sent dozens of planes and ships—and combat-equipped troops—to Latin American airports and seaports on an "urgent" basis in 1942 and early 1943 to pick up Japanese immigrants living in ten countries, most of them in Peru. That country's president, Ignacio Prado, wanted to get rid of all Japanese, including naturalized Peruvian citizens. Most of them were held by the Justice Department in Crystal City, Texas, or on U.S. Army bases in the Panama Canal Zone. In addition, Mexico agreed to put Japanese residents living near the U.S. border in a series of small concentration camps. Costa Rica interned Japanese residents on an island. The two Japanese residents of Paraguay were jailed in that country as well. By war's end eight hundred Latin American Japanese were sent to Japan, traded for U.S. diplomats and other American citizens who had been interned in Japan on December 7, 1941. After the war, Peru refused to accept the return of its citizens and former resident aliens. The United States then declared that they were all illegal aliens who had entered the United States without valid passports and began deporting them to Japan, a country most of them had never seen.

The government of Canada, which entered World War II with Great Britain against Germany in 1939, relocated 23,000 persons of Japanese ancestry after declaring war on Japan. They were moved to camps and abandoned mining towns in the interior of the country; three-quarters of those interned were Canadian citizens. Males sixteen or older were ordered to assembly areas as early as mid-January 1942. On February 27, the Canadian government issued an order for all Japanese in the western provinces to be moved inland. The evacuees' property was confiscated and auctioned off to help pay for the evacuation and internment. Former residents of British Columbia were not allowed to return to Canada's west coast until 1949. In Alaska, then an American territory, the United States evacuated 151 persons of Japanese ancestry to the relocation center at Minidoka, Idaho.

• • •

While thousands quietly entered the assembly centers and camps across the Americas, a few fought back. Masuo Yasui's son, Minoru, was one of them. He was an American citizen, a Phi

Beta Kappa graduate of the University of Oregon and its law school and an officer in the army reserve. He tried nine times, in uniform, to enlist in the regular army and was turned away nine times. When Minoru's father, Masuo, was sent back to jail after the interrogation about his younger children's Panama Canal drawings, Minuro went back to Oregon and decided to deliberately violate the 8:00 p.m. curfew for Japanese in Portland so that he could file a lawsuit. He walked the streets until 11:00 p.m., but foot patrolmen refused to arrest him, so he finally turned himself in at the Second Avenue police station. "Jap Spy Arrested" was the front-page headline in the *Portland Oregonian.*

Minoru Yasui was sent first to the assembly center at the North Portland Livestock Pavilion, where there were already more than three thousand people living in stalls built for cattle, hogs, and sheep. After being taken to the Minidoka camp in Idaho, he was brought back to Portland, where he was found guilty of choosing loyalty to Japan rather than the United States. The evidence, which put him in Multnomah County jail in solitary confinement for nine months, was that he had worked as a clerk in the Japanese consulate in Chicago, after being turned away by a dozen law firms in Oregon. He had quit his job at the consulate in Chicago on December 8, 1941.

Minoru's conviction would be appealed all the way to the U.S. Supreme Court. His case became one of four American Japanese challenges to the curfews and evacuations to reach the high court. The others were brought by Gordon K. Hirabayashi, Fred Korematsu, and Mitsuye Endo.

Gordon Hirabayashi, a senior at the University of Washington, was a Quaker whose parents had converted to Christianity in Japan. He had declared he was a conscientious objector before the war. He decided to defy the evacuation and curfew orders and went to an FBI office to report his deliberate violations—and was jailed on the spot. In a letter he wrote on May 13, 1942, he said:

This order for the mass evacuation of all persons of Japanese descent denies them the right to live. It forces thousands of energetic, law-abiding citizens to exist in a miserable psychological and horrible physical atmosphere. . . . It kills the desire for a higher life. Hope for the future is exterminated. . . . I must maintain my Christian principles. I consider it my duty to maintain the democratic standards for which this nation lives.

He was promised legal help from the American Civil Liberties Union in San Francisco, but ACLU national headquarters in New York and its founding director, Roger Baldwin, backed away from his case. A friend of President Roosevelt, Baldwin wrote to ACLU offices around the country in June of 1942 stating that he and the ACLU's national board wanted to keep the organization's name out of any filings by individual attorneys. "We cannot participate," he said, "except in challenging the evacuation order as it applies to Japanese Americans on the basis of race discrimination. . . . Local committees are not to sponsor cases in which the position is taken that the government has no constitutional right to remove citizens from military areas." Hirabayashi was convicted by the Federal District Court in Seattle and appealed the decision to the Supreme Court.

Fred Korematsu was born and raised in Oakland to immigrant parents who ran a floral nursery, and after high school graduation he worked as a shipyard welder until he lost his job after Pearl Harbor. Like many other Nisei, he was rejected when he tried to enlist, first by the U.S. National Guard and then by the U.S. Coast Guard. His parents and three brothers reported to the Tanforan Assembly Center on May 9, but he refused to go to the incarceration camps, deciding instead to go underground. He had minor plastic surgery to change the look of his eyes and planned to move to the Midwest with his Italian-American girlfriend, Ida Boitano. The plan fell apart; his surgery failed to make him look more European, and he and his girlfriend broke up. So, changing his name to Clyde Sarah on a forged draft card, he claimed to be of Spanish and Hawaiian descent and was hired as a welder at a navy shipyard near San Francisco, rising through the ranks to foreman.

Korematsu was arrested on May 30 on a street corner in San Leandro, California, and taken to the San Francisco county jail. Ernest Besig, director of the ACLU of Northern California, visited him in jail, and asked Korematsu if he was willing to be a test case to challenge the constitutionality of the mass evacuation. When Korematsu agreed, Besig and another ACLU lawyer, Wayne Collins, represented him in federal court in San Francisco—against the wishes of ACLU leaders in New York. Judge Adolphus F. St. Sure rejected Besig's argument that Korematsu, an American citizen, was being denied due process. St. Sure released Korematsu on $2,500 bail, pending an appeal. But as Korematsu left the courtroom, a military policeman holding a gun took him into custody and delivered him to the Tanforan Assembly Center. Korematsu was later convicted in federal court for violating Executive Order 9066. Represented by Collins, who left the ACLU, Korematsu fought his case through the courts and he, too, appealed to the Supreme Court.

Mitsuye Endo was from Sacramento and had been a California state employee before being removed to Tanforan and then the Tule Lake Relocation Center. She was contacted by a civil liberties attorney, James Purcell, about challenging her evacuation. She seemed to have a strong case: she was a U.S. government worker, her brother was in the U.S. Army, and she had no connections to the Japanese government. Purcell filed a habeas corpus petition on her behalf; when it was denied, her case was appealed and was eventually brought to the U.S. Supreme Court.

In a unanimous decision in 1943, the Court decided two of the four challenges, ruling against Hirabayashi's and Yasui's appeals, stating that the curfew was constitutional under the government's war powers. Korematsu's and Endo's cases reached the Supreme Court as well, but judgments were deliberately delayed until after the 1944 presidential election.

4

"KEEP THIS A WHITE MAN'S COUNTRY"

THE OPENING OF THE CONCENTRATION CAMPS:
MARCH 22 TO OCTOBER 6, 1942

On April 7, 1942, the governors of ten western states met with Milton Eisenhower of the War Relocation Authority and Colonel Bendetsen of the Wartime Civil Control Administration in Salt Lake City, Utah, to discuss the relocation of the West Coast Japanese from assembly centers to camps in the badlands of their states. "The people of Wyoming have a dislike for any Orientals and simply will not stand for being California's dumping ground," said Governor Nels Smith of Wyoming, shaking his fist at Eisenhower. "If you bring Japanese into my state, I promise you they will be hanging from every tree."

The governor of Arizona, Sidney Osborn, repeated the "dumping ground" line. Utah's Herbert Maw said he thought there was too much emphasis on constitutional rights. Then he stood up and shouted: "The Constitution could be changed. . . . If these people are dangerous on the Pacific Coast they will be dangerous here!" The governor of Idaho, Chase Clark, said, "The Japs live like rats, breed like rats and act like rats. I don't want them coming into Idaho." He later compromised, saying he would accept American Japanese "only if they were in concentration camps under military guard." The state's attorney general, Bert Miller, backed him up: "All Japanese must be in concentration camps for the remainder of the war. . . . We want to keep this a white man's country."

Only one governor, Ralph Carr of Colorado, said he would accept American Japanese in his state. "If you harm them, you must harm me. I was brought up in a small town where I knew the shame and dishonor of race hatred. I grew to despise it because it threatened the happiness of you and you and you."

Soon enough, the federal officials realized that the relocation of the *Nikkei* was going to be more difficult than first imagined. Finding the Japanese and Japanese Americans had not been difficult. Although for more than forty years the Census Bureau denied it—admitting the truth only in 2007—the 1940 census had just been completed and Census Bureau records were moved to the Presidio in San Francisco, so the army and the FBI had maps of where almost every Japanese family lived. The problem was where to put them, and how to move them. And there were still questions about who would be in charge of the relocation camps.

It was not only officials and bureaucrats who were wary or just plain scared about the evacuation. May and June of 1942 became one of the peaks of hysteria in the West, as reports reached the public of the fall of Corregidor, one of the last American outposts in the Philippines. More than seventy-five thousand starving Filipino and American troops, many of them crippled by disease, surrendered on the Bataan Peninsula and Corregidor, a rocky island in Manila Bay, in April and May of

1942 and were marched through eighty miles of jungle on their way to a Japanese prisoner of war camp. Thousands of Filipinos and hundreds of Americans died on the brutal march. Though the fall of Corregidor was reported in 1942, news of what would be called the Bataan Death March was kept from the American public until January of 1944.

The fall of the Philippines and the perception that Japan was winning the war turned some Issei and Nisei against each other. Charles Kikuchi was walking through the grandstands in Tanforan when he saw an old Issei smiling, talking to a friend about the Philippines. "About time, no?"

"It made my blood boil," said Kikuchi. He challenged the old man, who asked him who he was for in the war. "America," he answered. "The man," wrote Kikuchi, "called me and my friends fools, saying they could never become Americans. 'Only the *Ketos* [literally, hairy people] could become Americans.'"

One of the units captured by the Japanese army on Corregidor was the 200th Coast Artillery Battery, originally made up of eighteen hundred reservists from the New Mexico National Guard, more than a third of them Hispanic Americans or Native Americans. At least two hundred of them died on the march, some shot or bayoneted if they could not keep walking. In Santa Fe, where local families did not know much about the details of what was happening in the Philippines, telegrams were arriving announcing the deaths of their young men at the places called Corregidor and Bataan. Local residents armed with shotguns and hatchets marched on the nearby internment camp where hundreds of the so-called dangerous Issei were being held, determined to kill as many American Japanese as they could. They were talked out of it by officials who said that a massacre would invite retaliation on the rest of the American soldiers being held in the Philippines.

Other towns struggled with their own conflicting reactions to the movement of prisoners and evacuees to their areas. In Lone Pine, a ranching town of 1,071 people six miles south of the Manzanar Assembly Center and Relocation Camp, twenty-two local merchants signed a letter to the army requesting that small numbers of internees be allowed to shop at their businesses. Other townspeople, five hundred of them, then signed another petition asking that the evacuees be kept behind barbed wire. The town barber said, "We ought to take those yellow-tails right down to edge of the Pacific and say to 'em, 'Okay boys, over there's Toyko. Start walkin'." A county supervisor in Inyo County, which had a population 7,625, said, "A Jap's a Jap, and by God I wouldn't trust one of them as far as I could throw a bull by the tail." A flight instructor at a small local airstrip added, "It's a plain case of survival of the fittest. It's either us or the god-damned Yellow-bellies! What are we waiting for? The Army needs target practice on those sons-of-bitches."

Nine miles north of Manzanar, in Independence, the Inyo County seat and a town slightly bigger than Lone Pine, a store-keeper's wife said, "There's people in Independence who were just frightened out of their wits. They thought the Japanese were going to break out of Manzanar and we'd all be slaughtered in our beds." A former official at Manzanar added, "I can't remember the guy's name, but there was a man in Independence who formed his own militia and was training people. . . . They were going to save the women and children of Independence."

• • •

As the government wrestled with issues of authority, logistics, and statistics, the spring of 1942 was a time of anguish and uncertainty for American Japanese families and individuals in the three West Coast states. The army, with the help of civilian contractors, was still searching for relocation sites, usually on empty land already owned by the federal government. The military was designing and building—sometimes with the help of American Japanese volunteers—President Roosevelt's "concentration camps." Ten locations were finally chosen from the dry lake beds and lava fields in the far north of California to Arizona deserts and Indian reservations and swampland in Arkansas. By the summer of 1942, most of the Japanese and Japanese Americans had been moved or were in the process of being moved from the assembly centers, Santa Anita and the sixteen others. Most of the camps were ready—almost ready, anyway. Beginning on March 22, the army had begun moving people inland from the assembly centers. The long, slow, and dirty trains—171 of them—were alternately too hot and very cold, always dark, with window shades pulled so the evacuees could not see where they were going.

Estelle Ishigo, the white woman who chose to go with her husband, Arthur Ishigo, a Nisei, to the camps, wrote back her impression of the first relocation camp, Manzanar. "The sight of the barbed wire enclosure with armed soldiers standing guard as our bus turned slowly through the gate stunned us. . . . Here was a camp of sheds enclosed with a high barbed wire fence, with guard towers and soldiers with machine guns."

Manzanar opened on March 22 and became a relocation camp under WRA control, built to hold ten thousand "evacuees," or prisoners, from Bainbridge Island, Los Angeles, and San Joaquin County, California. Nine more camps opened between May 8 and October 6.

Poston, Arizona, was one of the first to open, starting on May 8. It was actually three camps—Poston I, II, and III—built on an Indian reservation near the California border. Its peak population was 17,814. People there came from all over California and southern Arizona and they called the camps "Roastin', Toastin', and Dustin'."

Tule Lake, California, a former Civilian Conservation Corps camp built on lava beds close to the Oregon border, opened soon after, on May 27, and accommodated a peak of 18,789 people from Sacramento, Oregon, and Washington. When a young opera singer well known in the Sacramento area, Fumiko Yabe, was headed for Tule Lake, she bought a bathing suit, not knowing that the lake had disappeared into a barren plain five hundred years before.

Early that summer, with seven of the ten relocation centers still to open, Milton Eisenhower left the WRA. He hated the job, earlier telling his boss, Secretary of Agriculture Claude Wickard, that he had intended to use the camps as platforms to move the evacuees into useful jobs around the country. In the end, his inclination did not matter. On June 17, when the Office of War Information director, Elmer Davis, offered Eisenhower the position of assistant director, he jumped at the chance.

Eisenhower, desperate to leave the WRA, had recruited his own successor: Dillon Myer, a lifetime civil servant who was serving as deputy director of the Department of Agriculture's Bureau of Soil Conservation Service. Eisenhower and Myer were friends. At a dinner one night, Myer asked Eisenhower one last time if he should take the job. "Yes, if you can do the job and sleep at night. I couldn't."

Eisenhower was offered a new position only eleven days after the U.S. Navy, with the crucial (and secret) help of Japanese American code breakers and translators, crushed the Imperial Japanese Navy at the Battle of Midway. It was the turning point of the Pacific War. Thereafter, there was almost no chance the Japanese military could approach the West Coast of the United States, much less invade California, Oregon, or Washington.

So, by the time Myer took over, "military necessity" was effectively dead as an argument for the camps. On that same day, June 17, 1942, the director of the American Friends Service

Committee, C. Reid Carey, told a church conference, "We are doing exactly the same things as the Germans."

Still, the camps were being built and continued opening. The openings under Myer were:

Gila River, Arizona, opened on June 20. The land, a reservation, was the home of the Gila River Indian Tribe and held a peak of 13,348 people from Fresno County, Sacramento, and Los Angeles.

Minidoka, Idaho, near the town of Hunt, opened August 10, with a peak population of 9,397, and held people from Seattle, Portland, and northwestern Oregon. One of the first arrivals there, Monica Sone, wrote, "We felt as if we were standing in a gigantic sand-mixing machine as the 60-mile gale lifted the loose earth into the sky, obliterating everything. Sand filled our mouths and nostrils and stung our faces and hands like a thousand darting needles."

Heart Mountain, Wyoming, with prisoners from Los Angeles and Santa Clara County, California, opened on August 12. Peak population was 10,767.

Amache (also called Granada), Colorado, built on a treeless prairie for prisoners from all over California, opened on August 24. Peak population was 7,318.

Topaz, Utah, with a peak population of 8,130 evacuees from the San Francisco Bay Area, opened September 11.

Rohwer in McGehee, Arkansas, opened on September 18. The camp held people from Los Angeles and San Joaquin, California. "It was a living nightmare," an evacuee wrote of Rohwer. "The water stagnated at the front steps. . . . The mosquitoes that festered there were horrible, and the administration never had enough quinine for sickness."

Jerome, Arkansas, was the last camp to open, on October 6, 1942. The people interned there were from the San Joaquin Valley and San Pedro Bay area, and the camp had a peak population of 8,497. Later on, Rohwer residents were moved to Jerome, and Rohwer was converted into a prisoner of war camp housing captured German soldiers.

The camps and various federal prisons, at their peak, held a total of 120,313 American Japanese, alien and citizen. Of those, 92,786 were Californians. Their new "homes" were described this way by the California Site Survey of the National Park Service:

> The camp interiors were arranged like prisoner of war camps or overseas military camps, and were completely unsuited for family living. Barracks were divided into blocks and each block had a central mess hall, latrine, showers, wash basins, and laundry tubs. Toilets, showers, and bedrooms were unpartitioned; there was no water or plumbing in the living quarters; and anyone going to the lavatory at night, often through mud or snow, was followed by a searchlight. Eight-person families were placed in 20-x-20-foot rooms, six-person families in 12-x-20-foot rooms, and four-person families in 8-x-20-foot rooms. Smaller families and single persons had to share units with strangers. Each detainee received a straw mattress, an army blanket, and not much else. Privacy was non-existent. Everything had to be done communally. Endless queues formed for eating, washing, and personal needs.

A conscientious objector named Don Elberson was assigned to meet each trainload of evacuees arriving at Tule Lake. "It was brutal," he remembered.

> Some days we had to process 500 or more people. . . . Nothing mitigated the moment I had to take them to their new homes. You'd have to take these people into this dingy excuse for a room, twenty by twenty-five feet at best. These

were people who'd left everything behind, sometimes fine houses. I learned after the first day not to enter with the family, but to stand outside. It was too terrible to witness the pain in people's faces, too shameful for them to be seen in this degrading situation.

His daughter, Marnie, was born while he was at Tule Lake, the first Caucasian child born there. In later years, when she changed schools as her family moved around after the war, teachers would ask where she was born and she would answer, "Tule Lake Japanese American Relocation Camp in California." Some of those teachers said there was no such place and the little girl learned to say, simply, "California."

The WCCA began moving ten thousand of the evacuees at the Santa Anita Assembly Center to the Manzanar Relocation Center or to one of the three relocation camps holding seventeen thousand people in Poston, Arizona, on May 29, 1942. The government estimated that within two to three months, all Japanese would be in one of the ten relocation camps, even though many of the barracks were not complete. Some of the letters sent to the Friends Service as Santa Anita closed down said things like, "I do hope the women can get better toilets and showers. They cannot bear the toilets where they must sit side to side and back to back (with strangers) and no partitions."

After they arrived at Manzanar, Jeanne Wakatsuki's mother, Riku, was one of the women who carried large unfolded detergent boxes to hide behind in the rows of toilet seats in the women's latrines. Many of the women would go into the latrines only late at night for a bit of privacy and to avoid the long lines of other women waiting outside.

Leland Ford, a California congressman with no love for the camp residents, had said from the beginning, "All Japanese, whether citizens or not, must be placed in inland concentration camps." Still, even he was a bit shocked when he saw Manzanar. "On dusty days, one might just as well be outside as inside at Manzanar."

Jeanne Wakatsuki later wrote that the evacuees Ford and other officials saw were "a band of Charlie Chaplins marooned in the California desert." The American Japanese, who were not told where they were going, had arrived in the high desert camp in the summer clothes of Southern California to find that nighttime temperatures were below freezing and then way below freezing in fall and winter. The army shipped in truckloads of surplus cold weather gear, including coats, hats, boots, gloves, and wool knit caps, all left over from World War I and all in sizes way too large for the evacuees. The floppy coats and pants did make them look like so many circus clowns. Finally the army responded to demands for sewing machines; for weeks, the women of the camp cut and sewed the oversized clothes. "They flopped, they dangled, they hung," said Miss Wakatsuki, until the clothes were remade into smaller and more fashionable slacks, coats, and capes by the women of Manzanar.

"Once the weather warmed up in the daytime, it was an out-of-doors life," she continued, "where you only went 'home' at night, when you finally had to: 10,000 people were on an endless promenade inside the square mile of barbed wire that was the wall around the our city."

The end of the trail for the Poston evacuees was Parker, Arizona, the town near the Poston Indian Reservation on the California border. The temperature was 102 degrees when Shizuko Tokushige, a new mother, arrived. She described the cruel end of her trip, transferring from a train to the camp bus.

A solider said, "Let me help you, put your arm out."
He proceeded to pile everything on my arm. And to my

horror, he placed my two-month-old baby on top of the stack. He then pushed me with the butt of the gun and told me to get off the train, knowing when I stepped off the train my baby would fall to the ground. I refused. But he kept prodding and ordering me to move. I will always be thankful [that] a lieutenant checking the cars came upon us. He took the baby down, gave her to me, and then ordered the solider to carry all our belongings to the bus and see that I was seated and then report back to him.

The new residents of Poston felt the same shock as those who got off the buses at Manzanar. "There is going to be a fence around the camp!" Tetsuzo (Ted) Hirasaki wrote from the Arizona Indian Reservation. "Five strands of barbed wire! They say it's to keep the people out. . . . What people? The Redskins!" He also heard claims that the fence was to keep out cattle. "Where in cattle country do they use five-strand barbed wire? If they don't watch out there's going to be trouble. What do they think we are, fools?"

Another former San Diegan, Kiyuji Alzumi, wrote of his impression of arrival: "Extreme heat that can melt iron. No trees, no flowers, no birds singing, not even the sound of an insect, sandy dust whirled into the sky, completely taking the sunshine and light from us."

Charles Kikuchi, the diarist, learned that he was headed for Topaz in Utah. In one of his last diary entries from Tanforan, he had written, "I ran across something interesting today. Down by the stables there is an interesting old rest room which says 'Gents' on one side and 'Colored Gents' on the other. . . . To think that such a thing is possible in California is surprising."

The Uchida family at Tanforan was also on the Topaz list. Their neighbors back in Berkeley, a Swiss family, drove to Tanforan to say good-bye once more with baskets of food and flowers.

But the children, both under sixteen, were not allowed inside the assembly center. Hearing that, the Uchida girls raced to the camp's main gate, where they saw their friends.

"Teddy! Bobby!" Yoshiko called, running to the fence. The four children reached through the barbed wire, squealing with delight, when a soldier lowered his rifle toward them, saying, "Hey, get away from the fence, you two."

Decades later, the Uchida children remembered this incident. They said they thought they were about to be shot.

The Topaz Relocation Camp, where the Uchido girls and their mother were incarcerated, was in the Sevier Desert, on a high and windy plateau in southwest Utah. It was a shock, to say the least, for the daughter of a successful American family. She was a Berkeley graduate, planning to be a schoolteacher.

After arriving in Topaz, the Uchidas and other evacuees were handed a list of camp rules, which, under the section called "Restrictions," included:

a. Stay within signs of limited area
b. Do not pick fruit
c. No fishing without license
d. Do not dig flower plants
e. No trespassing on farming areas
f. Help prevent fire hazards
g. Do not dig or damage trees
h. No wading or otherwise polluting creek water
i. Do not disturb birds or animals

Yoshiko Uchida chose to avoid the officials enforcing these rules. "Sometimes as we walked," she wrote, "we could hear the MPs singing in their quarters and then they seemed something more than the sentries who patrolled the barbed wire perimeters of our camp, and we realized they were lonely young boys far from home, too. Still, they were on the other side of the fence, and they represented the Army we had come to fear and distrust. We never offered them our friendship, although at times they tried to talk to us."

The lonely and bored young soldiers, probably just as disoriented, watched over the camp in this bleak landscape. Miss Uchida described her new "home" this way:

> The camp was one mile square and eventually housed 8,000 residents, making it the fifth largest city in the state of Utah. As we plodded through the powdery sand toward Block 7, I began to understand why everyone looked like pieces of flour-dusted pastry. In its frantic haste to construct this barrack city, the Army had removed every growing thing, and what had once been a peaceful lake bed was now churned up into one great mass of loose flour-like sand. With each step we sank two to three inches deep, sending up swirls of dust that crept into our eyes and mouths, noses, and lungs.

A great many of the residents were constantly sick, with upset stomachs and colds, especially in the winter. "Illness was a nuisance," she wrote, "especially after we began to work, for memos from a doctor were required to obtain sick leave. We had no idea when the water would be turned on, for its appearance had no predictable pattern. . . . People sometimes got caught in the shower covered in soap when the water trickled to a maddening stop."

She went on, "My mother is sick much of the time and her greatest problem was not being able to walk to the latrine. It was simple enough to find a makeshift bed pan, but it was embarrassing for her to use it, knowing the neighbors could hear everything but the faintest of sighs." They solved the problem by subscribing to the *New York Times*. They kept piles of the newspaper and it was Yoshiko's job to rattle them as noisily as possible to cover the noise whenever the bedpan was in use.

It was not always easy to maintain the resolve of the Uchidas. At the same time, Shizuko Horiuchi, interned at Minidoka in Idaho—a dust bowl in the wind, a mud hole when it rained—wrote to a Caucasian friend, "The life here cannot be expressed. Sometimes we are resigned to it, but when we see the barbed wire fences and the sentry tower with floodlights, it gives us a feeling of being prisoners in a 'concentration camp.'" He continued, "We try to be happy and yet, oftentimes, a gloominess does creep in. When I see the 'I am an American' editorials and write-ups, the 'equality of race' etc.—it seems to be mocking us in our faces."

● ● ●

In late August, Twentieth Century Fox released a feature film titled *Little Tokyo, U.S.A.* The plot was driven by a Los Angeles detective discovering Japanese spies, saboteurs, and murderers preparing for an invasion of the United States. The *New York Times* review called it "63 minutes of speculation about prewar Japanese espionage activities."

Filmed as if it were a documentary, using authentic news film of the roundups of California Japanese and Japanese Americans, the movie called for the evacuation of both loyal and disloyal *Nikkei* in the name of national security. The film ends showing Little Tokyo as a ghost town without people or lights. The Office of War Information responded by calling it "an invitation to the Witch Hunt" and began demanding that Hollywood scripts be shown to government censors before filming.

The *Santa Ana Register* could not match Hollywood in a publicity fight, but its publisher, R. C. Hoiles, continued his lonely crusade, calling for a rollback of Executive Order 9066. On October 14, 1942, he wrote:

> Few, if any, people ever believed that evacuation of the Japanese was constitutional. It was a result of emotion and fright rather than being in harmony with the Constitution and the inherent rights that belong to American citizens. The question we should consider is whether or not this evacuation will in the long run really help us win the war. If it will not, we should make every effort possible to correct the error as rapidly as possible. It would seem that convicting people of disloyalty to our country without having specific evidence against them is too foreign to our way of life and too close akin to the kind of government we are fighting.
>
> We need all the manpower we can obtain. To remove the Japanese from the place where they could serve our country by helping us furnish food and doing useful services weakens us in our defense by that amount. . . . If we are not willing to run any risks and cannot have faith in humanity and regard people innocent until they are proved guilty, we are on the road to losing our democracy. We cannot help but believe that we would shorten the war and lose fewer lives and less property if we would rescind the order and let the Japanese return and go to work, until such time as we have reason to suspect any individuals of being guilty of being disloyal to America.

Two weeks later the *Register* reprinted a long article from the *Christian Advocate*, a national journal. Clarence Hall of the *Advocate* reported on how, throughout occupied Europe, the American policy toward Japanese Americans was being compared to the Nazis' treatment of Jews, going on to say that Pierre Laval, the Nazi-backed prime minister of collaborationist Vichy France, "is said to have justified his deportation from France of 70,000 Jews by reporting what was happening in California. . . . Over in New Delhi, Jawaharlal Nehru sat down to write a letter to an American friend, citing his amazement of and concern over what the [American] action portended for India in its relations with the United Nations."

● ● ●

The peaceful endurance of many of the internees, particularly the Issei, was often seen by non-Japanese as an indication of passivity. Many American Japanese, instead, saw themselves as choosing *"gaman,"* a Japanese term that can mean "to persevere with dignity in the face of adversity," or "to suppress anger and refuse to take retaliatory action against hardships." Jeanne Wakatsuki also commented on how *"shikata ga nai"* was another common saying at the camps, meaning "it cannot be helped."

While the overwhelming majority of the American Japanese accepted their lot with little complaint, particularly in the beginning, tensions and a sense of injustice began to build among the *Nikkei*. A few resisted in the courts, others through violence. One of the first outbreaks of anger came at Santa Anita in early August of 1942, when evacuees were already being moved to Poston by the trainload. Fusa Tsumagari, scheduled to leave in five days, wrote to Miss Breed on August 9 about what happened.

> On Wednesday the army ordered our barracks searched. . . . Previous to this whenever such an order was given, [we were] notified of everything. This however was done abruptly with no reason given. Then, they closed certain

gates and would not allow people to pass unless they were searched. Then, to top that, they began to confiscate scissors and knitting needles. . . . Some of the police had the nerve to steal people's money and remove things from people's houses without allowing the occupants to see what was being taken. One policeman in particular aroused the people to such a degree that they began to mob him. . . . Unfortunately the mob of people were so aroused they chased him and beat him with chairs. . . . The Army took control for three days.

Her brother, Yukio, sent his own description: "The investigation created a frenzy in camp. A huge mob of infuriated people gathered to ask for the reason for such doings. Frightened by the large crowd and excited by pointed questions directed to him, the investigator drew his gun and threatened to shoot anyone who might molest him."

Charles Kikuchi knew some officials were trying to provoke the evacuees with exaggerated taunts and outright lies. When he became the editor of the Tanforan newspaper, a mimeographed sheet called *The Totalizer*, he sometimes was the first Japanese American to be told what would happen next. He was called to administration offices during the last week of August and was told, "Casa Grande."

"What's that?" he asked.

"Arizona."

"I asked a lot of detailed questions," Kikuchi wrote. "We are leaving next Tuesday at 6:45 in the morning. The train will leave from San Francisco at 3:15. I asked whether we would have any time to stop over in the city. [They] told me a scare story about how the Daylight Limited did not want any Japanese and that they were going to shoot us right on the train."

The information fed to Kikuchi was wrong on all counts. He ended up in Utah, in the Topaz Relocation Camp.

The troubles at Santa Anita were the beginning of ongoing complaints and sporadic violence in most of the assembly centers and camps. Administrators, many of whom had worked on Indian reservations, wanted to create community councils and such to mimic life on the outside. "Pioneer communities" was the officially favored name for people surrounded by barbed wire and by soldiers with guns and fixed bayonets. The idea was that the evacuees themselves would democratically elect "community councils" to deal with camp administrators. But all that was mishandled from the beginning. The men from the government immediately ruled that only Nisei, born in the United States, American citizens, could be block captains or hold other minor offices in the camps. That ignorant blunder set the Issei, the older, more mature, more experienced Japanese American evacuees, against their own children, undermining the traditional structure of the hierarchical Japanese society. That mistake compounded the family conflicts caused by army-style mess halls, which further separated families. "My own family, after three years of mess hall living, collapsed as an integrated unit," wrote Jeanne Wakatsuki. An Episcopal priest at Tule Lake, Daisuki Kitagawa, added, "The loss of the family table and the family kitchen was not simply a loss of opportunity to teach manners to growing children, but a forceful symbol of that human institution which transmits values from one generation to another."

If there had been a cohesive American Japanese community in California, it was breaking up along many fault lines. Despite what General DeWitt and others believed, the residents of the camps were as diverse as any other group of more than a hundred thousand people. City people were uncomfortable with country folk. The same was true of English speakers and monolingual Japanese. Buddhists and Christians often distrusted each other. Californians were generally disliked by Oregon and Washington people.

A small but growing number of Issei and *Kibei* hoped Japan would win the war. Some, not believing what they read and heard in American journals and on the radio, continued to think Japan was winning even as Allied forces were turning the tide. The great majority of evacuees were simply pained by the war—many had relatives in Japan—but supported the United States and cooperated with camp administrators. Soon enough, some of those people were seen as collaborators and called *inu*—"dogs"—by the pro-Japan faction.

Life magazine and other publications, using photographs supplied by the War Relocation Authority, portrayed the internees as model democratic citizens living a kind of resort life, but in fact, as early as August of 1942, many administrators were warning their bosses in Washington that the camps were likely to produce America-hating Japanese Americans. Dillon Myer, the new WRA director, was already talking, privately, about closing down the whole relocation camp operation. He instituted a liberal "leave" policy designed to begin that process. "Short-term leave" was allowed for a week or so to visit doctors or tend to personal affairs. "Work leave" was granted for camp residents willing to work on midwestern farms desperately in need of workers during harvest seasons. "Indefinite leave," already granted to students attending eastern and midwestern colleges willing to accept them, was expanded to include evacuees who wanted to take their chances on finding work outside. The presidents of the campuses of the University of California, led by Robert Sproul, president of the university, persuaded Governor Olson to write to Roosevelt saying, "Unless some special action is taken, the education of those who might become influential leaders of the loyal American born Japanese will abruptly be closed. Such a result would be injurious not only to them, but to the nation, since well-trained leadership for such persons will be needed after the present war."

The president may have agreed with that, but many American institutions of higher learning, including some of the most prestigious, Princeton and the Massachusetts Institute of Technology among them, refused to admit Japanese American students. Harvard offered to allow the army to train Japanese linguists on its campus, but wanted to charge more than double the rates offered by schools such as the University of Chicago. There was also a government restriction on Japanese American students: many universities were prohibited from taking evacuated students because of "secret" military training and research on their campuses, which usually merely meant that they had ROTC (Reserve Officers' Training Corps). Still, by the end of the war, forty-three hundred Nisei were enrolled in colleges and universities east of the West Coast states.

For those remaining in the camps, though, life continued to be a struggle. In some cases, events took a tragic turn. There had been numerous suicides and suicide attempts and more than a dozen Japanese men had been killed or wounded by soldiers guarding them in the relocation centers and in Justice Department camps and jails. On May 12, 1942, a man named Kanesaburo Oshima was killed by a sentry at Fort Sill, Oklahoma, a temporary center for the so-called dangerous aliens. The next day Ichiro Shimoda, a forty-five-year-old gardener from Los Angeles who had served in the Japanese army as a young man and was arrested on the day Pearl Harbor was attacked, was badly wounded by another guard at Fort Sill. He was known to be mentally unstable and had twice attempted to kill himself by trying to bite off his own tongue. An FBI report dated May 18, 1942, said he was shot twice while trying to climb over a camp fence.

On May 16, 1942, Hikoji Takeuchi was shot at Manzanar by a military police private named Edward Phillips. A WRA investigation report quoted his commanding officer, Lieutenant Buckner, as saying that guard service was so monotonous that MPs welcomed "a little excitement, such as shooting a Jap."

Frustration and fear were spreading in the camps—on both sides of the fences. On July 27, 1942, Hirota Isomura, a fisherman from San Pedro, and Toshio Kobata, a farmer from Brawley, California, were shot and killed by a guard, Private First Class Clarence Burleson. Both men, interned as "dangerous enemy aliens," were being transferred from a prison at Fort Lincoln, Nebraska, to one at Lordsburg, New Mexico. Two of 150 transferees, they were both too sick or tired to walk the mile from the Lordsburg train station to the temporary camp and were fired on as they arrived in a camp automobile at 2:30 a.m. at Poston I on November 18, 1942.

After a few months in the camps, the numbers of antiadministration or anti-American residents steadily increased. Young men, particularly young *Kibei*, organized as gangs and began to terrorize residents they considered spies or collaborators for the administration. They began traveling in groups during the day, then harassing and beating the residents they did not like, usually at night.

A community council member, Fred Tayama, was beaten almost to death for cooperating with camp administrators. The FBI was called into the camp to investigate and arrested two popular Nisei, young men hundreds of evacuees considered innocent. All of the members of the community council resigned and evacuees surrounded the small center stockade, determined to prevent the removal of the two prisoners to civil or military jails outside. The standoff lasted a week until the administration agreed to free one man and to allow an "evacuee court" to try the other one.

At Manzanar, the young toughs began wearing headbands with MANZANAR BLACK DRAGON ASSOCIATION written across them in Japanese. Camp administrators ignored them at first, saying it was up to the Japanese to settle things among themselves. When women started a work project that first summer, weaving and making camouflage nets for the army, they soon became a target. Young children, egged on by Black Dragons, began throwing stones at the women.

One of the Black Dragon leaders was Joseph Kurihara, the bitter World War I veteran, who was a college graduate and had been a successful businessman before the war. There were rumors of "death lists" of pro-American residents. Karl Yoneda, a former journalist and union organizer, was one of the names on a list, because he had met with Military Intelligence Service officers who were recruiting translators for the war in the Pacific. When the recruiters arrived on November 28, Dragons went door-to-door threatening men and their families, warning them not to talk to the army men. Yoneda, who said Kurihara threatened to have him killed if he met with the recruiters, was one of fifty men who applied. Fourteen, including Yoneda, a *Kibei* and a member of the Communist Party, passed language tests and were immediately sworn in as U.S. Army privates. Guarded by military police, the fourteen left Manzanar for MIS training at Camp Savage in Minnesota. Yoneda's wife, Elaine Black Yoneda, and their four-year-old son, Tommy, waved from behind the barbed wire. "Daddy, don't leave me," the boy cried. "I want to go with you and help beat up the Nazis."

Mrs. Yoneda, who was Caucasian, and her young son, along with sixty other relatives of the new privates, were moved into administration buildings for safety and then sent to an old Civilian Conservation Corps camp in Death Valley. After two weeks they were allowed to go home, even to San Francisco, where Mrs. Yoneda's parents lived. Her dark hair turned white in the three weeks after her husband left. In San Francisco, she was required to inform General DeWitt personally each month of her whereabouts and to report whether little Tommy had done anything to compromise national security.

At the same time, late in November of 1942, JACL officials in the camps were allowed out for a week to meet in Salt Lake City. The organization, which preached cooperation with administrators of the camps, was defined by its official hymn:

> There was a dream my father dreamed for me
> A land in which all men are free—
> The desert camp with watchtowers high
> Where life stood still, mid sand and brooding sky
> Out of the war in which my brothers died
> Their muted voices with mine cried—
> This is our dream that all men should be free!
> This is our creed we'll live in loyalty
> God help us rid the land of bigotry
> That we may walk in peace and dignity.

The main piece of business discussed by the JACL leaders in Salt Lake City was the determination of Mike Masaoka, who lived in Utah and was never in a camp, to petition the War Department to once again allow Nisei to serve openly in the armed forces. Returning to the camps, the officials were the targets of anti-American thugs. Saburo Kido, the JACL president, had backed Masaoka's efforts, and was attacked in his quarters at Poston by eight masked men, later identified as *Kibei* between the ages of eighteen and thirty. He was hospitalized for more than a month. The same thing happened to Dr. Tom Yatabe at Rohwer and to James Oda at Manzanar.

On December 5, 1942, at Manzanar, Frank Masuda, who had owned a restaurant in Little Tokyo and was a leader of the JACL, was badly beaten up by several other evacuees. He identified Dick

Miwa, a camp cook and a *Kibei*, as one of his assailants. Miwa was already known as one of the kitchen workers attempting to organize a union. He had also publicly accused the camp's chief steward, a Caucasian, of stealing rations and selling them outside on the black market. Joe Kurihara quickly organized a mass demonstration demanding Miwa's release from the jail in Independence.

One speaker after another attacked the "*inu*," shouting out their names and threatening to kill them. "We should not be afraid to die in this cause as our brothers are dying for justice and permanent peace and the new order in Asia," one said. Two nights later, on December 7, 1942, some Black Dragons rushed from a demonstration celebrating Pearl Harbor to the camp hospital looking for Masuda, intent on killing him. Masuda survived by hiding under a bed. The camp director, Ralph Merritt, called in 135 military policemen to block the protesters at the center jail, where Miwa and others were being held, and then declared martial law and called in more troops.

"Hold your line. Remember Pearl Harbor!" an army officer shouted as a crowd of camp residents grew bigger and angrier. The soldiers put on gas masks and threw tear gas canisters. One fired his rifle into the crowd and others began to shoot. Ten evacuees were wounded, eight of them requiring major surgery. Two died, James Ito, who was eighteen years old, and Jim Kanagawa, twenty-one. An official autopsy showed that each of them had been hit in the back or side.

Harry Ueno, a thirty-seven-year-old Hawaiian who had lived in Japan for eight years in the 1920s, and who later owned a couple of fruit markets in Los Angeles and Beverly Hills—his clientele included Darryl F. Zanuck, Douglas Fairbanks, and Tom Mix—was another principal organizer of the kitchen unit, which came to symbolize Manzanar's growing anti-JACL sentiment. He was among the most popular men in Manzanar, well known after he produced evidence, handwritten accounts, that Caucasian superiors were stealing sugar from the residents' supplies and selling it on the black market. After he was arrested on December 5, accused of attacking Fred Tayama, he was taken in handcuffs to the town jail in Independence. He was held there for a night, then brought back to camp and held in a barracks room used as a temporary camp jail. He watched the action from there and said:

> By the time the tear gas was clear, I could see one man, not more than ten or fifteen feet away, on the ground face down. Three men tried to take him into the police station. But when a man is dead, he's pretty hard to carry. I open the window and I jump out and helped them carry the body into the jailhouse and put it on top of the table. He was bleeding. He must have been hit from behind at close range. Shot running away . . . I knew the one we brought in. James Ito. He's eighteen years old. One man, very strong JACL, was sitting in the back of the table. He saw that dead man, and he pounded the table and he said, "I made a mistake! I couldn't believe the United States could do this!" He was not talking to me or anybody else. He was yelling to himself.

Masuda and twenty other JACL members whose names were on a Black Dragon "killing" list were quickly moved to the old Civilian Conservation Corps camp in Death Valley—and then freed to resettle wherever they chose to go. Miwa, Ueno, and Kurihara, classified as "aggravated troublemakers" along with ten others, were moved to another old CCC camp, this one a thousand miles away in Moab, Utah, hundreds of miles from any sizable town. It was a prison, really, with armed guards watching them shower and use the lavatories. The forty or so prisoners there were isolated from their families, and one wrote to his wife, "I shall be happy to die as a descendant of the Japanese race. I am quite satisfied even to get shot for not licking a white man's ass."

The "troublemakers," who had never been charged with anything, were moved on to an "isolation center" on a Navajo reservation near Leupp, Arizona. Even in official government correspondence, center officials were asking that the center, holding fewer than one hundred men, be closed down. "I should like to see a reexamination of the advisability of continuing the Leupp Center," said one government lawyer. "I think it is an un-American institution, corresponds to and is premised on Gestapo methods. I don't like the idea of individuals being sent to Leupp without being told why they are being sent." The center director, Paul Robertson, told WRA director Myer, "We have 67 men at Leupp Relocation Center. In reviewing the dockets of these evacuees, I was very much amazed at the lack of evidence."

• • •

Still, back in the relocation camps, most tried to do their best to endure. Louise Ogawa wrote to Miss Breed in September, "Poston would be a paradise if it were not for the dust, heat, wind and insects. . . . And it was not only insects flying around. Chinese pilots, being trained at an Arizona Army Air Force base, got their kicks by pretending to strafe the camps, flying so low that the barracks shook."

Then she added: "Life is beginning to settle down to the monotonous regularity that is truly depressing. . . . Not much sociable visiting going on at all. The afternoons are still too hot to do so. And who wants to walk in dust up to the ankles?"

But Louise Ogawa was not a person to stay depressed for long. She wrote to Helen McNary, Miss Breed's assistant:

I may have complained about my new environment but I know it will be difficult to adapt myself to the new surroundings right away. I am sure everything will brighten up soon and I will begin to love this place almost as much as my home in San Diego. When I stop to think how the pilgrims started their life, similar to ours, it makes me feel grand for it gives me the feeling of being a pure full-blooded American.

5

A DESERT CHRISTMAS

DECEMBER 25, 1942

Topaz, mockingly called "The Jewel of the Desert," was the new home for residents rounded up in the Bay Area. The camp was on a plateau forty-six hundred feet above sea level in Utah. No one had ever lived there. Yoshiko Uchida described the terrible windstorms that plagued the camp.

Soon barracks only a few feet away were completely obscured by walls of dust and I was terrified the wind would knock me off my feet. Every few yards, I stopped to lean against a barrack to catch my breath, then lowering my head against the wind, I plodded on. When I got to school, I discovered many children had braved the storm as well and were waiting for me in the dust-filled classroom.

I made an attempt to teach, but so much dust was pouring into the room from all sides as well as the hole in the roof that it soon became impossible, and I decided to send the children home before the storm grew worse. "Be very careful and run home as fast as you can."

As my mother, and sister, and I waited out the storm in our room, the wind reached such force we thought our barrack would be torn from its feeble foundations. Pebbles and rocks rained against the walls, and the newspapers we stuffed into the cracks in the siding came flying back into the room. The air was so thick with the smoke-like dust, my mouth was gritty with it and my lungs seemed penetrated by it. For hours the wind shrieked around our shuddering barrack, and I realized how frightened my mother was when I saw her get down on her knees to pray at her cot. I had never seen her do that before.

The wind stopped short of destroying our camp. . . . Although our barrack had held, I learned later that many had been blown out into the desert.

One of the soldiers there, a Caucasian named Roger Walker, was as shocked as she was, writing home that "the sheeting had cracks at least a quarter of an inch between each board. There was no insulation whatsoever. There were bare light bulbs, eight to every 120 feet of wire. . . . There is no concrete foundations under the barracks." He also wrote, "It is really difficult to see how they [the evacuees] survive."

The Uchida family had good news and a good laugh when their father was released from prison in Montana and allowed to rejoin them. Dwight Uchida, the former Mitsui executive, taken from a comfortable home in Berkeley, became a block captain and a leader of the men who met regularly with camp administrators. He would occasionally be allowed to visit surrounding towns and other camps. Sometimes he would return with treasures, butter, eggs, bacon—and stories. The best one was about coming back to Topaz in an army car and stopping, as required, at the gate. "There are six of us including Caucasians," said the driver. The guard put his head in the window and asked, "Which one of you is Mr. Caucasians?"

●　●　●

"I was the first Jap to knock at the gates of Poston," said Shig Nakashima of El Centro, California. He had led three carloads—eleven people—with three Caucasians to drive the cars back to California. They had a hell of a time finding the three Poston camps. Even locals, and there were few of them, gave them bad directions. If the desert folk were generous with directions, good or bad, none of the cafés along the way were. They refused to give the evacuees food and water.

When they had finally arrived at Poston on May 8, 1942, it was a total surprise to the WRA people working there, who scurried around looking for the right paperwork. After a couple of hours, Nakashima and the ten other evacuees were moved into an empty barracks building. Inside, four soldiers with tommy guns arrived to guard them. The evacuees and their guards were sitting around for hours talking about baseball and life in California. When dinnertime came, the evacuees, who had not eaten all day, were invited to dine with the staff. It was good: green salad, Virginia ham with candied yams, peas and carrots, apple pie, lots of milk—and more friendly conversation. One of the evacuees, Marva Maeda, thought camp was going to be a holiday.

But by the next evening seventy-five more Japanese had arrived by train and buses. One of them, a diarist, wrote "HELL can't be worse than this." The temperature was well over one hundred degrees. This time a mess hall was opened and the new arrivals were eating the mush produced by army cooks in training.

"The earth around Poston is not unlike parched flour; it is fine dust which the wind blows around readily," wrote a high school senior named Lawrence Yatsu. The camp was surrounded by barbed wire and harsh Arizona desert; temperatures could soar to 115 or 130 degrees in the summer. Masami Honda, another San Diegan, wrote of the twenty-five-mile desert bus ride to Poston: "It was so hot, over 110 degrees, that people, especially the older people and the kids, were getting sick. So we opened the windows. Immediately everyone was covered by dust. . . . I know you won't believe this, but it's really true, friends couldn't recognize each other."

Mary Sakaguchi Oda, who practiced medicine for forty-six years after leaving the camps, later described the impact on her family: "My older sister developed bronchial asthma in camp. It was a reaction to the terrible dust storms and winds. The asthma became intractable, and she died at the age of twenty-six." Kanshi Yamashita, a high school senior sent to Poston, wrote, "Those hot summer days and the things we learned! Self-appointed experts in the art of keeping cool, that's what we are! Saturate the floor with water, take off all clothing, dump all available bath towels in a bucket of water, drape them on oneself à la Gandhi, and there we were, just as hot."

• • •

Four days after Shig Nakashima arrived at one of the Poston camps, Isamu Noguchi arrived at another. At the time, the only American Japanese there were JACL volunteers helping to finish barrack construction. Noguchi, a New York sculptor, was a solitary volunteer. He was also one of the best-known Japanese Americans in the United States. His work was known around the world and his latest piece was the huge steel bas-relief over the entrance of the new Associated Press Building in Rockefeller Center. The illegitimate son of a famous Japanese poet,

Yonejirō Noguchi, and a young American woman, Leonie Gilmour, a Bryn Mawr graduate trying to make her way in the New York publishing world, young Noguchi had been a student of Constantin Brancusi in Rome, a friend of Alexander Calder and Man Ray in Paris, and a lover of Frida Kahlo in Mexico. Born in Los Angeles in 1904, he was back in California on December 7, 1941, driving south toward San Diego to inspect stone for his work when he heard the news of Pearl Harbor on the car radio.

He was tortured by what to do. He was a Nisei, a *Kibei*, and an American citizen living in New York. He considered himself American and was angry that his father, back in Tokyo, had become an important propagandist for Imperial Japan. He made the rounds of government and military offices in Washington and New York asking what he could do for the American war effort. He was routinely rebuffed. Finally, a friend, John Collier, director of the Bureau of Indian Affairs, suggested he go into the new relocation camps and teach art to the thousands of American Japanese headed for those camps.

So he did, voluntarily entering Poston. As a New Yorker, he was not subject to any evacuation orders. His new address was Room A, Barracks 7, Block 5, Poston Relocation Center. He wrote a letter to his half sister, Ailes, explaining what he was doing. She wrote back, saying, "Your very beautiful and moving letter reached me. . . . I can only urge you to leave as soon as possible. In that intense heat and with no fruit or vegetables or milk you will lose your health."

By mid-summer Isamu Noguchi realized he had made a mistake going into the camps. He set up an Arts and Handicraft Center in Poston but, really, no one came. He had great trouble communicating with his fellow residents. "I am extremely despondent for lack of companionship," he wrote to John Collier. "The *Nisei* here are not of my own age and are of an entirely different background and interest."

To another friend, he wrote, "The people here are for the most part farmers, completely unintellectual, and with little apparent interest in the policies or politics of democracy, other than resentment with their common lot."

Noguchi asked to leave on July 28. It was not that easy. DeWitt and Bendetsen of the Fourth Army thought him "a suspicious person." Secret intelligence files questioned his reasons for moving around California earlier in the year, when he tried to organize a group called Nisei Writers and Artists Mobilization for Democracy. He was being followed and army intelligence officers wrote that he was near military installations when he visited friends in Santa Barbara and Carmel.

Finally, on November 2, the army allowed his release. He had been inside for 184 days. Driving back to New York, he stopped in Wisconsin to see his friend the architect Frank Lloyd Wright. From there he wrote to his half sister Ailes, "Please let my various friends know that I am on my way. I feel like Rip Van Winkle."

• • •

The heat. The heat. The dust. Fathers dug foxholes under their barracks so that their children could lie in them for hours in the middle of the day. Spaces underground were sanctuaries in most of the camps. A professional photographer named George Hirahara actually built and equipped a secret darkroom under his "apartment"—ordering equipment from Sears Roebuck catalogs—at Heart Mountain in Wyoming. He took and developed more than two thousand photos.

The cold. Even in summer, the nights could be cold in the desert camps. The winters were terrifying. Charles Hamasaki, who was sent from Los Angeles to the Minidoka camp in Idaho, wrote, "Twenty-five degrees below zero man. I'm from Southern California. I had my moccasins—moccasins, not shoes—with me and just a tee-shirt and overcoat. When we got off the train there was a snowdrift ten feet high . . . and they have to line us up in the freezing weather to count the heads so nobody would escape."

Frank Emi, the twenty-nine-year-old grocer who had liquidated his family's little supermarket in Los Angeles, said this about the Heart Mountain Relocation Camp in Wyoming:

> It was in the middle of a dusty prairie. You could hardly see 10 or 25 feet ahead of you. . . . Course, it turned out dust storms were the least of our worries because the winter was the coldest in Wyoming history; it was 30 below zero. If you went to the restroom, which was located outside, and wet your hands or took a shower your head would be in icicles and if your hand was still wet it froze to the metal doorknobs. . . . We didn't even have topcoats when we arrived. We were California boys.

At the beginning of November, Tetsuzo (Ted) Hirasaki, writing from Poston to Miss Breed in San Diego, talked about the weather as well, describing the dramatic desert temperature swings: "Brrr to have to get up in the morning. It is about 38 degrees in the morning and in the middle part of the afternoon, it is about 80+. The mornings don't warm up until noontime."

Hirasaki had a tubercular lesion in his biceps, but he wrote in his letter to Miss Breed that his arm was all right—though not much helped by the camp medical facilities. "The medical situation here is pitiful," he reported. "The main and only hospital is at Camp I, 15 miles from here. Here in Camp III there is one young doctor with not too much equipment and one student doctor working in an emergency clinic. They are supposed to take care of 5,000 people!"

He scoffed, "And they (the Big Shots) wonder why we squawk. . . . If they don't watch out there's going to be trouble." He said that one of his close friends had "got to thinking—and he went crazy. He tried to commit suicide by slashing his wrists. His roommates found him bleeding and immediately gave him first aid. He is still alive but his face is like that of a wild ape caged for the first time." He went on, complaining again that the machine guns in the camp towers were pointing inside. "The Army had the gall to tell us that the purpose of the towers was to keep the white folk from coming to mob the Japs. . . . Ha, ha, ha. I'm laughing yet. . . . Enough of this before I go out and murder a white man by killing myself. God forgive us for the thoughts that are beginning to run amok in our brains."

Then he added: "I am sending you a few things in appreciation of all the things you have done, as well as my sister and all the rest. The lapel pins are for you. . . . Have a nice Thanksgiving dinner."

Ever cheerful, Louise Ogawa wrote back to San Diego that Thanksgiving dinner at Poston was wonderful. A couple of weeks later, as camp life became calmer at Poston, Louise wrote to Helen McNary, "After six weeks of school life in camp, everything has become similar to the life in San Diego."

Perhaps not quite. She described their work:

> I went cotton picking with my fellow school-mates to raise funds so the school will be able to have a school paper. We left home at 8:30 A.M. on a cattle truck. We were going bumpity-bump down the narrow dirt road when all of a sudden we came to a halt. We were surrounded by cotton plants. We flung the bag over our left shoulder and began picking the cotton. I often crawled on the ground to pick the fallen cotton. It certainly was a good thing that I wore slacks and a long sleeve blouse because you get scratched all over. . . . It certainly is a boring work. It is no wonder

that the Negroes have developed such a talent in singing.
I only picked 14 lbs. but I tried! . . . I see men with packs
on their backs walking toward the east to the plateau for
petrified wood or toward the west to the Colorado River
to fish. This seems to be the main activity for the older
folks.

• • •

On December 8, 1942, a year after the army first rejected him,
Ben Kuroki was finally overseas. The kid from Nebraska had
been scheduled to be left behind, peeling more potatoes or cleaning more latrines, when the Ninety-Third Bomb Group left the
United States. He went to the squadron's adjutant, Lieutenant
Charles Brannan, and pleaded his case, tears rolling down his
cheeks, begging again to fight. Finally, Brannan called in his secretary and said, "I'm going and Kuroki's going, too."

Now the Ninety-Third and its forty B-24 bombers were in
Huntington, sixty miles from London. Kuroki was in Communications as a ground-bound clerk, pleading with officers to let
him fly. Lieutenant Erik Larson, the armaments officer, listened
as Kuroki told his story one more time, ending, "I want to prove
my loyalty, sir. I can't do it on the ground."

"Are you sure you know what you're doing?" asked Larson.
He told Kuroki the average life span for members of B-24 crews
was ten missions. Kuroki was sure. He was sent to gunnery
school near London: five days of lectures about spotting enemy
planes and firing just ten rounds of a .50 caliber machine gun
on the ground. He was a gunner. Now he had to find a crew who
would take him.

There were many openings; gunners died in crashes, gunners
froze at their positions as German fighter planes buzzed around
them like deadly bees, gunners got "flak-happy," breaking down
with combat fatigue. Kuroki went back to Larson, who called

in Lieutenant Jake Epting, a Mississippian commanding a B-24 nicknamed "Red Ass"—its symbol was a mule kicking Hitler. He called his crew together and said, "If there is anyone here who objects to flying with Kuroki, let me know now." No one did. The next day the Red Ass was ordered to fly to North Africa on temporary duty, with Kuroki manning a machine gun.

● ● ●

As the first Christmas of the internment approached, Louise Ogawa sent Clara Breed in San Diego a handmade card with happy drawings and the words: "With our Friends, the Rattlesnakes, / Coyotes, and Scorpions / We send you / SEASON'S GREETINGS / from Poston / The Oasis of Arizona."

Fusa Tsumagari sent a more sobering report from one of the three Poston camps at the same time.

> I guess you have been hearing over the radio about the riot in Camp 1. The version I heard over the radio was quite unlike anything that I have heard in camp. . . . I'll tell you our version. The first outbreak occurred about two weeks ago on a Saturday night. A band of people were so sick and tired of "Stool-pigeons" going around and listening to private conversations and getting people into trouble that they went to the homes of the "Stools" and brutally attacked them. Then, two men were picked up on charges of "Attacking with Intent to Murder." They were going to be taken to Phoenix by the FBI for a hearing. The people in Camp 1 heard this and balked. They did not want these men to be taken to Phoenix and tried for two reasons: first, they did not believe these men were guilty of the charges against them; second, if taken to Phoenix they probably would not get a fair trial. The people built large bonfires near the police station and parked all night to be on guard

so that the men would not be taken out when everyone was asleep.

A week later, Tetsuzo Hirasaki sent Miss Breed a letter describing the end of the incident at Poston: "Because a Jap wouldn't have a Chinaman's chance in an Arizona court, the people of Camp I did not want the prisoner to be taken out, therefore the strike. After 5 days a compromise was reached and the man is to be tried here in Poston II with a Jap judge & jury." He went on to report, "Most of the trouble was caused by misunderstandings between the people and the Chief of Police, who is anti-Jap, a big blustery fellow who likes to push a small fellow around."

The Japanese American Citizens League was at the center of many of the troubles at the camps. Many internees scorned the league as a tool of the government and camp administrators, openly accusing JACL leaders and members of being spies and informants.

Still, the JACL continued to try to boost morale for those living in the primitive camps. Bent nails wrapped in old paper were given as gifts, valuable because the residents were building their own furniture with scrap wood left over from the hasty construction of barracks. In the autumn of 1942, the league sent out appeals to people and organizations to send more cheerful presents to the children in the camps. Thousands and thousands of Americans responded, especially through their churches. But there was a backlash, too. Newspapers around the country were bombarded with hate mail.

"Certainly the best present we give the Japs for Christmas would be a kick in the pants. Especially if they were near a large body of water. . . . Mae E. Collins"

> "I could never look another serviceman in the face if I were
> to extend Christmas greetings to a Jap. . . . A Sailor's
> Mother."
>
> "As to sending 40,000 Christmas presents to Japs, I feel that
> anyone who has the desire to do that should be living
> with the slimy devils. . . . A Mother"

Still there were thousands of Americans who obviously felt differently because packages were arriving every day. Before they were passed out, guards stripped paper, wrappings, and ribbons from the boxes; they looked and shook, searching for secret messages or contraband. Chocolates and other candies had to be scooped up with men's caps. As for cards, like all mail in and out of the camps, they were routed through a post office box in New York City, where more than a hundred censors opened and read every letter and card. The censors used scissors, so letters looked like Swiss cheese or paper dolls—one more humiliation.

Even without wrapping paper or ribbons, residents were cheered by the gifts. "Yesterday night I got a X'mas present from someone I don't even know," wrote a seventeen-year-old internee at Heart Mountain, Stanley Hayami, in a new diary. "I got it from a lady named Mrs. C.W. Evans who lives way over in Minominee, Michigan. I got the present via the Sunday School." All the presents sent to the camp, Hayami reported, were sent by the Presbyterian Union Church. "I really think it was a fine gesture," he wrote. "I'm going to write to the lady as soon as I can."

A few days later he wrote:

> Far away in New Mexico in an isolated spot, there are a
> few very poor Mexicans who attended a certain Mission.
> There, poor people were told by the priest that the kids in
> Heart Mountain wouldn't have a very good Christmas,
> because they didn't have an income, and because they were

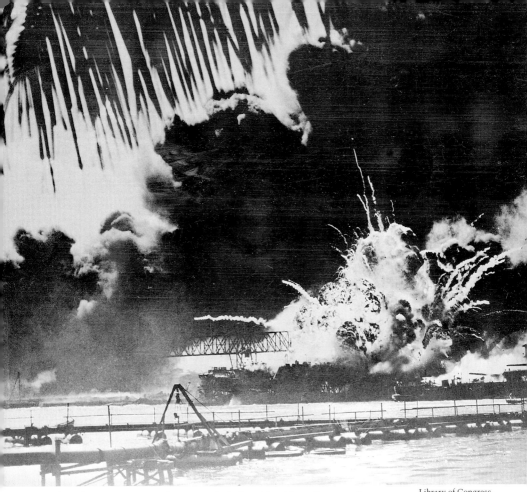

After the surprise attack on Pearl Harbor, President Roosevelt addressed Congress: "Yesterday, December 7, 1941, a date that will live in infamy, the United States of America was suddenly and deliberately attacked by naval and air forces of the Empire of Japan."

Within forty-eight hours of the attacks, FBI agents searched the homes of thousands of "Suspect Enemy Aliens." More than twelve hundred men were arrested without charges. The evidence against them ranged from membership in civic organizations to possession of any written materials with Japanese characters, including Bibles and knitting manuals.

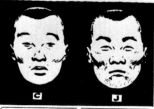

Milton Caniff, courtesy of American Social History Project, Center for Media and Learning, CUNY

Dorothea Lange, Library of Congress, LC-USZ62-3514

On February 19, 1942, President Roosevelt signed Executive Order 9066, which resulted in the incarceration of 120,000 West Coast American Japanese. Assembly notices were posted and American Japanese were registered for evacuation.

Hysterical rumors of invasion and sabotage swept the West Coast. Soon guides were printed on how to tell Japanese "enemies" from Chinese "friends." This cartoon by Milton Caniff was published in hundreds of newspapers in early 1942.

Like all evacuees, the Mochida children wore identification tags while they waited for their evacuation bus. War Relocation Authority (WRA) leaders removed anyone with "a single drop of Japanese blood."

Clem Aubers, photo © courtesy National Archives

At Santa Anita racetrack, the largest of the assembly centers where American Japanese were held while the concentration camps were being built, lines of soldiers faced off against the evacuees arriving by train.

Residents of Bainbridge Island, Washington, were among the first to be evacuated. The islanders were marched to a ferry and when they docked in Seattle, men waiting with shotguns spat on them.

While residents at Santa Anita joked they lived in the stall of the great Seabiscuit, evacuees suffered the filth, unsafe water, and persistent sickness typical of assembly centers, as shown here at Tanforan.

Dorothea Lange, National Archives

Lieutenant General John DeWitt insisted on sending the American Japanese to camps because there was no way to tell the difference between the loyal and disloyal, saying "A Jap is a Jap."

Army reserve officer Karl Bendetsen (left) was assigned to General DeWitt and conceived the legal strategy to hold the American Japanese for more than three years without charges.

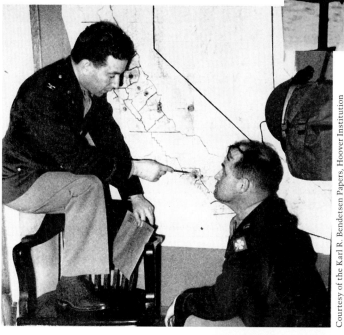

Courtesy of the Karl R. Bendetsen Papers, Hoover Institution

Secretary of War Henry Stimson (left) opposed the evacuation, but as "a president's man" he accepted his duties. His deputy John J. McCloy said, "Why, the Constitution is just a scrap of paper to me."

UPI/Bettmann

California attorney general Earl Warren pushed for the evacuation, claiming that the California Japanese had moved near airports and factories to commit sabotage—not mentioning that the Japanese had lived there long before those were built.

Walter Lippmann wrote in his influential column, which was published in more than 250 newspapers across the country, "The Pacific Coast is in imminent danger of a combined attack from within and without."

Theodor Geisel, the editorial cartoonist of *PM*, published a drawing showing hordes of buck-toothed American Japanese collecting dynamite. He signed the cartoon under his well-known pseudonym, Dr. Seuss.

Wayne Collins, a fiery civil liberties attorney, spent more than thirty years representing thousands of Japanese Americans threatened with deportation—sometimes literally pulling them off ships headed for Tokyo.

This photograph of Fred Korematsu (center) at his family's plant nursery before the war now hangs in the National Portrait Gallery's "Struggle for Justice" section. Represented by Wayne Collins, Korematsu was one of four Japanese American dissenters whose cases reached the Supreme Court.

The photographer Dorothea Lange, standing behind a crowd of evacuees, worked for the WRA after becoming famous for her photographs of migrant workers during the Great Depression.

The renowned photographer Ansel Adams sought to generate opposition to the camps, but he became frustrated when the incarcerated insisted on showing only the best side of their lives in camp.

Isamu Noguchi, the celebrated Japanese American sculptor, lived in New York and thus did not face evacuation. He volunteered to be interned and teach art to his fellow evacuees.

An Ansel Adams photo of Manzanar, taken from a guard tower. The landscape was harsh, but incarcerated farmers and gardeners were able to make the desert bloom.

The barbed wire and guard towers of Manzanar were secretly photographed by a well-known Los Angeles photographer, Toyo Miyatake, who built a camera hidden inside what appeared to be a lunchbox.

First Lady Eleanor Roosevelt visited Gila River Relocation Center with WRA director Dillon Myer in 1943. That same spring, Japanese American soldiers were hidden from view while her husband was touring western army bases.

The cheerfulness of Ansel Adams's camp subjects, as seen in his portrait of the Tsurutani family, irked the photographer, but served the government's purpose in portraying camp life as something like a long vacation.

Clem Albers, War Relocation Authority, National Archives

Mess halls broke up families, as children ate with their friends. In *Farewell to Manzanar*, Jeanne Wakatsuki Houston wrote: "After three years of mess hall living, [my family] collapsed as an integrated unit."

Many teenagers found freedoms in camp; Chiyo Kusumoto said it "was like a dream—going to the grandstands where there were records—and boys and dancing."

Hikaru Iwasaki, National Archives

Clara Breed, the children's librarian of the San Diego Public Library, met hundreds of young Japanese Americans and during the camp years she sent them letters, books, and gifts.

All the camps had boy scout troops. As boy scouts, the future senator Alan Simpson met the future congressman Norman Mineta when Simpson's Cody, Wyoming, troop came to visit Mineta's camp.

Christmas at Heart Mountain. Children tried to continue normal American life in camp; it was only years later that they began to ask their parents why they hadn't fought back.

Some internees, of course, did fight incarceration. Frank Emi led the Heart Mountain Fair Play Committee, protesting the fact that evacuees were eligible for the draft but were still denied their full civil rights.

Densho and Frank Abe

In 1943 the WRA, using confusing loyalty questionnaires, sent those deemed "disloyal" to Tule Lake. This photograph is of "disloyals" from Manzanar arriving at Tule Lake.

Courtesy of the National Archives

Tule Lake became a violent place, with pro-Japan activists terrorizing "loyals," and with troops and tanks regularly moving in to quell riots.

University of California Press, reprinted by courtesy of Wayne M. Collins

General John Weckerling recruited Private John Aiso as the first soldier to serve as a secret translator in the Pacific, saying, "John, your country needs you." Later, Aiso said, "No American had ever told me America was my country."

Harry Fukuhara (right) interrogating a Japanese prisoner of war in in Aitape, New Guinea. Major General Charles Willoughby said, "Never before in history did an army know so much concerning its enemy.... Those translators saved over a million lives and two years."

U.S. Signal Corps photograph, courtesy of the National Japanese American Historical Society

Military Intelligence Service recruit Kenny Yasui served in Burma and had swam alone to an island and persuaded the Japanese garrison there to surrender.

In Europe, German and Italian soldiers
surrendered in large numbers before the
ferocious fighting of Japanese American units.
A German officer captured by a Japanese
American shouted, "You're not an American.
You're supposed to be on our side."

Stanley Hayami kept a diary of life at
Heart Mountain Relocation Center,
agonizing over his high school grades and
ambitions before joining the army as soon
as he graduated.

Bud Aoyama, National Archives

Sergeant Ben Kuroki flew fifty-eight missions in Europe and the Pacific and toured America as a war hero. One of his stops was at Heart Mountain, where he thrilled young people, but he never heard the threats from some of the pro-Japan groups.

Lieutenant Daniel Inouye, a winner of the Medal of Honor as a platoon leader in Italy, returned home to Hawaii with a metal hook, replacing the arm he lost in combat. Standing here with his father, he later became a long-serving United States senator.

Courtesy of the Daniel K. Inouye Institute

Members of the American Legion Post in Hood River, Oregon, became a national symbol of prejudice when they painted over the names of Japanese Americans serving in Europe on the "Wall of Honor" at the local courthouse.

As the American Japanese returned to their homes after the war, a few found that their neighbors had helped preserve their businesses and farms. Far more were still treated as enemies.

Many of the evacuees, having lost everything, became residents of shoddy towns, trailer parks, and abandoned army barracks.

General Joseph "Vinegar Joe" Stilwell presented a Distinguished Service Cross to Mary Masuda in honor of her brother, who was killed while serving in Italy. Upon hearing about her family's difficult return home, Stilwell said he would be glad to form a "pick-axe" brigade to protect them.

President Harry S. Truman saluted the all–Japanese American 442nd Regimental Combat Team, the most honored combat unit per capita in American military history. Truman shook the hand of Private Wilson Makabe (left), who lost a leg in combat. He addressed the veterans: "You fought not only the enemy, but you fought prejudice and you have won."

uprooted from their homes and put into camp. Well these people were poor themselves but they wanted to help us anyway. They went to their priest and said that they didn't have much money and the nearest store was about fifty miles away, what could they do? The priest answered by going to that store and buying some gifts and bringing them back. He exchanged these gifts for chickens, vegetables and such that they could spare and took these back to the store in exchange for the gifts. I think that I'll remember this forever.

Hayami had begun his diary on November 29, 1942. Just a year before, he had been a sixteen-year-old junior at Alhambra High School in the San Gabriel Valley, ten miles east of downtown Los Angeles, before evacuation to the Pomona Assembly Center and then to Wyoming with his mother, father, two brothers, and a sister.

"It is no special day, but I have to start someplace," he wrote on the first page of the diary. He described his family, which included his thirteen-year-old brother, Walt, and his nineteen-year-old sister, Grace, nicknamed "Sach." He reported that Sach was trying to convince their parents to let her leave camp to study dress design. "Well I'll be darned they've finally decided to let Sach go to college; it's to be Washington U. in St. Louis, Missouri." He mentioned his twenty-two-year-old brother, Frank, an engineering student at Berkeley. Then Stanley Hayami closed out the brief diary entry, saying, "Well that's about all for now I guess. Gotta get up early tomorrow & get braced for the great bad news—report cards."

He was obsessed with his grades, not unusual for Japanese American students. He had been a straight A student back home, but now was getting some Bs. The competition was tougher at Heart Mountain; there were just too many smart kids in the camps. The report card he was waiting for had three As and two Bs.

Two weeks later, he wrote of hearing news of the troubles at Manzanar.

> Last Monday, December 7. The *Isseis* and *Kibeis* rioted at Manzanar. They were celebrating the Japanese victory at Pearl Harbor and some loyal American *Nisei* tried to stop them and they (rioters) killed one and injured several others. Among those that were injured and had to be taken away for his safety was Tad Uyeno. Tad lived across the street from us at San Gabriel and was our competitor. The internal police could do nothing so the Military Police were summoned into camp. The rioters charged the MPs with rocks so they threw tear bombs. When this didn't work they shot the rioters and wounded a few. Now Manzanar is under martial law. During the riot in which there was a mob of about 4,000, one group tried to haul down the "Stars and Stripes" but failed as fourteen boy scouts stood guard with rocks and repulsed the attackers.

At one of those meetings of hundreds of people, an administration informer reported that a *Kibei* said, "If you think you are citizens, just try to walk out of the camp past the sentry line. If the sentries don't shoot you, I'll believe you are a citizen." Two weeks before Christmas at Heart Mountain, Amy Imai walked along the fence with her five-year-old brother, who was chattering on about what Santa Claus might bring him that year. Amy couldn't take it. She pointed to a guard tower and the spotlights and said, "There is no Santa Claus here!"

Actually there was a Santa Claus at Heart Mountain. He was the star of a Christmas carol celebration in the main hall. Hayami wrote that little kids went up to shake hands with Santa and get some candy and nuts from him, and "they looked as if they were in a trance." They came back holding up their packages and looking intently at them.

There had been no snow so far in Wyoming, but "White Christmas" was a favorite song among the evacuees. Then at eleven o'clock the crowd started for their barracks. It was finally snowing.

Some of the carolers, almost as a joke, decided to go to the guard towers and continue singing. As Karo Kendo remembered the night, "I can still picture it. I was so cold and the [light] glistened on the barbed wire. After we sang, we heard this poor voice, almost choking with tears, saying 'Thank You!' How lonely he must have been up there."

● ● ●

"Dec. 25, 1942," wrote Hayami. "Merry Xmas!" He gave his mother five balls of wool yarn for crocheting, but "the presents I'm giving to Sach and Walt haven't come yet." He wrote:

> This morning I went to church then went to Nishioka's house with Walt, Tomo, George, and a bunch of other guys. We played a game of cards and Nishioka's mother served us cocoa, cake, candy, and soup. When we left at around 2 o'clock we were so full, we could hardly move. Walt and I went home and got our coats, because it was beginning to get a little chilly, and then we went to see the football game. The game was between Pomona and Santa Anita which ended in a 6 to 6 tie.
>
> After the game we came home and at four o'clock we had a nice turkey dinner; yum, yum!! At about 7:00 o'clock I went to our mess hall Xmas party. It was lots of fun! We played some games, one of which I had to eat crackers. Walt, Frank, and Dick Tomemura sang and played some Hawaiian songs . . .

The Christmas turkeys had been raised by residents, a good many of whom had been poultry farmers before the war. The same thing was true of all the trimmings. The evacuees made the western deserts bloom and drained some of the swamps of Arkansas. Many of the American Japanese, particularly the Issei, had real trouble eating American staples like macaroni and cheese, and other foods without vegetables. Many of them were farmers, extremely talented farmers, and they began growing vegetables and soybeans to make tofu. They created rice paddies in Arkansas. Men were catching fish in western rivers. Seeing what was happening, the WRA encouraged camps to exchange their most successful produce and soon enough local farmers were visiting the camps to find out how the Japanese were able to grow crops that had never been seen in their areas.

But when news of turkey dinners was picked up by newspapers around the country, readers reacted predictably. Letters to West Coast editors poured in from Americans outraged by the thought that the Japanese in the camps were eating better than American civilians suffering under rationing and combat soldiers who were getting by on packs of C rations. So when a group of ingenious young Nisei figured out how to capture wild ducks landing on a camp pond (they took the front windshield out of a small panel truck and drove headlong into the ducks, in the end trapping almost a hundred birds), camp administrators took the ducks. Three of the young men were accused of violating state fish and game laws and sent to the county jail.

Two days after the Christmas festivities, Hayami was already turning to more serious matters facing his fellow Nisei. He wrote of a Nisei who had joined the army immediately after the war started:

He was sent to Australia as an interpreter under General MacArthur. Soon he became tired of being a soldier with a pen, so he asked for a gun and permission to be sent into battle. At first they refused him because of the double danger he faces. He would be shot by the Japanese and because of his face he might be shot by his own men. Because of his persistence however they sent him to the battle zone. They assigned an American as a bodyguard to lessen the danger, but the danger he faces is still great. So tonight in some jungle he is risking his life, so he can teach his parents' people a lesson, and punish them for what they did. I don't know this certain *Nisei* soldier, but I feel proud of him and what he is doing. He is showing that *Nisei* are loyal Americans.

* * *

By the end of 1942, after Colonel Bendetsen received the army's Distinguished Service Medal for his legal work, exactly five hundred evacuees were released to return to their home communities on the West Coast under a Bendetsen-approved plan called "Mixed-marriage non-exclusive policy." The colonel had become concerned that the children of mixed marriages living in the all-Japanese camps were becoming "exposed to infectious Japanese thought." After the release, he reported that "mixed-blood adults predominantly American in appearance and thought have been restored to their families, their communities and their jobs."

At the same time, Governor Charles Sprague of Oregon asked Hugh Ball, the editor of the *Hood River Daily News*, to visit Tule Lake and tell him what the camps were like. Ball stayed a few days and then wrote a letter to the governor that began:

> For almost complete lack of objective, steady work, many of these young Japanese-Americans are rapidly degenerating into cynics, whose ideas are based upon what I believe is the utter hopelessness of their future. Some of them I have known for years, and in former days all white

Americans who knew them rated them as fine, loyal American citizens. Today, a number of them with whom I talked scoffed when I suggested to them that it would be entirely in their own interests if they would regard their internment as "water under the bridge" and take this opportunity to live up to the oath they took and publicized just prior to their evacuation.

Here are but a few of the comments to my suggestion that they cooperate in large numbers to go out and harvest the beet crop: "Why should I work for people who hate me because I am an American born of Japanese parents?" "We are not good enough to be accepted as American citizens, so why should we help Americans?" "They have branded us as traitors—well, if that is the way they want to think about us, let it be that way."

One of the young men there told him, "Just one year in this camp and we will all be bums."

6

UNCLE SAM, FINALLY, WANTS YOU

NISEI ENLISTMENT: JANUARY 29, 1943

At the beginning of 1943, the closed world of the imprisoned young Nisei changed completely. On January 29, 1943, Secretary of War Stimson issued a press release in Washington that began: "It is the inherent right of every citizen, regardless of ancestry, to bear arms in the Nation's battle. When obstacles to the free expression of that right are imposed, they should be removed as soon as humanly possible."

Four days later, President Roosevelt declared, in an official letter to Stimson, "The principle on which this country was founded and by which it has always been governed is that Americanism is a matter of the mind and heart; Americanism is not and never was a matter of race or ancestry."

Wonderful words, at last. But all they meant was that Nisei in the camps could enlist in the army (not the navy). But first, they would be required to complete a military form called "Statement

of United States Citizen of Japanese Ancestry." A loyalty oath.
The key questions in the army form were:

27. Are you willing to serve in the armed forces of the
    United States on combat duty or wherever ordered?
28. Will you swear unqualified allegiance to the United
    States of America and faithfully defend the United
    States from any and all attack by foreign or domestic
    forces, and forswear any form of allegiance to the Japa-
    nese emperor, to any other foreign government power
    or organization?

Dillon Myer of the WRA, who was determined to speed up
the closing of the relocation camps, quickly realized that the
form, with slightly altered wording, could be used to facilitate
the release of camp residents too old or too young to serve in
the military. The WRA began to print its own forms called
"Application for Leave Clearance" and required all evacuees to
declare their loyalty. The idea, in his mind, was to define "loyals" and "disloyals" and then separate them and allow "loyals"
to leave the camps—as long as they did not try to go to the West
Coast.

The War Department, pushed by Deputy Secretary McCloy,
who was in the process of changing sides in Washington arguments, realized as early as mid-1942 that the internment had
been a mistake. The notion of recruiting Japanese American soldiers from the camps had been debated, secretly, in the War
Department for months, with General DeWitt in San Francisco
repeatedly arguing for keeping all the West Coast evacuees
behind barbed wire. But McCloy's new position was being backed
by other officials, including Elmer Davis of the Office of War
Information, who told Roosevelt, "Loyal American citizens of
Japanese descent should be permitted, after individual testing,
to enlist in the Army and Navy." Part of Davis's argument was

that, in broadcasts from Tokyo, the Japanese were effectively using the American concentration camps in a propaganda campaign in other Asian countries, asserting that the war in the Pacific was essentially "a race war": Caucasians against all Asians.

• • •

The American people did not know it, but there were already hundreds and then thousands of Japanese Americans in the army. Even though more than two thousand Japanese Americans in the military were mustered out unceremoniously in January of 1942, others were kept in uniform by local commanders who innocently or deliberately ignored orders from Washington. One all-white army company in Hawaii reported that it had no Japanese Americans when, in fact, the unit's star softball pitcher was a Nisei. By the time of Stimson's announcement, a Nisei combat unit made up of former active-duty soldiers from Hawaii and members of the Hawaii National Guard was already training as the One Hundredth Battalion of the U.S. Army at Fort McCoy in Mississippi. Early in 1941, before the war, the military had been building a secret new unit, the Military Intelligence Service, quietly recruiting bilingual Japanese Americans from Hawaii and California to be used as translators and interpreters if there were a war with Japan. This was a difficult task: the army estimated that less than 3 percent of Nisei could speak much more than elementary Japanese and that perhaps one hundred Nisei were actually fluent in the language of their ancestors. Bill Hosokawa, a Nisei newspaper reporter before the war, described his MIS interview this way: "I thought I [had] a fair speaking knowledge of the language, but the interviewer quickly proved me completely inadequate. . . . First he asked me to read a high school text. I could make out perhaps two or three characters in a hundred."

The first instructor hired, in September of 1941, was a thirty-one-year-old army private named John Aiso from Los Angeles, a prewar draftee working as an army truck mechanic. A graduate of Brown University and Harvard Law School, Aiso must have been the most overqualified mechanic in the service. He studied at Brown on a scholarship financed by the government of Japan, as did his roommate who became a translator for Emperor Hirohito in Tokyo. Aiso had practiced law in Los Angeles, and also in both Japan and Manchuria where he worked for the British American Tobacco Company. He was fluent in Japanese, which had turned out to be a rare talent among the Nisei. Aiso, who wanted to return to his law practice in Los Angeles, initially turned down the MIS offer made by General John Weckerling. He changed his mind when Weckerling stood up, came around his desk, put an arm on Private Aiso's shoulder, and said, "John, your country needs you."

"No American," Aiso said later, "had ever told me America was my country." He also recalled, vividly, that on December 8, 1941, when he and his colleagues were on a trolley going to his office at the Presidio, a hysterical woman waved her arms toward him and yelled to white men in the car, "There's a Jap. Kill him! Kill him! What's wrong with you men?"

The work of Aiso and Weckerling was little known until after the war. In the end, more than six thousand Japanese Americans secretly served in the Pacific—almost all with distinction and almost unbelievable bravery—as translators and interpreters attached to the British and Australian armies, as well as to U.S. Army units.

The secrecy surrounding the Military Intelligence Service was doubled for a few hundred translators and interpreters in the navy and Marine Corps, which were still essentially segregated services. MIS training originally began at the Presidio in San Francisco, but General DeWitt demanded they be moved out of

California and the language school moved to Camp Savage and then Fort Snelling in Minnesota. People up there were different than the Californians. Minnesotans who lived near Camp Savage would wait outside the gates on Friday nights to invite the Nisei to their homes for dinner or the weekend.

When camp was over, though, their duty was among the most dangerous in the military. The linguists had to worry about friendly fire but also knew they would be executed as traitors if they were captured by Imperial Japanese soldiers. Nisei wearing American uniforms often were assigned white bodyguards in case American soldiers, trained to shoot first and ask questions later, mistook them for Japanese infiltrators wearing uniforms stripped from dead American soldiers. One of the Nisei, Sergeant Fred Tanaka, on a ship headed for the Solomon Islands, went from one white soldier to another saying, "Take a good look and remember me because I'm going in with you."

There was, of course, both hostility and confusion about the linguists, especially at the beginning. The first time Admiral William Halsey encountered Nisei, two of them, they were interrogating six Imperial Japanese pilots, badly burned when they were shot down by navy planes. They got no information. The two pilots who could talk kept repeating, "Kill me, please kill me."

"Goddamn you bastards," Halsey roared, not at the pilots but the interrogators. "What the hell did the government send you to school for?" Later the admiral would change his mind when Nisei intercepting Japanese messages helped guide the navy into some of the greatest sea victories in history. The MIS translators and interpreters were helped by the fact that the Imperial Japanese leaders believed their language was impenetrable. The Japanese military often used rather simple coding, accounting for two critical American intelligence achievements in the Pacific. On April 4, 1943, a Nisei, Harold Fudenna, intercepted a coded radio message detailing the flight plans of the Japanese Pacific commander Admiral Isoroku Yamamoto, the man who planned the attack on Pearl Harbor. In a bomber escorted by six A6M Zeros, fighter planes, Yamamoto was touring Japanese bases. His plane was attacked by eighteen American P-38s and shot down over Bougainville. Then, almost exactly a year later, his successor, Vice Admiral Shigeru Fukudome, was killed when his plane ran into a tropical storm and crashed near the Philippines. Local fishermen found a waterproof container in the water near the crash site and turned it over to Americans. The box, which contained the plans for Operation Z, the last major operation planned by the Japanese, was taken to Australia by submarine, where it was decoded and translated by two American Nisei. They were both *Kibei*, Yoshikazu Yamada and George "Sankey" Yamashiro, working at the Allied Translator Interpreter Section headquarters in Brisbane. Two months later, using the translated plans, American ships and planes destroyed much of Japan's dwindling navy and air force in the Battle of the Philippine Sea. Three Japanese aircraft carriers were destroyed in the battle as well as more than six hundred planes in what became known as the "Marianas Turkey Shoot." The U.S. Navy lost just twenty-three navy Hellcat fighters.

On the islands as the Allies moved toward Japan in one bloody battle after another, the MIS men learned tricks of their new trade. First, they needed captives and Japanese soldiers usually preferred death to surrender, but that began to change some when Nisei using megaphones promised them, in their own language, fair treatment as prisoners. Captured Japanese were obviously worth more alive than dead and word got around that the Americans were no longer shooting prisoners, as they had often done early in the war. The interrogators also learned, or knew from their own American Japanese families, that the key to dealing with the enemy was "honor" and "shame." One trick that worked was telling prisoners, in the most friendly way, that the Americans would ask the International Red Cross to inform their families back in Japan that they had been captured and were safe. That was the last thing some prisoners wanted—they were afraid of the shame that would envelop their families—and they began to talk about their units and battle plans.

Among the most valuable and dangerous work the MIS men did was "cave flushing." Thousands of Japanese soldiers and civilians hid deep in lava caves when Americans invaded one island after another on their route to Japan. Nisei volunteered to climb into the caves to try to talk the Japanese into giving up and coming out of the deep darkness. One flusher in Saipan, Corporal Bob Kubo, armed only with a hidden pistol, climbed down a rope and after hours of conversation persuaded 122 civilians and nine Japanese soldiers, trained and conditioned to die before surrendering, to climb out of the cave with him. It was a scene unimaginable to most Americans. As many of his comrades did, Kubo shared boiled rice with the Japanese soldiers, talking about home and family until they agreed to leave their weapons and come out. Most of the flushers were sergeants and corporals; Japanese privates bowed to them or to their rank as they entered the caves.

The other options, there and elsewhere, were to simply block the cave entrances or use flamethrowers to kill anyone inside, including civilians.

One irony was that the most desirable MIS recruits were *Kibei*, the young Americans educated in Japan who not only spoke the best Japanese but also better understood the thinking and culture of the Imperial soldiers they interrogated. Dillon Myer, the WRA director, later wrote that he overheard a conversation between two young men in a camp saying, "It's only the damned *Kibei* who can get into this man's army."

One of the *Kibei*, Kenny Yasui, who had gone to school in Tokyo, posed as an Imperial Japanese colonel and ordered sixteen Japanese soldiers to surrender—and they did. Takejiro Higa, a *Kibei* educated in Okinawa, was interrogating captured Japanese soldiers when he looked up and spotted two of his seventh grade classmates. "Goddamn it. You don't recognize an old classmate?" Higa said. Suddenly he began to cry and so did the two Japanese soldiers.

He wasn't the only one. Many of the MIS Japanese encountered old friends, teachers, and, most of all, relatives. The interpreters often asked for permission to visit prison camps holding Imperial soldiers to look for family members.

Staff Sergeant Roy Matsumoto, whose parents were incarcerated at Jerome, Arkansas, served in Burma and was noted for crawling into no-man's-land between American and Japanese troops at night and listening to the Japanese make their plans for the next day. On one occasion, he came back to American lines and supervised the setting up of a machine-gun ambush at the point he heard the enemy planned to attack. When the enemy came at 3:00 a.m., they were immediately pinned down by the machine-gun fire. Matsumoto, pretending he was a Japanese colonel, jumped up and screamed *"Susume!"*—Advance!—and the Japanese did, right into the American guns.

On the tiny island of Myitkyina, Sergeant Grant Jiro Hirabayashi called G-2 (Intelligence) one morning to say, "Captain, you're not going to believe this, but I've got about twenty females, I think Korean, and I need help." They were "comfort women" forced to sexually service Japanese soldiers. They were freed and flown out to India—after a going-away party where they sang Korean folk songs to a handful of Nisei from Hawaii.

After the war, Major General Charles Willoughby, General MacArthur's chief of intelligence, said of the work of the Nisei linguists, "Never before in history did an army know so much concerning its enemy prior to actual engagement, as the American army during the Pacific campaigns. Those interpreters and translators saved over a million lives and two years."

* * *

Ben Kuroki went to war in North Africa. The Red Ass was one of hundreds of American planes providing air support for the desert battles in North Africa between the troops of British Field Marshal Bernard Montgomery and Germany's Marshal Erwin Rommel. By then the farm boy from Nebraska was a top gunner with a nickname, "Most Honorable Son." The crew was based near the city of Oran in Algeria. Kuroki's first combat mission had been over the port of Bizerte in Tunisia on December 13, 1942, bombing German troops and equipment coming in from Italy across the Mediterranean.

Over Bizerte, black puffs of flak, the deadly chunks of metal scattered from antiaircraft guns, surrounded the B-24s. The Red Ass was one of the planes hit; flak from behind almost beheaded the nineteen-year-old tail gunner Roy Dawley. The plane and crew flew nine more missions—Kuroki took over as tail gunner, quietly vomiting on each run—bombing German installations on both sides of the Mediterranean. They served over Tunis, Bizerte again, Palermo in Sicily, Messina, and Naples. Before the first Italian raid, Kuroki said to the waist gunner Joe Fori, "Looks like we're going to knock spaghetti out of your ancestors."

"Yeah?" said Fori, an Italian American. "Wait'll we get to the Pacific and knock the rice out of your most dishonorable ancestors."

After the last Italian run, the B-24 was scheduled to go back to its base in England. It didn't make it. The Red Ass was lost in the clouds, the navigator could not figure out where they were, and the plane ran out of gas. The pilot Lieutenant Jake Epting spotted an opening in the clouds and dove through, landing somewhere in the desert. No one was injured and the men were jumping up and down, laughing, until they saw Arab tribesmen on camels coming over the dunes, waving guns and spears, surrounding the crew and their plane. They seemed distinctly unfriendly. Then the cavalry came over the hill to rescue the Americans. It was the Spanish cavalry. The Americans had come down in Spanish Morocco. Spain was a neutral country, bound by international law to detain them for the duration of the war.

The crew was taken to a Spanish air force base where they were held in a barracks watched by armed guards. After a few days, Kuroki told Epting he wanted to try to escape. He got the idea that if he wrapped himself in a blanket and wrapped a white shirt around his head, like a turban, he could pass himself off as an Arab. Fori asked him why he was so anxious to escape and Kuroki said that in California they were holding Japanese Americans in concentration camps and it was his job to prove their loyalty to the United States. He got out of the camp all right, then stumbled along in a heavy rain, falling into ditches and trenches. He was free—for about thirty-six hours. Local Arabs and then Spanish soldiers spotted him and he ended up in a cell with a dozen other men, local crooks. After a night in jail and hours of incoherent questioning in three languages, he was taken back to the Spanish air base.

The next day, he and the whole Red Ass crew were loaded into a German Junkers Ju 52 and flown to an airstrip near Alhama, Spain, a small town with a small, neat hotel. Suddenly they were being treated as guests. The beds had clean, starched sheets, the food was hot and so was the water in the bathtubs, and two maids, sisters, Carmen and Rosa Tomas, were fascinated by Kuroki. They had never before seen anyone who looked like him. There were twenty-one other "internees" in the hotel, mostly pilots, American, British, and two from New Zealand. A tailor from the town came by to make the latest American guests better suits than they ever wore back home. Their new friends told them that American or British diplomats came around every couple of weeks with money and cigarettes for the Spaniards—and were allowed to take away a couple of men to Gibraltar, then usually on to London.

The Air Corps was always determined to get detained airmen back into service—expensively trained crews were being killed or captured by the hundreds, month after month—and after three months the United States embassy in Madrid negotiated the release of the Red Ass crew.

The rumor was that the exchange rate for each man was a new Buick for Spanish officials in Madrid. True or not, Epting's crew, including Kuroki, had a new B-24 waiting in England. This one they named Tupelo Lass. They had learned that hometown newspapers would not print the name Red Ass. Now they named the B-24 after Lieutenant Epting's hometown of Tupelo, Mississippi.

Tupelo Lass and the rest of the Ninety-Third Group were sent from England back to North Africa one more time, but never told exactly why—except that they would be training for a secret mission. Day after day, the group flew low-level flights in formation, dropping dummy bombs on dummy targets. There was no room for error when screaming along at top speed ten feet above the desert—and more than one B-24 landed with bomb doors torn off and cradled in palm trees.

• • •

The Pearl Harbor day troubles in Manzanar and other camps in December of 1942 brought the evacuation and the camps back into the news—and, predictably, politicians reacted quickly. In Washington, Senator A. B. "Happy" Chandler of Kentucky formed a special investigative committee that held hearings in the Capitol and then went on a slapdash "fact-finding" tour of the relocation camps. With his wife in tow, he spent a couple of hours at each of six locations. At Manzanar, the camp director, Ralph Merritt, accompanied the Chandlers and sent a written report to Dillon Myer saying, "Mrs. Chandler took the opportunity to express her very vigorous opinion about all Japanese, which was summarized by the expression that they should be put on shipboard and be dumped in the ocean . . . and to various people she spoke vigorously against the whole WRA policy, mentioning the cost to taxpayers."

At the same time, Isamu Noguchi, the sculptor, back home in New York, wrote of the troubles in the camps in the February 1, 1943, issue of the *New Republic*, saying:

> I had been in Poston for a short time before the disturbance there, and I am afraid I must report that the newspaper interpretation of it—the rioters were merely pro-Axis elements—was oversimplified. Pro-Japanese sentiment and a hoodlum element in the center played a part in the trouble. But the situation of which the troublemakers took advantage was produced by other causes, chiefly two: the great sense of frustration, which all members of the camps feel; and the great cleavage between the first generation and the second generation, which has the American-born, who cooperate with the authorities, the subject of attack. . . . It must be remembered that these 110,000 people are presumably in the camps because they were unable to find places to go, voluntarily, before the mass-evacuation order was issued. They should not be confused with the 1,974 suspect enemy aliens in internment camps.

Methodist bishop E. Stanley Jones, a famous missionary, visited five of the relocation camps and wrote about the experience in *Christian Century* magazine.

Their spirits are unbroken. They took the pledge of allegiance to the flag at a high school assembly, and my voice broke as I joined with in the promise of loyalty "to one nation indivisible, with liberty and justice for all." Liberty and justice for all—how could they say it? But they did and they meant it. Their faith in democracy is intact. Their faith in God holds too, in spite of everything.

Maybe. Following President Roosevelt's change of heart, or leading it, General Marshall, the army chief of staff, ordered the formation of a second segregated Nisei unit, the 442nd Regimental Combat Team, on February 1, 1943. The army teams of recruiters sent to the camps quickly discovered that patriotism was one thing, but enthusiasm for service was another.

The army, distributing its questionnaires in Hawaii and in the camps in February of 1943, called for 1,500 Japanese American volunteers from Hawaii and 3,000 from the mainland. An overwhelming 10,000 men from Hawaii crowded recruitment offices on the islands, many of them racing on their bikes or just running to the army offices. The announcement was met with less enthusiasm on the mainland, where, of course, the vast majority of draft-age men of Japanese ancestry and their families were behind barbed wire. Only 1,256 volunteered from the camps during the initial call for volunteers, so the army had to change the numbers: calling for 2,900 men from Hawaii and 1,500 from the mainland.

"Last Tuesday night I went to a meeting held by the army concerning the new order opening voluntary enlistment in the army," wrote Stanley Hayami. He reported that the event was put on by "a lieutenant, two sergeants & a Japanese-American sergeant." The Japanese American sergeant was Ben Kuroki, the farm boy from Nebraska. The Army Air Corps hoped he could encourage more enlistments from the camps.

Hayami described the meeting.

> They gave a lot of talks telling us how we would benefit if we volunteered. And answered a lot of questions. Said that the reason why they wanted to put us in a separate combat unit was for publicity.
>
> A lot of people wanted to know if they could have some guarantees so that after the war was over, they wouldn't have their citizenship taken away, & the lands they own taken. They answered that we would be protected by the 14th amendment in the Constitution.
>
> Then one man says "Well the 14th also is supposed to have kept us out of camp, what about that?" The army men answered by saying that "In time of war the 14th and such do not hold & the army has control & can do practically anything."
>
> Then one man says "What the heck, are we going to get kicked out every time a war comes up." Then the army man said that he agrees that a great injustice was done us when we were kicked out, but he says that the army has realized that what they did was probably wrong, and is now trying to help us to make up for it.

Hayami described how, that Wednesday and Thursday, the young men from his block gathered to discuss the recruitment. "The *Nisei*," he wrote, "wanted to join provided that they got certain guarantees, including citizenship and the ability to own land. However the *Issei* opposed the recruitment, saying, 'Why bother? We want to go back to Japan after the war anyway.' The *Nisei* brought up with American ideals just naturally opposed the *Kibeis* brought up with Japanese ideals & each thought the other dumb & grew more hate between themselves."

Most of the questions the army men heard were from young men asking why they should fight for a country that had imprisoned their parents—to say nothing of destroying family farms and businesses. Also, the thought of a segregated unit was abhorrent to many. At Topaz camp in Utah, young internees hammered away with a single question: Why couldn't the Nisei simply serve as other Americans? Why should they be singled out when there was no all-Italian or all-German unit?

The camps were in an uproar. Babe Karasawa, interned at Poston, told his father, "Me and the guys are going to volunteer." His father's answer was, "That's stupid! They put you in a place like this? And you're going to volunteer?"

When Mitsuo Usui, whose family had been forced to sell their nursery in Los Angeles for just $1,000, told his father he planned to serve, they shouted at each other in the first argument they had ever had. "We lose everything—the property, the business, our home," his father said. "It's like a kick in the pants and now they're saying come in and shine my shoes." The old man physically kicked his son out the door. Mitsuo slept that night in a furnace room. When he woke, his mother was standing there. She said, "If you feel that strongly about your country, then you volunteer and go. . . . I'll take care of Papa."

The enlistment program was a failure in all the ten camps. Dillon Myer, the director of the War Relocation Authority, had predicted that there would be as many as 2,000 volunteers in Heart Mountain. The army fudged the results: it was announced that 3,000 had volunteered. In fact, in the end, most of the American Japanese who volunteered were from Hawaii, where there was no massive internment. The actual number at Heart Mountain was 38. The enlistment numbers from other camps were: Minidoka, 308; Poston, 236; Granada, 152; Topaz, 116; Gila River, 101; Manzanar, 100; Tule Lake, 59; Jerome, 42; and Rohwer, 40.

At Heart Mountain, the camp director, Guy Robertson, tried a harsher, more threatening tone than the army teams, writing to Nisei evacuees, "I would like to ask if the parents realize that a life-long stigma may be borne by their children who fail to recognize and live up to their responsibility." He went on to state that their final choice on whether or not to cooperate would permanently affect not just their own lives but "the whole future of American Japanese people who wish to make their future home in America."

Robertson told American Japanese, "Your government has asked outright that you express your loyalty. . . . Question 28 gives everyone the opportunity to make a definite statement regarding his loyalty or friendship. Your government has offered the citizen an opportunity to volunteer in the armed forces of the United States."

He went on to scold the evacuees:

> The response to these sentiments at Heart Mountain has been very, very disappointing. May I ask the citizen group how they expect to approach their government in asking concessions, whether it is restitution, reparation, or whatever you may ask, when you have more or less repudiated your government by failing to indicate a fair average of enlistment comparable to other relocation centers. In view of the fact that you have not offered your wholehearted support to your government's program, you will be judged by the answer you have made and the attitude it expresses. If you have reacted favorably, you will be considered favorably. If you have reacted unfavorably, you will, in all probability, have unfavorable consideration. Surely you understand that you cannot hope to force any issue with the government of the United States.

The recruiters were frustrated, but their frustrations were minimal when compared to the outrage among many American Japanese. The loyalty questionnaires were insulting on many counts, but two questions were particularly divisive. Question 27 had rubbed salt in the wounds of young men whose parents' lives had been ruined. Question 28 was worse: it assumed all Japanese and Japanese Americans were loyal to the emperor of Japan. The Issei, whose average age was fifty-nine and who were still considered citizens of Japan—they had been barred from applying for American citizenship since 1924—would become stateless persons if they answered yes.

More than 65,000 of the Nisei of draft age answered yes to both questions. Thirteen thousand answered no to at least one question. A total of 6,733 answered no to both questions. They were immediately called the "No-No Boys." Others said yes, then wrote in complaints or caveats such as, "If my parents are allowed to go home." Most of those who answered either question with a no were classified as "disloyals."

• • •

James Hatsuki Wakasa was shot and killed at Topaz just before sunset on April 11, 1943, by a sentry named Gerald B. Philpott. Wakasa was in his sixties and had come to the United States in 1903, studying for two years at the University of Wisconsin. During World War I, he was a civilian cooking instructor at Camp Dodge, Iowa. The army said that he was trying to escape and that he had ignored Philpott's warnings. According to the army report, Wakasa was shot while crawling under the camp's outer fence. WRA employees later determined that Wakasa was inside the inner camp fence when he was shot. A postmortem examination of the entry and exit wounds also found that Wakasa was facing the soldier who shot him.

Eiichi Sato, a social worker for Block 36, where Wakasa lived, went to inspect the scene the next morning with four other prisoners. They were approaching the fence and when they were approximately thirty-five feet away an army jeep came speeding by and, upon seeing them, came to an abrupt halt. The driver stood up from his seat and grabbed the submachine gun from his companion. Sato recalled that the driver then "jumped off the jeep and came dashing to the fence pointing his gun at us and said: 'Scatter or you'll get the same thing as the other guy got.'" Philpott faced a court-martial two weeks later and was found not guilty.

Two days later, on April 13, General DeWitt testified before a House Naval Affairs subcommittee, saying, "You needn't worry about the Italians at all except in certain cases. Also, the same for the Germans except in individual cases." But when it came to the American Japanese, he said, "No Jap should come back to this coast except on a permit from my office. . . . We must worry about the Japanese all the time until he is wiped off the map."

Once again he added, "A Jap is a Jap," which prompted a *Washington Post* editorial response.

> The general should be told that American democracy and the Constitution of the United States are too vital to be ignored and flouted by any military zealot. The panic of Pearl Harbor is now past. There has been ample time for the investigation of these people and the determination of their loyalty to this country on an individual basis. Whatever excuse there once was for evacuating and holding them indiscriminately no longer exists.

The *Post* also recognized the long-term damage the evacuation was doing to the nation itself, editorializing two months later, "The outright deprivation of civil rights which we have visited upon these helpless and for the most part, no doubt, innocent people may leave an ugly blot upon the pages of our history."

Many WRA officials might have agreed with the *Post*'s editorial. From the top down, they realized that evacuation was not only expensive, but it was destroying people's lives and accomplishing little that was worthwhile. Dillon Myer, director of the agency, said, "It saps the initiative, weakens the instincts of human dignity and freedom, creates doubts, misgivings and tensions." The War Relocation Authority had two goals, often in conflict: to maintain order and to get as many of the internees back to a semblance of normal lives, in part by giving the boys furloughs to harvest crops across the Midwest and encouraging girls to apply for admission and employment at schools, offices, hospitals, and factories away from the West Coast.

Many residents were released for good, officially or unofficially, to work in the East and the middle of the country, where there were serious labor shortages. The WRA received more than ten thousand requests from Chicago firms and institutions seeking to fill jobs left open as young men went off to war, and as other Americans, men and women, moved on to higher-paying jobs in defense industries. Seabrook Farms in New Jersey, the country's largest producer of frozen food, was actively recruiting labor at all the camps. The army, too, needed more men and some women, mainly nurses. Others had been and were being released to attend colleges that would have them. Camp administrators were also lenient about leaves because they saw that young Japanese behind the fences were being goaded and threatened by so-called pro-Axis elements. Hundreds of frustrated and angry young American loyalists were turning against camp administrations and the United States government itself.

Ted Hirasaki was on work release in a bakery in Klamath Falls, Oregon, a small city east of the Cascades, washing pots and pans nine hours a day—and walking in wonder through the straight high pines of the area. Others were happy working for the meager wages in the camps. Hisako Watanabe wrote to Miss Breed back in San Diego that she was enjoying working in the camp as secretary to the school business manager. Louise Ogawa was in the same office. They both thought about applying for work outside but worried about who would take care of their parents.

"My sister is in Minneapolis, Minnesota, with her husband doing domestic work," Fusa Tsumagari wrote. "My brother Yuki is working on a farm in Milwaukee but has not lost his ambition to be a doctor." Then she added: "Yesterday I finished reading, *Lost Horizon*. The points that interested me were: (1) the isolation; (2) doing everything in moderation; (3) the feeling of wanting to go out, and on the other hand wanting to stay in this leisurely place. Some feel as Mallinson in the story the strong urge to get out—to do things—anything to get out of here. . . . I guess this place could be called a second Shangri-La—if you like this type of living."

The living did not seem so bad for many teenagers; they were mostly optimistic and motivated young people. Louise Ogawa wrote about the first graduation at Poston.

> The student body president was called to the stage. He was asked which he liked better, chocolate, candy, or a Coke. He happens to like a girl nicknamed "Coke" and replied "Coke." So they brought out a bottle of Coca-Cola. Everyone screamed with surprise and hunger at the sight of a bottle of Coca-Cola. He had to get down on his knees and propose to the bottle of coke. Ben Honda, the M.C. replied, "Yes, Coke will be yours." How we all envied him!!

Fusa Tsumagari had more teenage news for Miss Breed in another letter.

Gee, it's hard for me to write this letter, it's so overdue. This time I have an excuse. The day I was going to write you, my b.f. from Layton, Utah, dropped in. I was needless to say more than surprised and all agog! He is a fellow I went around with at Santa Anita . . . but it wasn't very serious. But now that I've seen him again and realize he came all the way from Utah I feel like that song, "It Started All Over Again—the Moment I looked into his eyes," etc. . . . It seems to me, "I've got it bad and that ain't good." . . . He's about 5'8", dark, got a nice-shaped head—looks like Ronald Reagan in a crude sort of way.

Overall life in the camps had largely settled into a routine for many residents, a kind of shadow of life in an American town. Schools were built, teachers were imported, the boys played baseball and, in Boy Scout uniforms, raised the American flag each morning. The Boy Scouts were one of the few organizations that brought together the evacuees and local townspeople. Scouts from Cody, nine miles away, and Heart Mountain would hold joint programs, with the locals often staying over for weekends. Pup tents were shared. One was assigned to a Cody boy named Alan Simpson, who later became a Republican senator, and Norman Mineta, who later became the mayor of San Jose, California, and a Democratic congressman. Mineta would also come to serve in two cabinets as secretary of commerce under President Bill Clinton and secretary of transportation under President George W. Bush. A couple of American kids, Boy Scouts. They became friends for life, and unlikely partners across the aisle when they served in government.

Mineta's father, Kunisaku, was sent from Heart Mountain to the Military Language School at the University of Chicago early in 1943 to join other bilingual Japanese Americans teaching American soldiers in language classes. When his family was later allowed to join him there, they caught a bus along

Wyoming Route 20 in front of the camp and rode to Greybull, Wyoming, and then to Billings, Montana. While waiting for the train east, they had dinner in a Billings restaurant. Norman, by now thirteen years old, stood up and began walking around the table, stacking the dishes.

"Norman," his mother said. "You don't have to do that anymore."

The exodus from the camps was continuing, but it was still a one-by-one process. In the spring of 1943, Stanley Hayami was worrying about his grades, but he was also writing about his friends at Heart Mountain leaving the camp for school or work. Almost every day through the spring of 1943 there were new notations in his diary. Some were about his grades but most of them were about friends leaving the camps for school or work. "Today James Nakada got his release to Chicago. He's going all by himself and he's only 16, too. He's going to get a job as a houseboy or something." In a way, Hayami was also getting chances to interact with the world outside the camps: "Today I helped clean the school grounds. In the afternoon went to play Lovell. Our first game with the outside. We beat them 18–5."

Then, on April 25, Easter Sunday, he wrote of dressing and going to church with his friend Jimmie Yada. "I got baptized," he wrote. "So now I am a real Christian. I hope I can live up to that name."

Easter Sunday of 1943, the day Stanley Hayami became a Christian at Heart Mountain, the First Lady, Eleanor Roosevelt, was visiting Gila River and other camps. Traveling separately, President Roosevelt was at Fort Riley, Kansas, part of a nineteen-stop presidential tour of military installations around the country. There were more than 15,000 soldiers training at Riley, 160 of them Nisei who had completed their basic training and were given menial jobs around the installation, mowing lawns, chopping weeds, working in the motor pool. Although they had completed basic training, they were not issued helmets or firearms. Thirty of them were shoveling horse manure fifteen miles from the fort at the Cavalry Replacement Training Center. On the day of the president's visit, forty-two of the Nisei were ordered to mend fences and dig postholes ten miles away from their base. The rest were lined up and marched twenty minutes to a large hangar, which served as the Motor Mechanics School Building. Guarded by soldiers with machine guns, they were ordered to sit in bleachers, staring straight ahead and maintaining silence. After four hours, with Roosevelt long gone, they were dismissed. A private named Fred Sumoge from Hood River, Oregon, whose parents were at Tule Lake after losing their seven acres of strawberry fields because they could not pay their property taxes from the camp, said, "They treated us like prisoners. I wasn't sure that I would live through it." Then he began wondering if the reason American Japanese were concentrated in camps was that it would make it possible for the Air Corps to bomb them.

Still, no matter how they were treated, most of the American Japanese were still instinctively loyal to the United States. Masuru Ben Kahora, a Seattle businessman arrested on December 7 and held in Santa Fe, wrote to his family at Minidoka, urging them to buy U.S. war bonds. His wife, Kikuko, wrote back, "I am determined to become a part of American soil in order to bring up a new American generation. I am willing to take part in patriotic duties such as school PTA. My one point is to make an American of our daughter and a true one."

• • •

Once General DeWitt finally concluded that all Japanese, including American citizens, were the enemy, he stuck with that position. With Bendetsen as his spokesman, the West Coast commander continued to insist that there was no way to determine the loyalty of American Japanese—even the men who were now wearing the same uniform he wore. When McCloy, questioning and playing down his own role in the evacuation of 1942, began arguing that those Nisei soldiers must have the same rights as any other Americans in uniform, including a furlough before induction or before being shipped overseas, DeWitt countered by demanding that the Nisei soldiers from California would have to wear their uniforms, carry a permit issued by his command, and would be allowed to visit only two places in California, Manzanar and Tule Lake. Earl Warren, now the governor of the state, was no different than DeWitt, saying as late as June of 1943, "We know that submarines have been hovering off our coast and could send saboteurs into California. If we permitted Japanese to return to this combat zone, how could we tell between them?" He went on to state that "large numbers of Japanese in the relocation centers are Japanese army reservists and others have been taught sabotage."

"There isn't any such thing as a loyal Japanese and that loyalty just can't be determined," DeWitt said to McCloy and to General Marshall. McCloy's answer now was:

> We are going to send him to North Africa, we've got to let him have the same benefits as any soldier. . . . These fellows are going to war. They volunteered to fight for the white man. . . . These fellows, lots of them are Oriental in only one sense—they have that blood in them, but they have been born in California, chew chewing gum and go to American movies, played on basketball teams . . .

After DeWitt's testimony before Congress, on April 15, 1943, the War Department was forced to issue a directive ordering the Western Zone commander to allow Japanese American soldiers on furlough to visit anywhere in the West Coast states. The next day, the general called a press conference and said that he would follow orders. Then he added, "The War Department says a Jap-American soldier is not a Jap; he is an American. Well, alright. I said I have a Jap situation to take care of and I'm going to do it."

The number of Japanese Americans who had left the camps for jobs, schools, and the army since the beginning of the evacuation reached almost 20,000 before the end of 1943. By then, just more than 1,000 Nisei from the camps had volunteered and been accepted for military service. In Hawaii, the number was 2,686; a crowd of more than fifteen thousand people cheered as they were loaded onto ships in Honolulu.

On the mainland, Washington and the WRA continued to try to find ways to release more evacuees and make plans to close most of the camps as soon as possible. But there was opposition to that by the new governor of California, the former attorney general, Earl Warren, who had practically ridden to office on the backs of Japanese, alien and citizen alike. He won 57 percent of the vote on November 3, 1942, defeating Culbert Olson. During the campaign, Warren promised that the first thing he would do as governor would be to fire Carey McWilliams, director of the Division of Immigration and Housing. McWilliams was an Olson official hated and feared by California's big farmers, and he had also become a critic of the Japanese evacuation after visiting assembly and relocation centers.

Once in office, Warren did just as he promised. McWilliams, the author of highly praised books, particularly *Factories in the Field* detailing how white farmers treated migrant farm workers, went to New York, where he became editor of the *Nation* magazine.

Then, the new governor refused to negotiate with the WRA about the return of Japanese to their homes in his state. Warren stated his reservations in a press conference on the day after he was elected.

> I firmly believe there is positive danger attached to the
> presence of so many of these admittedly American-hating
> Japanese in an area where sabotage or any other civil disor-
> ders would be so detrimental to the war effort. I have
> always felt that the concentration of these Japs [in Califor-
> nia camps]—the reason for their concentration is based on
> military necessity and the Army, which is charged with
> the external security of our country is the only agency
> thoroughly familiar with the Jap and his machinations. . . .
> The Army should control the whole situation.

The same day that Warren spoke out, there was unrest at the Tule Lake camp, and soon the army came in to manage the situation. Oregon's largest newspaper, the *Portland Oregonian*, wrote, "With tanks, tommy guns, rifles and bayonets, the army moved into the Tule Lake segregation center, where Jap chauvin-ists had disregarded the civilian authorities and created a situa-tion pregnant with dread." The paper went on to praise the army for "quelling the disorder without firing a shot," remarking that "had that camp been an American camp in Japan, and had Japa-nese soldiers been summoned to abate a similar uprising, the ground would have been drenched with blood. The Jap, as a soldier, revels in the slaughter of unarmed human targets."

An editorial in the *Denver Post* added, "There is just one word to describe the situation which is being uncovered by investiga-tion of the Jap mutiny in the Tule Lake segregation center. That is 'Rotten.'" The *Post* went on to complain about how "White employees of the camp were under instructions from the War Relocation Administration not to give orders to Jap internees but merely 'Make suggestions.'"

The *Post* was further alarmed that WRA director Myer had been quoted in the *Seattle Star* "as saying the postwar problem of handling the Japs in this country is no problem at all because 'We can within three generations assimilate them.'" The editorial went on to say, "The only way the Japs in this country could be assimilated is through intermarriage with white Americans. Is that what Myer is advocating? Does he want to mix yellow and white blood?"

Kentucky's Senator Chandler reentered the scene, saying, "These disloyal Japanese have no place at all in the American way of life." He went on to accuse the WRA of "coddling" the inmates. He added that "disloyals" should be transferred to the Aleutian Islands off Alaska, two of which had been occupied by the Imperial Japanese in June of 1942. They were driven off by American troops a year later. Representative John Costello, a California congressman heading a congressional subcommittee investigating conditions at Tule Lake, told the *Times Herald* in Washington, D.C., that he had discovered reports indicating that the disturbances in the camps were ordered and directed by shortwave radio from Tokyo.

• • •

The press continued to attack the WRA and the camps throughout 1943—not because the camps were un-American but because officials were "soft" on the inmates. The *Los Angeles Times* published editorials like this one directed, the paper declared, at "sappy Jap-lovers": "Tokyo is protesting against our treatment of Jap internees. It is true that it has been scandalous—the scandal being that the Nips under this soft restraint have been better fed, housed, and otherwise more privileged than a great many free Americans." The paper then parroted the now oft repeated phrase, "As Gen. DeWitt remarked: 'A Jap is always a Jap.'"

"Soft restraint" or "coddling" the evacuees had been an issue, fed by rumors, from the very beginning. Such complaints drove the WRA to cut money allocated for food at Topaz from 39 cents a day to 31 cents. In the West, locals resented the fact that the camps had hospitals and their small towns did not. In Arkansas, the poorest of states, residents were enraged when local school-teachers, being paid $900 a year, were quitting to take Civil Service positions at the camps for as much as $2,000 a year. (Japanese American teachers were still being paid $16 a month.) In the areas around the camps, farmers picking up garbage and slops for pigs claimed that ham and fruit and other scarce and rationed items were being thrown away by well-fed prisoners. That was not true, but many Americans believed it. One of them, Congressman J. Leroy Johnson of California, said that there were "numerous reports and rumors of huge shipments of eggs, butter, sugar, and coffee" that were being delivered to the camps, and that classes in "art, dancing, rug-making are being offered the confined Japs."

The *Denver Post* published a six-part series on food surpluses at Heart Mountain, under the headline: "Food Is Hoarded for Japs in U.S. While Americans in Nippon Are Tortured." On December 6, a day before the second anniversary of Pearl Harbor, the *Los Angeles Times* published what the paper called a "Survey of Opinion," a straw vote collected from readers over two months. There were seven questions and more than twelve thousand responses.

1. Do you think the War Relocation Authority has capably handled the problem of Japanese in the United States? . . . "yes"—369; "no"—10,773

2. Do you favor Army control of Japanese in this country for the duration? . . . "yes"—11,203; "no"—372

3. Do you approve of the policy of freeing avowedly loyal Japanese to take jobs in the Midwest? . . . "yes"—1,139; "no"—9,750

4. Would you favor "trading" Japanese now here for American war prisoners held in Japan if it could be arranged? . . . "yes"—11,249; "no"—256

5. Do you favor a constitutional amendment after the war for deportation of all Japanese from this country, and forbidding further immigration? . . . "yes"—10,598; "no"—732

6. Would you except American-born Japanese if such a plan as the above were adopted? . . . "yes"—1,883; "no"—9,018

7. Would you permanently exclude all Japanese from the Pacific Coast states including California? . . . "yes"—9,855; "no"—999.

The *Times* then published an editorial titled, "Public Demands New Policy on Japs in the U.S." A cartoon showed West Coasters turning thumbs down on "Jap-Molly-Coddling."

7

"LOYALS" AND "DISLOYALS"

TULE LAKE: SEPTEMBER 1943

After his Easter conversion, Stanley Hayami returned to his diary, now worried by newly published stories of Japanese Imperial Army atrocities in the Pacific. Most of them had actually happened in 1942—the Bataan Death March and the execution of the airmen captured after Colonel James Doolittle led a dramatic bombing raid on Tokyo on April 18, 1942—many of the stories had been censored for more than a year for fear of their effects on American morale at home.

"It seems that since the 'murder' of the Doolittle bombers who were captured by the Japanese, public feeling seems to be pretty strong against us," wrote Hayami. "Every time the Japs over there do something bad, we over here (who have nothing to do with it—and who don't like it any more than anyone else) get it in the neck. Phooey!"

That same day in a speech on the Senate floor, Senator Tom Stewart, a Democrat from Tennessee, demanded that the citizenship of Japanese immigrants be rescinded. "They cannot be assimilated," he said. "There is not a single Japanese in this country who would not stab you in the back. Show me a Jap and I'll show you a person who is inherently deceptive." The national president of the American Legion's Women's Auxiliary said, "Let us long realize what the Japanese are. We have leaned over backward to care for the Japs who were sent to relocation camps. We might just as well realize now that they are not and never will be Americans."

Senator Chandler, the Kentucky Democrat who was chairman of the Senate's Military Affairs Committee, got some more publicity by holding hearings that concluded that as many as twenty thousand Japanese American young people were loyal to Emperor Hirohito. The senator was perceptive enough to understand that the camps were turning many evacuees against the government, and he considered the internment camps to be a failed experiment. The senator blamed Myer and his staff, stating: "I may say that generally, from the top, that is from Mr. Myer on down through each one of the officers, these people are sincere and God-fearing, honest, well-meaning American citizens, but they are theorists, they are professors, they are making a social experiment of this thing."

Because of Chandler's speeches on the Senate floor and interviews he gave to California newspapers basically saying the army should take over the camps, Myer asked Eleanor Roosevelt, whom he knew, if she could persuade her husband to see him. The WRA director was invited to lunch at the White House and told his story, saying Chandler was making a bad situation much worse, that if Chandler's committee report repeated officially what the senator was telling reporters, there would be more trouble in the camps. The president replied that he could take care of that—and he did. Calling other senators, Roosevelt said he wanted the Chandler report toned down when it was made

public. In the end, the Kentucky senator satisfied himself by rec-
ommending that "loyal" Nisei should be allowed to join the army
and "disloyals" should be segregated in a single camp—decisions
the War Department and the WRA had made months before.

By then, though, West Coast newspapers had begun oppos-
ing any release from the camps. The *San Diego Union* attacked
both American Japanese and the War Relocation Authority. Writing in a June 9, 1943, editorial that repeated General DeWitt's
"A Jap's a Jap" language, the paper editorialized, "The American people may soon find an invasion force of 119,000 Japs has
been landed by the WRA." The *San Francisco Chronicle*'s editorial was headlined "DeWitt Is Right" and advocated suspend-
ing the Bill of Rights. The *Los Angeles Times* headline was
"Stupid and Dangerous" over an editorial declaring, "As a race,
the Japanese have made for themselves a record for conscience-
less treachery unsurpassed in history."

In a smaller California paper, the *Santa Maria Courier*,
Edward Trebon, the editor and publisher, wrote a front-page col-
umn attacking a Caucasian reader's letter defending Japanese
Americans, writing:

> In the first place, you're a dirty, rotten, low-down, pusil-
> lanimous SNEAK. You haven't any more decency about
> you than the dirty yellow-bellied Japs you are upholding
> and fighting for—enemies of America—the race that would
> make you a disgusting foreigner in your own home-
> land . . . but you wouldn't understand that, because you're
> just a Snake . . . you weasel . . . you mangy baboon, you
> warty lover of Hirohito.

Then he ended by saying that he had met many Japanese Americans who were "truly loyal to America" and said he had no quar-
rel with them.

. . .

High school graduations were important events at all of the camps, complete with caps and gowns, diplomas, flags, guest speakers, and, perhaps most important of all, valedictorians. At Amache Relocation Center in Colorado in 1943, the valedictorian, Marion Konishi, said in her speech:

> Sometimes America failed and suffered. Sometimes she made mistakes, great mistakes. America hounded and harassed the Indians, then remembering that they were the first Americans, she gave them back their citizenship. She enslaved the Negroes, then remembering Americanism, she wrote out the Emancipation Proclamation. She persecuted the German Americans during the First World War, then recalling America was born of those who come from every nation, seeking liberty, she repented. Her history is full of errors, but with each mistake she has learned. . . . Can we the graduating class of Amache Senior High School believe that America still means freedom, equality, security, and justice? Do I believe this? Do my classmates believe this? Yes, with all our hearts, because in that faith, in that hope, is my future, our future, and the world's future.

And Stanley Hayami, at Heart Mountain? He still had a year of high school left and, one more time, he did not raise his grades and wrote, "Well, today was the finish of one year of hard schoolwork. I got the same grades as last semester: English—A; History—A; Advanced Algebra—B; Chemistry—A; Spanish II—B."

He was also missing more friends. On the seventeenth of August, Stanley wrote, "Kei Bessho who sat in front of me in Chemistry class last year went to Chicago 2 weeks ago. Mits

Inouye and Ralph Yanari, also in my chemistry class, and Albert Saijo, who worked in mess hall 5 with me back in Pomona, went together to work in the hospital at the Univ. of Michigan at Ann Arbor."

In late August and early September, he wrote again of one Nisei after another, family and friends, leaving Heart Mountain. His cousin Eddie left for the University of Cincinnati; his sister, Grace, nicknamed "Sach," left for Chicago. Stanley described her leave-taking: "It was windy—Sach had some tears in her eyes—though she tried hard to fight them back—don't blame her." She was headed to the American Academy of Art, planning to work for a doctor's family while she attended school.

Even Hayami's brother Frank had left Heart Mountain. Frank was released in August 1943, as by then, he wrote, "the government had decided that I was no longer considered dangerous to the public safety, and that I could leave camp to any destination in the United States with the exception of the area under the Western Defense Command which included the entire Pacific Coast." He packed one suitcase and, carrying a railroad ticket and $100 in cash, he departed for New York City "to seek my fame and fortune." At the time, he was carrying a 4C draft card, 4C meaning "enemy alien," even though he was a native-born American.

"I traveled without too much trouble from authorities or confrontations from the white Americans since they all took me for an American Indian or a Hawaiian because of my deep tan," he wrote. "The only work I could find was in restaurants, bussing the dishes off of the tables and slopping them into the garbage cans. My 4C draft card did not help me to get any work in the engineering field since most of that work was of a military nature."

• • •

All the policies that allowed anyone out of the camps were vehe-
mently opposed by General DeWitt and Colonel Bendetsen. Both
men, the architects of evacuation, were dealt with in the army
way: they were quietly relieved and promoted upward to avoid
any chance of national publicity or unrest about the camps. In
September of 1943, DeWitt was transferred to duty in Washington, D.C., and was replaced by General Delos Emmons, the martial law commander in Hawaii. Bendetsen, an extraordinarily
lucky man, was sent to London and then France, where he served
as deputy chief of staff of the forward communications zone in
Normandy.

While some Nisei were being released from the camps, the
state where most had originated, California, did not want them
back. Governor Warren said that the evacuees being released to
jobs and schools in other states were all "potential saboteurs"—and
he wanted none released in California. That same week, the San
Diego City Council formally called on the federal government
to stop releasing evacuees.

The state legislature took the same line as Governor Warren and began forming committees again to try to prevent the
American Japanese of California from returning to their home
state. Senator Herbert Slater, called the "dean of the California
Legislature" because he had served more than thirty years, traveled the state holding hearings designed to build public support
for preventing Japanese and Japanese Americans from returning
to their old homes. The committee invited parents of white
Americans fighting in the Pacific, leading to exchanges like this
with Mrs. Margaret Benaphfl, representing the Gold Star Mothers of California.

"We want to keep the Japs out of California," she said.

"For the duration?" asked Senator Slater.

"No, for all times."

"That's the stuff."

Pearl Buck, the author, also appeared before the Slater committee, praising the contributions of Asians to American life, but most California newspapers did not even report her presence, much less her hour-long testimony.

A state assembly committee, headed by Chester Gannon, questioned Mrs. Maynard Thayer of Pasadena, a member of the Daughters of the American Revolution, who was a leader of a pro–American Japanese organization called the Pacific Coast Committee on American Principles and Fair Play. Mrs. Thayer cited the Bill of Rights and this time the committee questioning was hostile.

> GANNON: What do you know of the Bill of Rights? The Bill of Rights has no application to state legislation and we know you attacked the American Legion and the Native Sons. When was the Bill of Rights written? What is it?
>
> THAYER: Of course, it's the first ten amendments of the Constitution.
>
> GANNON: You're like all these people who prattle about the Bill of Rights and don't know a thing about it. The Bill of Rights is not such a sacred thing after all. Don't you know at the time the Bill of Rights was written that we had 150,000 slaves in the U.S.? What did the Bill of Rights do about that—nothing. Slavery was accepted. And yet you talk about the rights of minorities being protected by the Bill of Rights.
>
> THAYER: I think we've made some progress in our interpretation since then. Our committee will back any groups whose constitutional rights are threatened. It is of the greatest importance that in time of war we do not get off into race hatred.
>
> GANNON: Are you a Communist? This sounds like Communist doctrine.

THAYER: I have been a registered Republican for thirty years.

Governor Warren then appointed a new committee, this one on race relations in the state. Leo Carrillo, an actor who was of Mexican descent, was appointed a member of this committee. He traveled California making speeches that included this line: "When people in Washington say we must protect American-Japanese, they don't know what they're talking about. There's no such thing as an American-Japanese. If we ever permit those termites to stick their filthy fingers into the sacred soil of our state again, we don't deserve to live here ourselves."

A few notable figures tried to use their reputations and talents to push against the anti-Japanese sentiment, including photographers Dorothea Lange and Ansel Adams.

Dorothea Lange, already famous for her work during the Great Depression in the 1930s, was hired by the War Relocation Authority to photograph the American Japanese evacuation and internment. She dedicated herself to the project, working seven days a week from the first roundups in March through the summer of 1942.

The army first limited her access and then confiscated her photos for the duration of the war.

Lange later wrote, "The internment is an example of what happens to us if we lose our heads. . . . What was, of course, horrifying was to do this thing entirely on the basis of what blood may be coursing through a person's veins, nothing else."

Adams, the visual poet of the west, had tried to enlist in the army in 1942 but was rejected because of his age, forty. He was invited to take photos at Manzanar by the camp's director, Ralph Merritt, an old friend from the Sierra Club.

Merritt was a man who knew the rules—and how to bend them. Internees were not allowed to use cameras, but Toyo

Miyatake, who had been a student of Edward Weston and was a well-known photographer back in Los Angeles, had smuggled lenses into the camp and used scrap wood to build a camera that looked like an ordinary lunch box. When Merritt realized what was going on, he arranged to have Miyatake's cameras, three of them, taken out of storage. He personally handed them to Miyatake, saying, "Use them!"

When Merritt invited Adams to Manzanar, the photographer agreed and came in September of 1943. He was a passionate man who hated the idea of the camps and thought that he could generate sympathy around the country for the hardworking and loyal Japanese and Japanese Americans being held behind wire fences and guard towers.

He spent a week in Owens Valley photographing the internees at work, at school, and in church. He was frustrated, however, by internees' insistence on showing only the best side of their lives behind barbed wire. They wore their finest clothes and smiled with their families. They were anxious to pose for the kind of photographs released by the government to try to picture camp life as happy and normal. He put together a book of photographs with the title, *Born Free and Equal: The Story of Loyal Japanese Americans*. "It is," he wrote of the book, "addressed to the average American citizen, and is conceived on a human, emotional basis accentuating the realities of the individual and his environment rather than considering the loyal Japanese as an abstract, amorphous, minority group."

Both the book and an exhibit of the photographs at the Museum of Modern Art in New York were commercial failures. In Adams's own words, "People refused to buy it." It was too soon. To many citizens, the faces of the camp still looked like the enemy.

• • •

During 1943, the population of the camps dropped from a peak of about 107,000 in January to 93,000 in December. With many of the better-educated evacuees gone, there was less leadership of the evacuees and a good deal more violence, beatings, and attempted murders of evacuees, who were now being called the "disloyals" and the "loyals."

The number of young men who answered no to questions 27 and 28 on leave application questionnaires, the "No-No Boys," had shocked camp administrators—and their bosses in Washington. On July 3, 1943, the U.S. Senate had reacted to their answers by passing a resolution urging segregation of the "disloyals" in a separate camp. Within days, the WRA announced its segregation policy for "persons who by their acts have indicated that their loyalties lie with the Japanese during the present hostilities or that their loyalties do not lie with the United States." The segregation had been proposed and backed by the same men who devised the evacuation after Pearl Harbor, including General DeWitt, Colonel Bendetsen, and Governor Earl Warren.

In effect, the government and its sloppily worded questionnaire had manufactured a new crisis in the camps. At the beginning of September, Tule Lake, where 42 percent of young men either failed to register for the draft or answered no to question 28, was selected as the segregation camp for "disloyals" and was converted to a maximum-security facility.

WRA director Myer specified the "disloyals" as:

- those who had applied for expatriation or repatriation to Japan and had not withdrawn their application before July 1, 1942;
- those who answered no to the loyalty question or refused to answer it during registration and had not changed their answers;

- those who were denied leave clearance due to some accumulation of adverse evidence in their records;
- aliens from the Department of Justice internment camps who the agency recommended for detention, and family members of segregants who chose to remain with their families.

As the transfers began, hundreds, then thousands of Tule Lake residents voluntarily declared themselves "disloyal" to avoid the breakup of their families or to avoid the chaos of one more move in sealed trains.

The plan, not publicized, was to strip "disloyals" of citizenship—the Constitution be damned!—and deport them to Japan when the war was over. A battalion of combat-ready troops, 899 men, backed by six tanks and a dozen armored cars, patrolled the fences of Tule Lake as the transfers of "disloyals" began. The first transfer started late in September of 1943 with 500 "disloyal" internees from Heart Mountain being sent to Tule Lake and 400 "loyals" sent from Tule Lake to Heart Mountain. There were more transfers to come: the WRA, with army help, came to move 6,289 more Tule Lake "loyals" to other camps and more than 9,000 "disloyals" to Tule Lake.

Chief Judge William Denman of the Ninth Circuit Court of Appeals described Tule Lake, after it became the segregation camp for "disloyals," during legal hearings.

> The barbed wire surrounding the 18,000 people, including thousands of American citizens, [made the camp look] like the prison camps of the Germans. There were the same turrets for the soldiers and the same machine guns for those who might attempt to climb the high wiring. The buildings were covered with tarred paper over green and shrinking shiplap—this for the low winter temperatures of the high elevation of Tule Lake. . . . No Federal

penitentiary so treats its adult prisoners. Here were children and babies as well. . . . To reach the unheated latrines, which were in the center of the blocks of 14 buildings, meant leaving the residential shacks and walking through the rain and snow—again a lower than penitentiary treatment, even disregarding the sick and the children.

At its peak, Tule Lake was "home" to 18,700 "inmates," twelve hundred combat-equipped soldiers, and 550 administrative personnel. The number of soldiers and administrators assigned to the segregation camp was more than ten times the average allotment of three officers and 124 soldiers to the other camps.

The extra contingents of military guardians of Tule Lake had been moved there in October 1943, after a truck carrying twenty-eight workers rolled over, killing one resident and severely injuring seven more. The workers were outside the gates headed for twenty-nine hundred acres of the farmland that provided food for the camp and for military bases in the west. The dead man was named Kashima, recently arrived from Topaz in Utah. Raymond Best, the camp's director, denied evacuees permission to hold a public memorial service for the victim. He shut off the camp's public address systems, but more than five thousand internees gathered anyway and declared a work stoppage, leaving $500,000 worth of vegetables to rot in the sun. The Tule Lake farm workers demanded improved safety and working conditions, and Best responded by firing them. He secretly brought in eight hundred farm workers from other camps, who were paid a dollar an hour, making more money in two days than Tulean workers made in a month.

Trouble became the norm at Tule Lake. WRA director Myer came to Tule Lake in November 1943. When word got out that the director was there, hundreds of internees surrounded the administration building for three hours. Led by "disloyals," most of them *Kibei*, they shouted demands for more food and better pay for their labor. The situation was bad enough to be brought to the attention of President Roosevelt. In a memo, which exaggerated what had happened, Attorney General Biddle wrote, "Serious disturbances have recently taken place at a relocation center of the War Relocation Authority at Tule Lake. . . . Japanese internees armed with knives and clubs shut up Dillon Myer and some of his administrative officers in the administration building for several days. The Army moved in to restore order."

On November 14, Raymond Best scheduled an Army-WRA rally at Tule Lake to support the camp administration. Colonel Verne Austin, commander of camp troops, was the principal speaker, but not a single evacuee appeared at the parade ground. The colonel gave his unity speech to rows of empty benches.

Martial law was declared the next day, as soldiers went from barrack to barrack trying to find out, without much luck, who were the ringleaders of this soft rebellion. Six barracks, fenced off, had been designated a "stockade" and were soon filled, though not necessarily with actual rebels. Then a stockade inside the stockade was built for suspect "disloyals" who were then forced to live in tents. A twelve-foot-high beaverboard wall was built around this inner sanctum, hiding the fact that the prisoners were denied visits, medical care, or mail.

The news of the army takeover became exactly what the military wanted to avoid: a national story. The *New York Times* referred to the Tule Lake riots in an editorial, saying, "We can't give leeway to possible spies and saboteurs because we simply want to believe that human nature, including that which is wrapped in a saffron-colored skin, is inherently good."

Another typical editorial was from the Huntington, West Virginia, *Herald-Dispatch* on November 8, 1943.

It's something of a relief to learn that Army forces—some of whom are veterans of the fighting in the Pacific area—have taken over at the Tule Lake internment center for disloyal Japanese and presumably have the situation well in hand. The War Relocation Authority policy of coddling and kid-gloving these treacherous, fanatical, insolent prisoners has finally resulted in an incident which promises to clean up the whole mess. Protecting the nation from the thousands of disloyal Japanese rounded up after Pearl Harbor is a military policing job, not a welfare workers' tea party.

In fact, Tule Lake was a citizen prisoner of war camp and a fearful place for most families. A 7:00 p.m. to 6:00 a.m. curfew was enforced by armed troops inside and outside the fences. As in many prisoner of war camps, the army protected the administration but let prisoners terrorize each other. At Tule Lake, there were gangs armed with clubs and homemade knives, including fanatic pro–Imperial Japan groups called *Hokoku Dan* and *Hoshi Dan*, The Young Men and Young Women's National Defense Association to Serve the Mother Country, which specialized in midnight raids and savage beatings of anyone they suspected of cooperating with WRA or military officials.

Jim Tanimoto, classified as "disloyal" because he had refused to answer questions 27 and 28, described a night at Tule Lake.

> Maybe twelve o'clock, two o'clock, this soldier comes running through our barrack and he's shouting as loud as he can, says, "Get your ass out of bed and get outside." We could see a line of soldiers ten, fifteen yards apart. There was probably ten or eleven of 'em. On one side, say there were five soldiers, loading their guns. And there was a machine gun right in the middle of the line. There was another five or six soldiers on the other side. . . . We're

standing there, middle of the night in our night clothes, and you begin to wonder, man, this is it. . . . We can see their faces, we can see their reaction, like "Hey, let's shoot 'em. These guys are animals." And then the officer in charge stepped forward, he comes forward and says nobody's going to escape while he's in charge. And he said that several times, real loud voice. . . . Next morning we heard that some soldier thought he heard someone planning to escape and that's why we got awakened.

Most nights, the fear was not of soldiers but of other residents. Tadayasu Abo, an American citizen from Tacoma, Washington, who had registered for the draft before being sent to Tule Lake, testified: "I would have been willing to swear unqualified allegiance to the United States if the government had assured me and my wife and children that we would be free and safe like U.S. citizens." But he felt that the government didn't care what happened to the American Japanese. He and his wife witnessed others being beaten, and he lived in fear that his family would be attacked by the gangs at the camp.

California's former immigration commissioner Carey McWilliams, long after he had praised the army for its efficiency when the camps had first opened, had become an important critic of the evacuation. He reported from the scenes of the new American Japanese exodus.

I witnessed the departure of the segregants from some of the centers for Tule Lake, and it was my most fervent wish that the entire membership of the Native Sons of the Golden West might have been present to see for themselves the anguish, the grief, the bottomless sorrow that this separation occasioned. They might have been convinced—although I doubt even those scenes would have convinced them—that the Japanese are not an inscrutable, unemo-

tional, stoical, or mysterious people. The evacuees realized that those who were going to Tule Lake were
destined to be deported, someday, to Japan; and this was a
final separation, a fateful farewell. Parents were being
separated from children and children from parents;
brother from brother, sister from sister. In those scenes was
the stuff of timeless tragedy and excellent documentation
for man's inhumanity to man.

On New Year's Day 1944, 207 Tule Lake stockade prisoners
began a hunger strike. Residents found a way to telegraph the
Spanish consul in San Francisco. Spain, officially neutral in the
war, was designated to handle Japanese affairs in the United
States. Spanish diplomats passed the Tule Lake complaints to the
War Department in Washington. The complaints were officially
rejected, though conditions improved somewhat at the camp.
But, then, stories began to appear in foreign newspapers, including Japanese papers, and Radio Tokyo, which reported that "the
American Army has entered the Tule Lake Center with machine
guns and tanks, and is intimidating the residents." Then the Japanese government, accusing the Americans of gunning down
innocent evacuees, permanently ended prisoner exchanges and
exchange negotiations. Before the November incidents, 4,724
camp occupants, including 1,949 American citizens, usually
children, were deported to Japan in exchange for American diplomats and businessmen and their families, six thousand of
whom were still in Japanese custody, many of them only under
house arrest.

• • •

On January 14, 1944, the War Department announced that
young Nisei were again eligible to be drafted. As a group their
status changed overnight from 4C to 1A. The rules had changed

again and this created another sharp and obvious divide in the camps. JACL leaders and members were ecstatic; others were furious.

Many young Nisei worried about who would take care of their parents if they joined the military. At Minidoka in Idaho, Robert Mizukami enlisted, telling his younger brother, Bill, to stay in the camp and take care of their parents. Then, when he was in basic training at Camp Shelby in Mississippi, one of the first men he ran into was Bill. "I thought I told you to stay home," said Bob. They were both in H Company of Battalion 2 in the 442nd. They served together in Italy before Bill was killed in action on July 11, 1944. The night before the brothers were talking and Bill said, "Boy, some of those shells are getting awfully close." Bob laughed and said, "Well, what do you want me to tell them when I get home?" He regretted the wisecrack for the rest of his life.

At the same time, more and more of the young people in the camps continued to head for colleges and jobs east of California. But there were catches: they could not go to school within twenty-five miles of a railroad line, nor could they go to any university with military connections, including Reserve Officers' Training Corps—which included almost every male-only or coed college in the country. Mary Sakaguchi Oda, who had been in medical school in California before the war, wrote: "When I heard that they were allowing students out of camp, I applied to ninety-one medical schools. When I received the replies, several of them stated that they could not consider my application because they had military installations on their campus. The implication of my return address—Manzanar—was that I was a potential spy or saboteur." Eventually, she was accepted by a women's medical school in Pennsylvania, becoming one of the more than forty-three hundred students released to continue their educations. The young Nisei were enrolled in six hundred colleges, none of them on the West Coast, though Robert Sproul, chancellor of the University of California, was the single most important figure in arguing for the release of students.

The Uchida family was among the luckiest in getting their children into colleges. With the help of church groups, particularly the American Friends Service Committee, a Quaker organization, Kay was offered a job as a teaching assistant at a nursery and day care center operated by Mount Holyoke College in Massachusetts. Yoshiko, the Berkeley graduate, was offered a full scholarship as a graduate student at Smith College, also in Massachusetts. At the same time, because of their father's work as a block captain reporting to Topaz administrators, a job that was becoming more and more dangerous, the WRA decided to allow their parents to relocate in Salt Lake City. Still, on her way east by rail, Yoshiko was confronted by the conductor who took her ticket. "You better not be a Jap," he said, "because if you are, I'll throw you off the train." She said she was Chinese.

● ● ●

Earlier in 1943, Sergeant Ben Kuroki flew in Operation Tidal Wave, one of the largest bombing raids of the war. This was his twenty-fourth combat mission in Europe; he had only to fly one more in order to go home. This was the secret mission that Kuroki and the rest of the crew of the Tupelo Lass were training for; the target was the oil fields and refineries of Ploeşti, Romania, guarded by hundreds of antiaircraft guns. Back in North Africa, at a base near Benghazi, Libya, the Tupelo Lass and the rest of the Ninety-Third Group were alternating between days of treetop flying practice and bombing raids over Italy. The commander of the Ninth Air Force, Lieutenant General Lewis Brereton, came to Benghazi to tell the flight crews, "You're going on the most important and one of the most dangerous missions in the history of heavy bombardment."

August 1, 1943, was a beautiful Mediterranean day. The Tupelo Lass and 177 other B-24s took off at dawn in North Africa. The round-trip flight from Benghazi to Ploeşti and back would take thirteen hours. Of the 177 bombers that took off together, 58 were shot down. Only two of the nine planes in Kuroki's squadron made it back. In all, 310 American airmen were killed. The survivors and the press were told the mission was a success—but it was not. Ploeşti oil continued to fuel German aircraft and tanks at the same rate as before the raid.

Kuroki continued on, undeterred by those losses. After he had flown the twenty-five missions in Europe necessary to go home, he volunteered for five more, writing home that he wanted to do that for his brother, Fred, who had been pushed out of the Army Air Corps. Epting, now a squadron commander, and others told him he was crazy. But he did it, racking up thirty missions before taking a boat back to New York and then being flown to the Edgewater Beach Hotel, a rest and recreation station on the ocean in Santa Monica, California. He figured that made him the first Japanese American to get to California in two years. Local folks stared at him—some ran away, some called police as he walked the beach and town with white airmen.

Now the army put him in the public relations business full-time, including visits to three relocation camps to urge young Nisei to enlist. Kuroki was to begin his tour on the popular NBC radio show of singer Ginny Simms, but one minute before the show in Hollywood started the army called and ordered him not to go on, fearing reaction across the country. He did appear, however, at the Commonwealth Club of California, in San Francisco, one of the country's most prestigious forums. Six hundred members crowded a luncheon to see and hear him on February 4, 1944. But when Staff Sergeant Ben Kuroki was introduced, no one applauded—the room was silent.

"I'm just a farm boy from Nebraska . . . " he began.

He spoke for a long time from twelve single-spaced typewritten pages. He told his story, beginning in Hershey and the farm the family had worked since 1928. He told them about the loneliness and fear of looking like the enemy, of peeling potatoes and begging officers to let him fight, then talking about his first mission and the flak slicing into Dawley's head, and the terror of flying fifty feet over Ploeşti. "We were," he said, "flying through a furnace." He continued his story, saying:

> I learned more about democracy, for one thing, than you'll find in all the books, because I saw it in action. When you live with men under combat conditions for fifteen months, you begin to understand what brotherhood, equality, tolerance, and unselfishness really mean. Under fire, a man's ancestry, what he did before the war, or even his present rank, don't matter at all . . . you're fighting for each other's lives and for your country, and whether you realize it at the time or not, you're living and proving democracy. . . .
>
> The tunnel gunner . . . was Jewish. I'm a Japanese-American. The bombardier of our crew was German. The left waist gunner was an Irishman. . . . We had a job to do and we did it with a kind of comradeship that was the finest thing in the world. . . .
>
> I nearly got it on the 30th mission, my last one. We were over Munster in Germany and a shell exploded right above the glass dome of my top turret. It smashed the dome, ripped my helmet off, smashed my goggles and interphone, but I didn't get a scratch. Things like that aren't explained just by luck. . . .
>
> I certainly don't propose to defend Japan. When I visit Tokyo, it will be in a bomber. But I do believe that loyal Americans of Japanese descent are entitled to the democratic rights which Jefferson propounded, Washington fought for, and Lincoln died for.

The crowd, almost every one of them white men, stood and applauded for ten minutes. Some were crying, including Henry J. Kaiser, whose shipyards, including the one on Terminal Island in Los Angeles, had been essential to the rebuilding of the U.S. Navy after Pearl Harbor. The speech and the boy from Nebraska were a sensation. He was interviewed by *Time* magazine and the *New York Times*. His photograph was in a dozen California newspapers and in the window of Brandeis's of Omaha, the biggest department store in Nebraska. A crew from WHO, the big radio station in Omaha, traveled to the farm outside Hershey to interview his family. The Office of War Information had the Commonwealth Club speech translated into Japanese—a language Kuroki could not speak or understand—for propaganda broadcasts. And he was invited back to the *Ginny Simms Show* and had dinner with the star at the Brown Derby in Beverly Hills.

But it was not that way at the three camps he visited. To most of the evacuees, particularly younger ones, he was a hero—Kuroki was cheered and mobbed by young people wanting his autograph—but he heard boos and hisses as well. He was considered a fool and a traitor by many. He had no idea that, by then, large numbers of men in the camps hated him, hated the idea of a Nisei serving with the army holding them as prisoners. Kuroki was booed when he said, "If you think that Japan is going to win, you're crazy. We're going to bomb them out of existence."

Frank Emi, the Los Angeles grocer at Heart Mountain, was not impressed by Kuroki. He was one of group of three hundred or so young evacuees who boycotted Kuroki's speech. "We just thought he was an asshole," said Emi. "A Nebraska boy who never knew anything about the camps, never was forced out of his home and for him to come to these camps and try to influence the people there to respond to the draft was totally stupid of him." Another hostile evacuee, Jack Teno, added, "He was lucky to get out of here alive."

That was not an empty threat. Beatings of evacuees were common in several camps; the victims were usually JACL members accused of spying on their own people and informing camp administrators. At Poston, the national chairman of the league, Saburo Kido, the lawyer from San Francisco, was beaten twice with planks and baseball bats and was in the hospital for weeks.

Then Kuroki received a letter from his family back in Hershey. His best friend at home, his hunting buddy, Gordy Jorgensen, a marine, had been killed by the Japanese in the Solomon Islands. Kuroki's reaction was to ask to go overseas again, to the Pacific Theater, and to train on the country's new superbomber, the Boeing B-29 Superfortress. Kuroki's request was denied. There was a specific War Department regulation stating that no Japanese Americans could fly in combat zones in the Pacific. He decided to write to members of the Nebraska congressional delegation, asking them to intercede for him with Secretary of War Stimson. He made the same request of the important men he met at the Commonwealth Club, particularly Monroe Deutsch, the vice president of the University of California at Berkeley, who sent a telegram to Stimson and recruited other prominent Californians to do the same. Dillon Myer of the WRA sent one as well.

It worked. Stimson sent a telegram to Dr. Deutsch saying, "I am happy to inform you that, by reason of his splendid record, it has been decided to except Sergeant Kuroki from the policy to which I earlier referred."

That was the end of it—almost. The crew of the B-29 to which Kuroki was assigned voted to call the plane the Honorable Sad Saki, a play on the names of a cartoon character called Sad Sack and the Japanese rice wine. As the crew prepared for takeoff from their training base in Nebraska, army intelligence officers and an FBI agent, claiming he was a reporter, tried to trick Kuroki into getting off the plane. His new pilot, Lieutenant James Jenkins, and the bombardier Lieutenant Kenneth Neill, confronted the agent with a copy of Kuroki's orders and the Stimson telegram. Neill yelled, "Stay there Ben. You don't have to say a damn word to them." Jenkins and Neill climbed aboard the Honorable Sad Saki. "Gun it!" yelled Jenkins. "Gun it!" And the Superfortress roared into the sky, headed for Tinian Island, fifteen hundred miles from the Japanese mainland.

Two days later, the Sad Saki was on Tinian, which was being used as a platform for B-29s dropping incendiary bombs on major cities in Japan. A plane called the *Enola Gay* was parked down the silver line on the forty-eight-square-mile island. It was being secretly refitted to carry a new kind of bomb, the atomic bomb. There were still Japanese soldiers hiding on the island, so Kuroki was ordered to wear a helmet at all times and never walk alone—one white man walked ahead of him and one was behind him because his superiors were worried that he would be shot, not by the Japanese but by American marines. If those guys spotted a Japanese face, they were trained to shoot first and ask questions later.

If shot, Kuroki would not be the first Japanese American killed by his own men. Sergeant Frank Hachiya was an MIS graduate from Hood River, Oregon—"the most beautiful place on earth," he would tell anyone who'd listen. He was a *Kibei* whose father was at Tule Lake and whose mother was still in Japan. He had volunteered to parachute onto Leyte in the Philippines to gather intelligence on Japanese positions as U.S. Marines prepared to invade. Hachiya was shot on December 30, 1944, and died four days later. The fatal shot was apparently fired by a marine, who saw Hachiya bringing Japanese maps back to American lines.

8

"IS THAT THE AMERICAN WAY?"

HEART MOUNTAIN DRAFT RESISTANCE: FEBRUARY 1944

I n the first week of January 1944, Anne O'Hare McCormick, a *New York Times* foreign correspondent and columnist, visited the three Poston camps in southwestern Arizona. On January 8, 1944, she wrote as if she were in another country, a country of "the homesick." She described a strange city with lush gardens and farms that had emerged "like an oasis in an endless desert of sand, sage, mesquite and huge cacti," a town that looked like "a cross between an American military camp and an Oriental town."

McCormick reported that when these American Japanese settlers first arrived in 1942, "the population had little in common . . . but its race and its fate. It was composed of aliens and citizens, rich and poor farmers, and professional people." While their isolation tended to make the interns turn inward and become "more ingrown, more Japanese," overall "they put an extraordinary cheerful face on their tragedy."

She went on to stress that "both they and the government know that there is no solid legal reason for holding them in detention. If they were politically organized and less frightened they would fight for their civic rights."

That column, along with the new newspaper attacks on American Japanese in California and increasing violence in the camps, had become a great worry in the White House. The 1944 presidential campaign was about to begin and Roosevelt intended to run for an unprecedented fourth term. He did not want the incarceration and treatment of American Japanese to be a campaign issue. The WRA was becoming a target for both sides in the ongoing debate inside the government that had begun immediately after Pearl Harbor.

Without the usual fanfare, Roosevelt, on February 17, 1944, issued an executive order placing the WRA under the control of the Department of the Interior, led by a critic of the evacuation, Harold Ickes. From the beginning, in private correspondence, Ickes had called the whole idea "fancy-named concentration camps."

By that spring, the War Department began—in secret, of course—to propose to the president that they end the evacuation of the American Japanese. Secretary of War Stimson brought the subject up at a cabinet meeting on May 26, 1944. But the closing of the relocation camps was not going to happen just yet. As Attorney General Biddle wrote in his notes of the meeting, "Secretary of War raised the question of whether it was appropriate for the War Department, at this time, to cancel the Japanese Exclusion Orders and let the Japs go home. War, Interior, and Justice all agreed this could be done without danger to defense considerations but doubted the wisdom of doing it at this time before the election." Harold Ickes, now officially in charge of the WRA, was the strongest voice in the room, telling

President Roosevelt, "The continued retention of these innocent people would be a blot upon the history of this country."

He added that the Japanese children "are becoming a hope-
lessly maladjusted generation, apprehensive of the outside world
and divorced from the possibility of associating—or even seeing
to any considerable extent—Americans of other races."

At the same time, the general who replaced General Emmons
in DeWitt's old job in San Francisco, C. H. Bonesteel, cabled the
War Department, writing, "My study of the existing situation
leads me to a belief that the great improvement in the military
situation on the West Coast indicates that there is no longer a
military necessity for the mass exclusion of the Japanese from
the West Coast as a whole."

After the meeting, the undersecretary of state Edward Stet-
tinius wrote to President Roosevelt, saying, "The question
appears to be largely a political one, the reaction in California,
on which I am sure you will probably wish to reach your own
decision."

Exactly. The president made it clear to his men that they
should do nothing until after the election in November. Two
weeks later Roosevelt refined his thoughts in a memo to Stet-
tinius and Ickes: "The more I think of this problem of suddenly
ending the orders excluding Japanese Americans from the West
Coast the more I think it would be a mistake to do anything dras-
tic or sudden. As I said at Cabinet, I think the whole problem,
for the sake of internal quiet, should be handled gradually." Ickes
and the others knew what he meant: after the elections.

● ● ●

That spring, while Washington debated and evaded the issue of
closing the camps, frustration and violence continued behind the
barbed fences of the relocation centers out west. On May 24,

1944, thirty-year-old Shoichi James Okamoto, who had been born in Garden Grove just south of Los Angeles, was shot at Tule Lake by Private Bernard Goe. He died the next day.

There were eight witnesses to the incident, both Japanese and Caucasian. The official report of the Army Investigation Committee released on July 3 read:

> Okamoto was driving Truck #100-41 at the order of the construction supervisor to get lumber piled across the highway from the old main gate, which is called Gate #4. . . . Harry Takanashi accompanied Okamoto on this assignment. Eleven boys from the heavy equipment crew were waiting for an Army escort. . . .
>
> According to Takanashi, the new sentry had just come on duty. Word has it that the new sentry was in a disagreeable mood and was known as one of the tougher sentries. The two on the truck went over the line a bit. The sentry, on Okamoto's side of the truck, could see Takanashi's badge, but could not at first see Okamoto's because of the high side door of the truck, and because of the sentry's short stature. . . . Okamoto showed the pass, was allowed through, and returned in a few minutes. . . . While he had been waved through the gate a few minutes before, he was halted. It is claimed Okamoto said words to the effect of, "Well, here's the pass." Perhaps this sounded cocky to the already irritated guard. The sentry ordered him off the truck and commanded Takanashi to drive. Without a driver's license, the latter explained he could not drive a truck. The sentry, it is said, was infuriated at this delay. From then on, commands were well peppered with curses. . . . To Takanashi's answer the guard is said to have replied, "You Japs and your WRA friends are trying to run the whole camp." He then turned back to Okamoto. . . . Heavy equipment boys, not many feet away, were talking among themselves of the sentry's aggressive

manner. "This one has it in for 'Japs,' etc." Okamoto, too, was apparently apprehensive by this time.

Takanashi and other witnesses said that the sentry then cocked his gun and went around via the front to the other side of the truck where Okamoto was standing. The sentry then ordered Okamoto to the back of the truck. This would have been just outside the gate. Okamoto started but hesitated for an instant. . . . The suspicion is that the guard wished to shoot him outside the gate. "Shot while trying to escape." The sentry struck Okamoto on the right shoulder with a rifle-butt. Okamoto raised his right arm and moved his body slightly back to ward off any further blows. While in this defensive position, the guard stepped back one pace and from a distance of four or five feet fired without warning. In all eyewitness testimony, the act was looked upon as an unprovoked attack. . . .

The sentry cursed, seemed nervous, and it is said, swung the rifle in [the heavy equipment crew's] general direction. More cursing. "You people get the hell out of here"—and they fled.

Six weeks later, military officers held court-martial proceedings for Private Bernard Goe. The private was charged and acquitted of manslaughter after an hour's deliberation. He was fined one dollar for the unauthorized use of government property: the bullet.

Both the actions of the army and the WRA questionnaires increased the tensions between guards and guarded; they not only divided the camps but also goaded residents to organize and resist in ways they never had before. At Heart Mountain, Frank Emi, the grocer from Little Tokyo, and Sam Horino, who had made the soldiers carry him out of his family's home in Gardena on the day they were relocated, formed a so-called Fair Play

Committee with other "No-No Boys" in February 1944, soon after draft notices arrived in the camp.

When Emi read question 27 of the leave application—"Will you go into combat duty wherever ordered?"—he thought, "It was very stupid and a very arrogant question to ask us, after we were thrown out of our homes and put in these concentration camps, without even a word about our citizenship rights or civil rights or constitutional rights being restored." He thought question 28—"Will you forswear allegiance to the Emperor of Japan?"—was just senseless. "We had never sworn allegiance to the Emperor of Japan," he told camp administrators. "And for our parents to forswear allegiance to Japan, that would have left them without a country," since Issei were not allowed to earn U.S. citizenship.

Emi himself was not eligible for the draft or military service. He was thirty-two years old and had two children. But when he first read the questionnaire, he had stayed up all night working out his response: "Under the present conditions and circumstances, I am unable to answer these questions." Then, with his brother, they put those words up on latrine doors under the headline, "Suggested Answers to Questions 27 and 28":

> We the members of the FPC are not afraid to go war—we are not afraid to risk our lives for our country. We would gladly sacrifice our lives to protect and uphold the principles and ideals of our country as set forth in the Constitution and the Bill of Rights, for on its inviolability depends the freedom, liberty, justice, and protection of all people including Japanese Americans and all other minority groups. But have we been given such freedom, such liberty, such justice, such protection? NO! Without any hearings, without due process of law as guaranteed by the Constitution and Bill of Rights, without any charges filed against us, without any evidence of wrongdoing on our part, one hundred and ten thousand innocent people were kicked out

of their homes . . . and herded like dangerous criminals into concentration camps with barbed wire fences and military police guarding it. . . . Is that the American way? NO! . . . THEREFORE, WE MEMBERS OF THE FAIR PLAY COMMITTEE HEREBY REFUSE TO GO TO THE PHYSICAL EXAMINATION OR TO THE INDUCTION IF OR WHEN WE ARE CALLED IN ORDER TO CONTEST THE ISSUE.

The Japanese American Citizens League members in camp accused the Fair Play leaders of sedition. So did the camp newspaper, the *Heart Mountain Sentinel*.

Emi and a friend, Min Tamesa, a millworker from Seattle, continued to protest and decided to walk out of the camp, knowing they would be stopped. They wanted to then use the incident to prove that they were not free citizens, if they ever ended up in court.

On the day of their planned walkout, the guards stopped them and asked for identification.

"Well, we don't have passes," said Emi. "We're American citizens."

The soldiers repeated the request for passes.

"Well," replied Emi, "what will you do if we don't get a pass and walk out?"

"Well, I'll just have to shoot you," said the guard.

A grand jury in Wyoming indicted Emi, Horino, and sixty-one other Heart Mountain Nisei who had refused to sign up for Selective Service. It was the largest trial in Wyoming's history and all of the resisters were found guilty and sentenced to three years in federal penitentiaries on McNeil Island, Washington, and in Leavenworth, Kansas.

Later, the same grand jury indicted seven Fair Play leaders again, including Emi and Horino. The charge this time was trying to organize a draft resistance movement. James Omura, a columnist for the English-language *Rocky Shimpo* in Denver, was indicted as well for writing columns urging the Heart Mountain leaders to exercise their rights as American citizens. Omura was found not guilty because of the First Amendment of the Constitution protecting free speech in the press.

After their second indictment, Frank Emi and other leaders of the Fair Play Committee at Heart Mountain were taken into custody by the FBI in the middle of the night on July 21, 1944, and taken to the jail in Cheyenne. This time the men were charged with conspiracy to violate the Selective Service Act.

On October 27, 1944, Emi and the other Fair Play leaders from Heart Mountain went on trial before a jury in Cheyenne. They denied nothing, said what they did and why they did it. They were found guilty and taken to Leavenworth, Kansas. Emi got four years this time. He served eighteen months before his conviction—and those of the others—was reversed by the Tenth Circuit Court of Appeals after the war was over.

Before the trial, Frank Emi and others had asked the American Civil Liberties Union to provide them with attorneys, but the ACLU refused, probably because the organization's founder and president, Roger Baldwin, still did not want to do anything that might embarrass his friend the president. But then an ACLU attorney from Los Angeles, A. L. Wirin, agreed to defend the seven as a private attorney.

In spite of the ambivalent attitudes of Baldwin and some other national officers of the American Civil Liberties Union in New York, the director of the San Francisco office, Ernest Besig, had been trying for more than a year to be allowed to see the camps, particularly Tule Lake, and talk to the residents. He was finally granted permission to visit on July 10, 1944. He was not, however, allowed to speak alone with residents. Camp administrators insisted on being present at all interviews. Even so, women in the camp learned that he was there and told him about the camp's "stockade," and the fact that they were not allowed to visit their husbands and sons in the makeshift prison.

Raymond Best immediately ordered Besig and his secretary to leave the camp and return to San Francisco, five hundred miles away. It was a rough ride. Someone had poured two bags of salt into Besig's gas tank. It was not hard to figure out that administration people were behind that bit of sabotage; Besig's car was parked in the "whites only" housing area outside the camp.

Shocked by all that he saw and heard in two days, Besig reported to New York: "Instead of being a center for disloyal Japanese, Tule Lake is really the dumping ground for misfits, anti-administration leaders, embittered youngsters, and a lot of old people who just want to go back to Japan. The administration under Best is so stupid that it succeeds in uniting all these elements against itself."

Besig was pressured by the ACLU board in New York to be supportive of the government and government power, but he was determined to find a way to defy New York. As he had before, Besig went to Wayne Collins, who was working out of a tiny office in San Francisco, to once again represent Korematsu against the orders of ACLU superiors in New York. No longer an ACLU employee, Collins, who had founded the San Francisco unit, was free and determined to ignore the calls, telegrams, and letters from New York that were prohibiting Besig from going back to Tule Lake.

Among other things, ACLU founder Roger Baldwin considered Collins incompetent and something of a wild man—and so did many who knew him. Besig said his friend Collins was "like a fox terrier," a fast-talking, angry Irishman who came to cases as if he had a shotgun, ready to blast in any direction. Many of his shots were at the Japanese American Citizens League, which he considered a partner in the evacuation.

> I detest them. They're nothing but a bunch of jackals. . . .
> The JACL pretended to be the spokesman for all Japanese
> Americans but they wouldn't stand up for their people.
> They led their people like a bunch of goddamned doves
> to the concentration camps. . . . I still feel bitter about
> the evacuation. It was the foulest goddamned crime the
> United States has ever committed against a wonderful
> people.

Whatever his skills and however deep his rage, the passionate and persevering Collins was already trying to represent the American Japanese behind the stockade fence at Tule Lake, the prison within a prison at Tule Lake. He was demanding to see the segregation camp and to get inside the stockade. Hoping to keep the attorney away, Best offered to come to Collins's office in San Francisco with other WRA officials. Collins greeted them by saying he would file a writ of habeas corpus for all four hundred prisoners if the stockade was not immediately shut down. Three days later, he drove to Tule Lake. There was no sign of the barbed-wire and plywood enclosure. The stockade was gone.

• • •

Back in Washington, Congress was in the process of passing Public Law 78-405, the Denaturalization Act of 1944. Signed by President Roosevelt on July 1, 1944, it allowed American citizens to renounce that citizenship in a time of war. Whatever the wording, there was only one group of citizens targeted: the residents of Tule Lake. The Justice Department believed that the law would provide a constitutional rationale to keep those citizens incarcerated, by pushing them to voluntarily become aliens. As always, there was also pressure from western politicians who used the chaos at Tule Lake as reason for barring American Japanese from returning to the West Coast. Representative Clair Engle of California, for instance, was saying, "We don't want those Japs back in California and the more we can get rid of the better." Engle, a Republican, was among those who believed the way to calm the camps was to tell inmates that they would be able to go to Japan after the war—a place most of them had never been.

Though only 117 evacuees, all *Kibei*, initially signed up for renunciation, Raymond Best and the Tule Lake administrators decided to deliberately ignore the growing pro-Japan organizations, gangs, and schools being put together by the true anti-Americans in the camp. They decided to turn a blind eye to these elements as a way to frighten residents into renunciation. As 1944 went on, "Japanization"—not the original idea of "Americanization"—effectively became the new Tule Lake policy. The gangs and their thugs were free to run wild, pressuring "loyals" to become openly disloyal—and thousands did, afraid of the violent disloyal gangs—and becoming convinced that they would be in danger outside the camp. It seemed the inmates were running the institution, a chaotic situation that led to the murder of the manager of the camp's co-op store, Yaozo Hitomi, who was openly pro-administration. He was found on July 2, with his throat slit.

Even "Americanized" Nisei were intimidated into learning Japanese ways and language—and waving Japanese flags. There were classes in martial arts, traditional Japanese tea ceremonies, and flower arranging. What went unnoticed in the camp was that the leaders and loudest voices of the pro-Japan groups—the Nisei and *Kibei* who were chanting for renunciation and expatriation—often were not themselves renouncing their American citizenship.

By end of the year, the number of Tule Lake prisoners applying for renunciation and expatriation had grown to almost two thousand. The camp was a nest of suspicion, terror, and confusion. Hundreds of the most fanatic young pro-Japanese *Kibei* joined with the so-called Sand Island Tough Boys transferred in from a Hawaiian internment center. The pro-Japan gangs were coercing residents with stories that the twenty military officers who processed the applications were telling the residents that they had two choices: renounce your citizenship or be sent out of the camp. As the government began making announcements about closing the camps, more and more Tule Lakers, afraid of going outside, applied for renunciation papers. As elders became more and more terrified that they would be in danger and separated from their families if they were outside, they were ordering or begging their children and grandchildren to renounce.

Finally realizing what was happening, the Justice Department announced at the end of the year that only American Japanese over the age of seventeen could renounce their citizenship. But it was too late—no one inside the camps believed the government anymore. In the end, 5,589 Tuleans, Americans, signed away their citizenship—and their rights as Americans. Seventy percent of the Nisei at Tule Lake were among the renouncers, most under unbearable pressure from the *Kibei* gangs, American soldiers, and their own alien parents in their closed, barbed-wire world.

The Justice Department continued to blunder through the end of the year. In the early morning hours of December 27, while soldiers surrounded the camp, forty armed border patrol officers pulled seventy suspected pro-Japan *Hokoku Dan* leaders out of their beds. They were dragged to Gate 3 and taken away in trucks, sent to Justice Department internment facilities, prisons, around the country. Predictably, even the most moderate of residents saw the seventy men as martyrs or heroes. More than a thousand people rushed to the gate, shouting "Banzai! Banzai!" and chanting about "the honor of internment."

John Burling, the assistant director of the Justice Department's Alien Enemy Control Unit, who had opposed the renunciation law, wrote in a Justice Department report, "It seems, at least in the light of hindsight, foreseeable that this group could be whipped up into a sort of hysterical frenzy of Japanese patriotism." Sympathetic or not to the pro-Japanese *Hokoku*, hundreds of male residents, some as a means of self-protection, shaved their heads in the bozu style of the Japanese Imperial Army.

Conditions at Tule Lake were dismal at best and, at the time, renunciations of U.S. citizenship, forced or voluntary, seemed irreversible. Despite opposition from ACLU headquarters in New York and Los Angeles, Wayne Collins, the driven San Francisco attorney, eventually represented more than five thousand Japanese Americans incarcerated in the Justice Department prisons and WRA camps—including the hopeless people who had given up their American citizenship. Even in the ensuing decades, Collins's style and accomplishments made an impression: in a 1985 issue of the *Pacific Historical Review*, John Christgau wrote on Collins in a piece aptly titled "Collins versus the World: The Fight to Restore Citizenship to Japanese American Renunciants of World War II."

"These renunciants whom I represent," Collins argued in a letter to the attorney general's office in Washington, "have submitted to gross indignities and suffered greater loss of rights and liberties than any other group of persons during the entire history of the nation, all without good cause or reason. They have been misunderstood, slandered, abused and long have been held up to public shame and contempt . . . and now these internees, faced with the loss of citizenship rights, are confronted with a threatened involuntary deportation to Japan."

In court, he argued, "Herr Hitler was guilty of abusing segments of [his] own citizenry for racial reasons. We are inured, however, to a like abuse of our own citizens by our own government."

• • •

Though more and more American Japanese were leaving the camps, their departures were not always easy. Regulation piled upon regulation as camp administrators were overwhelmed by paperwork coming from all directions. One of the first rules was showing evidence that Japanese Americans would not be living or working within twenty-five miles of a railroad line.

And for many of the evacuees, even younger ones, leaving the camps was almost as traumatic as leaving their homes. George Nakamura, who had been a student at Berkeley before being sent to Tule Lake and becoming an editor on the *Tulean Dispatch*, wrote, "Now that I have made plans to leave the project, I feel like staying a little longer. Life here has made me soft and indolent. I'm clothed, sheltered, and don't have to worry about where my next meal is coming from. I feel I've become part of the dust."

The old Issei, building Japanese gardens and pools framed by delicate little bridges, were caught between two worlds. The oldest evacuees, women and men who had worked from dawn to dusk all their lives, suddenly had something they never knew before, leisure. They had time now to relax and gossip and knit as they talked—or sip homemade sake and play the ancient Japanese board game Go.

One Issei at Heart Mountain, a man who had been wealthy, said:

> I guess I'll just have to go. I don't want to go. I sort of like
> it here. My work is interesting. I have time for golf and

fishing. I have lots of friends. I have no worries. My wife likes it here alright. My daughter has her friends. We're used to it.

Difficult as it was for some to leave camp life, the departures continued. The breakup of the Matsuda family, the farmers from Vashon Island, Washington, began two weeks into June 1944. The Matsudas, their twenty-one-year-old son, Yoneichi, and daughter, Mary, had all signed "yes" on the Application for Leave questions 27 and 28. So as "disloyals" from other camps were being sent to Tule Lake, they had been moved from Tule Lake. Yoneichi Matsuda, who considered himself a Christian pacifist, still felt he had to fight and left for basic training in Florida in June. On his last day in camp, his mother prayed in front of the family.

> God, this is a difficult time for all of us. We know Yoneichi-san carries the burden for our family and for all other Japanese families to fight with courage and bring honor to our community. Guide and protect him. May his battles be fought with a pure heart. We know You will be with him wherever he goes. . . . Amen.

Mary cried for a day, thinking, "My only brother goes off to fight a war for a country that is keeping us imprisoned like criminals."

A month later, she applied for training in the United States Cadet Nurse Corps and was accepted at Jane Lamb Memorial Hospital in Clinton, Iowa. Before she was scheduled to go to Clinton, her parents told her that they had applied to be transferred to Minidoka because they had Japanese friends nearby in Idaho, Japanese who had not been incarcerated because they lived away from the West Coast. Mary and her parents took a bus east to Pocatello, Idaho, before her parents boarded another bus to Minidoka.

While walking down a street in Pocatello, Mary was attacked in front of a barbershop—there was a NO JAPS ALLOWED sign in front—and the barber came rushing out and grabbed her in a choke hold, holding something against her throat, saying, "I oughta slit your throat from ear to ear you goddamned Jap!" She thought he was going to do it, but a friend of his across the street shouted, "Hey, Ken, knock it off!"

A month later, finally on her way to Clinton, Mary suddenly realized she was free, writing back to her parents, "It was like being in heaven. . . . It was incredible—the sense that I could walk anywhere I wanted to, and enjoy the flowers, the grass, and hear the birds."

Soon after that, Mrs. Matsuda, who was fifty-two, was offered a job at a vegetable cannery in Ogden, Utah. Her husband, sixty-seven, said that she should go and she did, holding her leave pass and crying and praying at the camp gate. In November, Mrs. Matsuda wrote to Mary, who had just turned twenty, "This afternoon when I opened your letter, your picture dropped out. It was such a wonderful picture showing how you are getting along so fine with your white friends. . . . I will watch you become a great nurse. That is all I ask."

Granted leave before being shipped overseas, Yoneichi traveled, illegally, to Vashon to check on the family farm. He could not find Mack Garcia, the Filipino workman, or Sheriff Hopkins. The place was run-down, but it was still there. He then went to Minidoka. He and Mary were both visiting at the same time. They were both in U.S. Army uniforms and camp residents could not stop staring at them. Then Private Matsuda was off for Maryland and then a nineteen-day freighter trip to Marseille, France, as a replacement in the 442nd Regimental Combat Team.

Other young people at the camps were also looking ahead to the rest of their lives. Stanley Hayami graduated from the Heart Mountain High School on May 11, 1944, and, at last, he got all As on his final report card and made the school's honor roll. He wrote, "Man, do I feel swell! 'member I thought I had T.B. or something, well I don't! Dr. Robbins looked my X-ray over and told me that there's nothing wrong with my lungs—so I guess I'll go on to college! Or the army."

Hayami remained an enthusiastic and optimistic young man, writing, "I made up my mind on something else, too—I'm going into the artist-writer field. And I'm going to be the best artist in the world. (Even if my I.Q. is low.)" After his planned college graduation, he figured, "I'm going to bum my way around the world—So the world better watch out—Hayami is going to the top!"

Stanley Hayami put the 1944 valedictory address by his friend Paul Mayekawa in his diary. It was titled "Citizenship Carries Responsibility," and in Mayekawa's speech he asked, "What are we, you and I? Are we Japs, simply in a sense as General DeWitt declared, 'A Jap is a Jap?' . . . As evidenced by General DeWitt's remark, there are some Americans who judge us only by our appearances." Despite the color of their skin, Mayekawa asserted that "by right of birth in the United States, we are Americans."

Still, Mayekawa went on to say that "evacuation has proved, however, that we cannot take citizenship for granted. We, the Japanese-Americans, in not establishing ourselves as firmly in the American way of life as we had thought, must now reaffirm our loyalty to our country and prove ourselves worthy of our citizenship." Yet, at the same time, he warned his audience not to forsake their Japanese heritage, since their heritage "may be the means by which we . . . further develop and enrich the American culture, for is not America made up of the various cultures of many nations?"

He acknowledged that graduates would be going their separate ways soon, to work or to college, though he stressed that "there are also those among us who will go into the armed forces. These persons, besides hastening the day of final victory, will constitute what I believe will be the greatest single factor in the re-establishment of the Japanese-Americans in such a definite and permanent place in the American life that issues, such as the evacuation, shall never again be necessary."

The class of 1944 at Manzanar High School graduated that same June. Their yearbook, *Our World*, looked almost exactly like any other yearbook in the United States. It was seventy-six pages long, gave short bios of the 169 graduates, including names of the high schools they attended before being forced to leave their homes. There were photos of all the teachers, athletic teams, cheerleaders, and clubs. The kids were all Japanese Americans, of course, boys growing out of their suits and bobby-soxers in saddle shoes.

The first pages of the yearbook began, "Since that first day when Manzanar High School was called into session, the students and faculty have been trying to approximate in all activities the life we knew 'back home.'" On the drama class page there were photographs, taken by Ansel Adams during the weeks he had spent at the camp, of student actors in *Growing Pains* by Auriana Rouveral. The play was described in the program as "the story of a typical American home."

There was a page devoted to a letter from Ralph Merritt, the director of the camp. He wrote, "Each of you can find a place in this country for normal living as free citizens. Of course this depends on your cooperation and courage and initiative. . . . Never was your future as bright as now."

There were no soldiers, or guns, or fences shown until the last two pages of the yearbook. There were no words on those pages, just one full-page photograph that showed a hand with garden shears trying to cut the barbed fence and another of a guard tower along the barbed-wire fences enclosing the camp.

That same summer, Ted Hirasaki, who had graduated from San Diego High School six years before, was moved after witnessing a Poston camp graduation. He wrote to Clara Breed about this, the first graduating class of Parker Valley High School. That day, graduates "marched into the partially constructed school auditorium and received their diplomas. They looked splendid in their caps and gowns. The boys were in blue and the girls, in white."

Hirasaki reported that Poston III High School had become an accredited high school that spring, and the name was changed to Parker Valley High School. "If I am not mistaken I believe Parker Valley High School is the only relocation center high school that has been so honored. It is magnificent the way the students have striven for higher education."

He went on to describe the growth of this school, writing how in the first year students had made do in makeshift barrack classrooms, but then:

> When construction of the school began the whole community volunteered in making adobe bricks for the school buildings. Even school children helped so that school could open in time for the fall semester of 1943–1944. Yes, the students can rightfully be proud to say "It's my school" for they built it with sweat and toil. The class gift was a beautiful American flag.

Many of the young graduates were anxious to adjust to new lives outside the barbed wire and watchtowers. "This will probably be my last letter written to you from the fair city of Poston, Arizona," Fusa Tsumagari wrote to Miss Breed that spring. "My mother is going to join my father in Crystal City

Texas. It is now almost 2½ years since we last saw him." Crystal City, originally built as a migrant labor camp, was one of the few Justice Department facilites that held both Japanese and German aliens—and, after late 1943, their families. The population there, more than three thousand, included the 1,500 Japanese seized in Latin America, mostly in Peru, as well as more than 1,000 Japanese aliens and almost 900 American Germans.

There was great irony in Tsumagari's next paragraph: the Japanese men on the FBI's "potentially dangerous" lists, and Germans on similar lists, were often treated much better than the confused innocents sent to the high deserts of the West.

> Crystal City, according to various letters we received, is a very wonderful place. It is quite an improvement over Poston. The buildings are white (not this black tar paper), each family cooks for themselves, have a shower in each barrack to be shared by the families occupying the barrack, well furnished, and a nice canteen. So much is allowed per person per day for food and this amount is given them in certain coins only good at the local store, and they tell us food is ample.

Tsumagari was not joining her parents in Crystal City; she headed to Minneapolis, Minnesota. Her next letter, in June, reported on her new life. "As you know, I am living with my 'sis' and her husband. All three of us are working; they in Heinrich Envelope Co., and I in L.S. Donaldson Company, a dept store." Tsumagari was working there as a typist in the mail-order division. She reported, "The work is monotonous and rather tiring at times, but I enjoy it. There are lots of things to learn, people are nice, and my typing has increased in speed and my accuracy is getting better. We're slightly swamped with work and consequently have little time to fool around, like in camp, but time passes fast."

Tsumagari was planning to attend business school and then aiming to take the civil service exam. As she looked ahead, she still thought of the past. She wrote, "Last Sunday Ikuko Kuratomi (do you remember her?) called me. She is living in St. Paul and attending Hamline University. She is coming over this Sunday for dinner and we hope to do some reminiscing and [put together the] patchwork of our life pattern."

While some young workers compared their lives after camp to their earlier lives behind barbed fences, others compared their fates with those signing up with the army. Ted Hirasaki wrote to Clara Breed in the summer of 1944, "I had hoped to be a barber at Camp Savage, Minn. I had an offer. In a routine checking of the arm, the doctor advised me that the arm bone is in a rather dubious state and that it would take some time before the condition would clear up. I could have walked under a snake's belly, I felt so low." He was hit hard by that blow, and had started to feel sorry for himself. Still, he couldn't help but look to other Nisei: "Then I read some articles in the Pacific Citizen, the JACL newspaper: It told of the heroic deeds of the *Nisei* soldiers, of the hardships they suffered—I woke up." He realized that what he was going through was "nothing compared to the fighting man on the front. I am back in training now. I am taking weight-lifting to condition my body."

The drafting of young evacuees continued to be the major topic of conversation—and conflicts—in the camps. Many aging Issei parents thought their sons' first obligation was to them, not to the country that imprisoned them. And many young men decided to defy any military orders as long as their basic rights were being mocked. "I am a No-No boy," said one teenager who refused to answer questions 27 and 28. "I am going to say 'no' to anything as long as they treat me like an alien. When they treat me like a citizen, they can ask me questions that a citizen should answer."

"Those of us who volunteered were ostracized," said another. "There were catcalls and we got into fistfights. The *Kibei*, those born in America but educated in Japan, threw food at us in the kitchen, and my poor mother, with three sons who had volunteered, was castigated mercilessly."

The talk and the situation were about the same in all the camps, except for Tule Lake. "Speaking of the draft problem," wrote Louise Ogawa from Poston to Miss Breed in San Diego, "quite a number of boys are being called for the army and together with the relocation this camp is slowly becoming empty. There are quite a number of boys refusing to appear for induction. I just can't imagine young boys just out of school being picked up by the F.B.I. and taken to jail. It just doesn't seem right." Ogawa went on, writing, "Maybe I am too Americanized to see their view point but on the other hand I know I should respect them for their decision and determination to carry out what they believe should be."

Tom Kawaguchi at Topaz, like many other Nisei, enlisted in the army against his parents' wishes. "I joined," he said, "because I always felt very strongly about patriotism. I felt that this was my country. I didn't know any other country." To him, his choice was straightforward. "When war broke out with Japan, I was ready to fight the enemy, and I had no qualms about whether it was Japanese or German or whatever. This was my country and I was ready to defend it."

Stanley Hayami felt the same way. His older brother Frank was already in the army, and after graduation Stanley was ordered to report for his army physical in Denver. "After taking the exam," he wrote in his diary, "Mits Kawashima, Calvin Kawanami, Lloyd Kitozono, and Mas and I roamed around town, ate a big T-bone steak, saw [the film] 'Guadacanal Diary,' then we went to a hotel to sleep."

By August, Hayami was headed to active duty. He wrote in his diary on August 20, "Probably this shall be the last time I will write in this book in a long time." In this entry, he described the news of the past three months of the war: "Well, France has been invaded and the allies are now close to Paris. Saipan Island in the South Pacific has been taken with the result that Premier Tojo and his entire staff was forced to quit. Hitler has been almost killed."

He wrote about American Japanese fighting in Europe, as well. "In Italy the Japanese-Americans are doing a wonderful job. The 100th is the most decorated outfit in the army."

Like many others who departed the camps, Hayami felt an odd nostalgia.

> Heart Mt. has been a dead place, a wonderfully live place too. Dust has blown through it and snow storms too. Some-day, from a foreign battlefield I shall remember it with homesickness. Mother, Father, brothers, sister, friends, mess hall, movie theatres, ice skating, swimming, school, weightlifting—all shall try to well up in my throat at once.

On August 22, 1944, Hayami reported for induction at Fort Logan, Colorado. Within ten days, Private Hayami was in Florida, complaining about the heat and sweat in his letter to his family. It was his first full day after arriving and "already they had us drill all morning and then this afternoon they gave us our rifles. I spent most of the day cleaning it."

"Today I got my sharpshooter's medal, but I don't feel like wearing it," Stanley Hayami wrote to his parents that fall. "In a regular *hakujin* [Caucasian] company a sharpshooter is rated very high, but in our company it is doing just average. In fact it is doing below average because almost half of our company got experts medals. . . . Our company did so damn good that we broke the Camp Blanding record!"

Back "home" at Heart Mountain, Private Frank Hayami, Stanley's older brother, was on furlough for Thanksgiving, but it was a sad time. Ted Fujioka, the first student body president of Heart Mountain High School in 1943, had been killed while "on a special mission" in France. Stanley, his basic training cut short, was at Heart Mountain for Christmas, one of twenty-one soldiers on holiday leave at the camp. By then more than five hundred Heart Mountain families had little flags with blue stars in their windows, indicating they had sons in the service. The Fujiokas were the first to display a gold star, indicating a son had been killed in combat.

Stanley was there on December 30, 1944, when the *Heart Mountain Sentinel*, the camp paper where he had worked, announced that Japanese and Japanese Americans were free to return to California. But it was too late for many of them: they were afraid and they had nothing left back there.

Some American Japanese, like Stanley's sister Grace, studying at Hunter College in New York City, were building new lives in the Midwest and farther east. While many of those younger people missed the charms of the West Coast, they also shared the fears of their parents of the hatred along the Pacific.

Louise Ogawa had moved to Chicago and was cheered by her new life. "Chicago is certainly a large city. It seems like a world all by itself! It's a wonderful feeling to be able to walk the streets side by side with all creeds of people again!" She was enjoying her job doing office work at A. C. McCluy & Co. in the Correspondence Department, and anticipating what she hoped would be her first white Christmas, having never experienced snow back in Southern California.

But as winter came, Ogawa was thinking of San Diego, writing, "I have heard people are returning to California. I am so happy that we are being accepted again in our cities where we spend much of our happy moments. I, too, would like to go to San Diego and yet hesitate." Ogawa paused. "With public sentiment as it is, I think it might be best to start life anew in a new community. Life would be so wonderful if all this hatred and racial discrimination was abolished from the earth."

"GO FOR BROKE"

THE LOST BATTALION: OCTOBER 30, 1944

When Pearl Harbor was attacked, there were 1,432 American Japanese in the Hawaii Provisional Battalion, a National Guard unit. They were American citizens defending the nation, even though they were denied voting rights. On May 28, 1942, they were activated and protected from discharge by the clever (and probably illegal) bureaucratic maneuvering of the military commander of the islands, General Delos Emmons. They were transported to San Francisco on June 5 and designated the One Hundredth Infantry Battalion—"One Puka Puka," to the Hawaiians—of the United States Army.

Nikkei in Hawaii were never evacuated, although several hundred Issei, community leaders called "possibly dangerous," were on FBI lists and interned without charges in prisons and camps. Islanders were subject to martial law but there were just too many Japanese on the islands, more than 150,000 people who made up more than 40 percent of the territory's population, to be considered for evacuation. There was no way they could be evacuated or incarcerated without destroying the economy of the islands. Besides, despite Pearl Harbor, Hawaii was not ripped by the racism, the political hysteria, and the white greed that swept the West Coast. The One Hundredth's next stop was Fort McCoy in Wisconsin, where their exceptional performance in training did not go unnoticed in Washington.

Because of the One Hundredth's training success, there were plans being debated inside the War Department to form a combined Hawaii–West Coast Japanese American segregated regiment to fight in Europe. The United States needed more combat troops and Elmer Davis, director of the Office of War Information, again told President Roosevelt that the incarceration of Japanese Americans continued to be an important propaganda tool of the Axis powers. Asian press and radio controlled by Imperial Japan brought up the camps whenever Americans or the British talked of death marches or the murderous conditions in Japanese prisoner of war and slave-labor camps in the Pacific.

To be sure, there were American Japanese, Ben Kuroki among them, already serving in the army, usually secretly. Many local commanders ignored or bent Washington rules that barred service for Japanese Americans. Hundreds of invaluable MIS translators were already in the Pacific. Twenty-six Nisei attached to the One Hundredth were secretly billeted for five months on Cat Island, Mississippi, in the Gulf of Mexico, for smell tests conducted by Caucasians using dogs; the theory was that Japanese smelled different from white soldiers.

When Secretary of War Stimson ruled in early 1943 that "loyal" Nisei could serve in the military, army statisticians had estimated that 2,900 to 3,000 Nisei in the mainland camps would volunteer for the combat team. Questions 27 and 28 of the army's loyalty tests, distributed in February, destroyed that calculation. Only 1,208 Nisei volunteered from the camps where their families were living under the shadows of guard towers. Knowing nothing of this, more than ten thousand Hawaiians volunteered for combat. The army took three thousand of them, disappointing the thousands of others in crowds of young men listening outside recruiting offices as each name was called. All over the islands, men had run through the streets to the offices of their draft boards. For the men who were selected, there were parties everywhere, girls placed flower leis around the boys' necks, and relatives and strangers pushed $5 bills into their pockets as they marched through Honolulu on March 28, 1943, to board the ships that would take them to San Francisco. After arriving in California, they were loaded on sealed trains and sent on their way to training and war.

One of the men chosen for service was nineteen-year-old Daniel Inouye. He was a premed student at the University of Hawaii who had quit school along with dozens of his classmates when they learned medical students were exempt from the draft. They wanted to fight. They were desperate to fight.

Inouye recalled that when he was leaving for the service his father told him, "America has been good to us. . . . It has given you and your sisters and brothers education. We all love this country. Whatever you do, do not dishonor your country." He stressed to his son, "Remember: Never dishonor your family. And if you must give your life, do so with honor."

Not surprisingly, the white officers who ran Camp Shelby in Mississippi, where the new Hawaiian recruits and men from the relocation camps began their basic training, did not trust the Japanese Americans. For one thing, they couldn't get over how small they were; the average height was five foot three and their average weight was 125 pounds. Their average shoe size was 3½ and the Hawaiians went barefoot whenever they could get away with it. They were issued toy wooden guns. Their mail home to the internment camps was secretly opened and read at Shelby.

It was the tone of those letters, the passionate patriotism, that convinced the commanders that trust in the Nisei was warranted, and real guns and ammunition were issued to them. By August of 1943, the One Hundredth was on its way to North Africa.

Commanding officers training both the Hawaiians and the mainlanders were surprised, though, by one thing: the two groups of Japanese American trainees did not like each other. The Hawaiians were dark-skinned and spoke a rapid pidgin language, a mix of English, Japanese, Chinese, Hawaiian, and Filipino. *Puka* meant "hole" or "zero," *S'koshi* meant "little bit," "'Ass why" meant "That's the reason." To the Hawaiians, the better-educated mainlanders sounded like white men. The Islanders were a carefree bunch who loved to drink and gamble away free time. They had money, including the envelopes of cash handed them by islanders bidding them "Aloha!" Dan Inouye ran a crap game and claimed he was making as much as $1,500 a month. "Go for Broke!" which became the motto of the 442nd, came from those crap games. It was also part of the fight song the Hawaiians sang to drumbeats.

> One-Puka-Puka . . . We're the boys from Hawaii nei. . . .
> We'll fight for you and the Red White and Blue . . . And go
> to the front . . . And back to Honolulu–lulu. Fighting for
> Dear Old Uncle Sam. Go for broke! Hooh! We don't give a
> damn! We'll round up the Huns at the point of our guns,
> and victory will be ours! Go for broke!

The motto of the One Hundredth when it was a separate (and segregated) unit was "Remember Pearl Harbor."

The mainlanders had lighter skin and were better educated, a more restrained bunch. They spoke good English and sent all their money back to their families in the relocation camps. The Hawaiians called themselves Buddhaheads, a slang term referring to pumpkins, and they called the mainlanders Kotonks, mimicking the sound of a coconut falling from a tree and hitting the ground. *Buddhahead* had a double meaning. *Buta* was the Japanese word for "pig," so *butahead* could mean "pigheaded." Fistfights and beatings became a major problem. In Washington, there was serious debate about breaking up the Nisei units.

At Shelby, Colonel Charles Pence got an idea for a way to help ease the tensions between the islanders and mainlanders. He decided to take busloads of Hawaiian officers and sergeants from the Mississippi army base to the Arkansas relocation camps, Camp Jerome and Camp Rohwer. One of the Hawaiians who saw the Arkansas camps, Sergeant Inouye, was one of the men who took the first trip on July 4, 1943, for what was called a "social weekend" at the Arkansas camps. He remembered it this way:

> Arriving, we saw formations of barracks, then turned in and saw high barbed wire, machine guns and bayonets, towers. We thought it must be a secret base. Then we saw people who looked like us. It didn't take long to figure out what was going on. . . .When we got back, I assembled my squad. I told them it was beyond imagination out there. This was where these mainlanders had come from, they were brave men.
>
> Up until that point I had no idea that these men had come from these camps. But on our way back from there, something haunted me and it's haunted me forever. Would I have volunteered if I were from that camp?

Sergeant Inouye, the young man who as a teenager had run through the streets of Honolulu to enlist, admitted he didn't know if he would have joined up if he had been interned or evacuated. "When we got back, they became our brothers. Blood brothers. You know, these guys, the mainlanders, were special, that even under these extreme circumstances they would volunteer. They were better than us."

As the mainland volunteers from the camps trained as the 442nd, elements of the One Hundredth were already in North Africa to prepare for the Allied invasion of Italy. They were then shipped to Salerno ten days after the Allies invaded the Italian port city. Within six weeks they took 25 percent casualties, with 3 officers and 25 enlisted men killed in action; 239 more were wounded.

The 442nd left Shelby and shipped out from Hampton Roads, Virginia, for the invasion at Anzio in southern Italy, landing there on May 1, 1944. The One Hundredth had already suffered almost a thousand casualties before the two Japanese American units, still segregated, were combined in Italy. The First Battalion of the 442nd had stayed at Fort Shelby to train new Nisei draftees as replacements. The One Hundredth, which kept its separate designation, took the place of the 442nd's First Battalion.

On June 6, 1944, as Allied troops landed on the Normandy coast of France, the all-Nisei One Hundredth Battalion was the American unit closest to Rome, just six miles south of the city. They were ordered to stop there by General John Harmony. They camped and then stood by for more than a day on the side of the main route to the city, Highway 7, as the Caucasians of the First Armored Division caught up and marched triumphantly past them into the first Axis capital captured by the Allies.

Then the men of the One Hundredth were loaded on trucks and moved to an area north of the city. A week after that, farther north, the One Hundredth, mostly Hawaiians, was officially merged into the 442nd Combat Unit, most of them mainlanders from the West Coast. Three weeks later, on June 26, 1944, with the One Hundredth Battalion veterans in the lead, the combined 442nd went into battle for the first time, surrounding the German-held town of Belvedere di Spinello. It was a bloody fight and the Americans suffered nine hundred casualties, winning a Presidential Unit Citation, which read:

> All three companies went into action boldly facing murderous fire from all types of weapons and tanks and, at times, fighting without artillery support. . . . The stubborn desire of the men to close with a numerically superior enemy and the rapidity with which they fought allowed the 100th Battalion to destroy completely the flank positions of the German Army. . . . The fortitude and intrepidity of the officers and men of the 100th reflects the finest traditions of the Army of the United States.

The 442nd Combat Regiment was designed as a self-contained battle force of 3,800 men, backed up by its own artillery, medical, and engineering units. The regiment spent the rest of the summer engaged in bitter battle after battle as they made their way through northern Italy. By mid-July, the 442nd, under constant attack from dug-in German units in Cecina and Castellina, would, according to United States military records, report 1,100 enemy kills and 331 captures. The campaign continued until the 442nd reached the Arno River on August 31, 1944. The combat team by then had lost 239 men, killed or missing, and another 972 wounded.

On July 11, 1944, George Saito of the 442nd wrote to his father about his brother Calvin: "I believe the War Department has notified you of our loss of Calvin . . . it happened so soon, on the 12th day of combat. . . . He happened to be one of the unlucky ones—his passing was instantaneous."

George Saito continued, as he wanted to be sure that his father understood his and his brother's decision to join the 442nd, "Dad, this is not the time to be preaching to you but I have something on my chest that I want you to hear—In spite of Cal's supreme sacrifice don't let anyone tell you that he was foolish or made a mistake to volunteer. Of what I've seen in my travels on our mission I am more than convinced that we've done the right thing in spite of what has happened in the past—America is a damned good country and don't let anyone tell you otherwise."

Three months later, George Saito was killed in action.

In September of 1944, the 442nd was moved by ship to France, landing at Marseille and then traveling five hundred miles by train and foot through the Rhône Valley for an assault on the German-held French town of Bruyères, a German stronghold in the Vosges Mountains. The battle in the black forests of northeastern France began on October 15. The terrain and weather were the worst the men of the 442nd had seen so far. Many of them still wearing summer gear, they crawled up steep and muddy slopes and were battered by cold winds and soaking rain. The Germans fought well, as if they were defending their own homeland. The fighting raged for nine days with heavy casualties on both sides. The people of the town had lived underground in cellars, with little food and water. When the firing ended and villagers emerged in the daylight, they were stunned to see what one of them called "little men with yellow skin and slanted eyes." Some guessed the men in strange uniforms were "Hindus" of some kind. Private First Class Stanley Akita remembered, "They didn't believe we were American soldiers. I don't think they knew what a Japanese looked like."

It was not over, though. The Germans counterattacked over a hill east of the town. At one point, they fired on medics wearing Red Cross armbands, killing a wounded American, Sergeant Abraham Ohama, on a stretcher. Enraged soldiers of the 442nd charged up the hill yelling "Banzai!," fighting hand to hand for a half hour. They killed fifty Germans and captured seven more.

Next the Nisei units were ordered to take Biffontaine, a few miles away, another German strongpoint, guarded by four hills. They captured the town after taking the hills and then engaging in eight days of door-to-door fighting. Stanley Akita was captured by the Germans during that fight. A German interrogator said, "You're supposed to be fighting with us, not against us. What makes you think you're an American?"

• • •

After the Bruyères and Biffontaine battles, the 442nd was pulled back for two weeks of rest and recreation in a secured town called Belmont, where the attractions included hot showers, hot food, and dry socks. That lasted for two days. They were called back for one of the most difficult jobs of the French campaign: rescuing the First Battalion of the 141st Regiment of the Thirty-Sixth Infantry Division, the "Alamo Regiment," originally a Texas National Guard unit, which was cut off and surrounded. That was "The Lost Battalion," soon to be famous across the United States.

They actually were never lost; they had just outrun other units on their flanks. American commanders knew exactly where they were, on a hilltop east of Biffontaine, behind German lines in a grim pine forest that was foggy during the day, pitch-dark at night. They were 275 men with no food, and their only water was scooped from muddy foxholes. They were running out of ammunition, and they were surrounded by at least seven hundred Germans with tanks and heavy armor. The battalion was now led by a lieutenant from Jersey City, New Jersey, Marty Higgins, the highest-ranking officer still alive. Each day they sent out radio messages, but only twice a day in order to conserve battery power for their only link to the world beyond their small hilltop: "Send us medical supplies," "We need rations," "Please we need fresh water," "I need radio batteries. My wounded need plasma." Army Air Corps P-47 fighter-bombers attempted to drop supplies, but most of them ended up in German hands. A rocket with its nose cone filled with chocolate buried itself so deeply in the mud that it could not be pulled free.

Several rescue missions had already failed, including a break-out attempt by the Lost Battalion itself that left fifty men missing in action. To the 442nd, which was never told the nature of the mission, this was just taking another hill for no particular reason. They moved out at 3:00 a.m. on October 27. In fog, rain, and snow, they moved up muddy forest slopes, each man holding the pack of the man in front of him. Again, neither the "T-patchers," as the Texans were called, nor the Nisei knew of each other—nor of the fact of the rescue mission. The 442nd began to move up the hills two kilometers from the T-patchers. After taking heavy casualties in savage fighting for five days, the Nisei units were blocked and under heavy fire from German artillery units on a ridge above them. It was only then, five days into hell, that the 442nd was told what the mission actually was: the Germans were about to capture a depleted American battalion—and it was their job to rescue their comrades.

The men of the 442nd were barely able to advance in the heavy rain up steep and slimy terrain and through the tangles of trees. The mined and booby-trapped land was dotted with German machine-gun nests and snipers. Second Lieutenant Edward Davis, the only officer left in his company—most of the 442nd officers were Caucasians at the beginning—stood up, turned to Sergeant Wataru Kohashi, and asked the Nisei sergeant to follow him. The two of them began a hopeless charge. Then, one after another, the Nisei stood and charged up the hilltop, shouting the battle cry, "Banzai! Banzai!" One of them was Private First Class Mickey Akiyama, who had been the first Nisei to volunteer at Manzanar when the army came looking for recruits. He was shot in the head during the charge, but then he bandaged himself up and put his helmet back on. In the helmet he kept the photograph of his baby daughter, Mariko Ann.

"We didn't care anymore, we were like a bunch of savages," said Private First Class Ichigi Kashiwagi. The 442nd took the hill in an hour. The next morning, October 30, was strangely quiet, until American artillery blanketed the ridge between the 442nd and the T-patchers. When the Nisei advanced again, there was little response. They saw discarded German equipment and uniforms; the enemy had moved out during the night.

At the end of the battle, the One Hundredth had been reduced from 1,432 men a year earlier to 260. The combined 442nd and One Hundredth, with 42 men killed in the rescue, was down to 800 men. The number of T-patchers rescued was 211. The first Nisei to break through, Private First Class Matsuji Sakumoto, saw a mud-blacked Texan, Sergeant Ed Guy, with his lips quivering in shock. Sakumoto said the only thing he could think of, "Want a smoke, soldier?" Hiro Endo found a wounded T-patcher in a foxhole, pouring something dark from his canteen. Endo thought it was chocolate dropped by P-47s, but it was just muddy water gathered from rain in the foxhole. "I offered him my canteen of water," said Endo. "And I saw tears running down his cheeks."

"Chills went up our spines when we saw the *Nisei* soldiers," said Marty Higgins. "Honestly, they looked like giants to us." The Lost Battalion's final radio transmission was, "Patrol 442 here. Tell them we love them."

The rescue of the Lost Battalion was an irresistible story for the American press, particularly because the battles of the south had become "The Forgotten Front" after the Normandy invasion seized the world's attention. Dozens of newsmen and cameras were waiting for the T-patchers who came down from the hills. The 442nd was moving in the other direction, deeper into the forest. While the T-patchers were celebrated, the Nisei were only finally issued mountain winter gear—coats, sweaters, gloves, and waterproof boots—on November 4, to replace the summer combat uniforms they were wearing before the mission.

For most of the American reporters, the rescued not the rescuers, white men not Nisei, were the focus of the story. The *New York Times* account of the deadly drama in France, an Associated Press article, was published on November 7. The headline read, "Doughboys Break German Ring to Free 270 Trapped Eight Days."

The article did not mention that the "doughboys" were Japanese Americans. The 442nd was not mentioned in the AP report. The accompanying photograph, supplied by the Army Signal, showed Marty Higgins shaking hands with Lieutenant C. O. Barry of Williamstown, Pennsylvania, "of the relief unit." There was no Lieutenant Barry in the 442nd.

Time magazine was an exception to most home-front journalism, writing: "From a cautious experiment the army has received an unexpectedly rich reward. A group of sinewy oriental soldiers, only one generation removed from a nation that was fanatically fighting against the U.S., was fighting just as fanatically for it."

After the press was gone, General John Dahlquist, commander of the Thirty-Sixth Division, a controversial leader who would be accused of using the Nisei as "cannon fodder," called a parade to honor the 442nd for the rescue mission at a ceremony on November 12. Looking out at the detachment, he angrily asked his adjutant why so few soldiers assembled when he had ordered a mass formation. The adjutant, Lieutenant Colonel Virgil Miller, answered, "This is all there is." He shouted at Miller again, when Companies I and K of the 442nd marched by. "I ordered everyone out today." There were only eighteen still standing from Company K and eight from Company I—twenty-six men out of the four hundred who went into battle.

The 442nd, exhausted and undermanned—the casualty list was over two thousand wounded and killed in just four weeks in the Vosges campaign—was taken off the line on November 17 as replacements began to arrive. The Nisei still standing were rewarded with what they called the "champagne campaign," spending four months in light combat in the hills behind Nice, along the Riviera border between France and Italy. There was time off to check out the Mediterranean beaches and bars of the Côte D'Azur—and shock French men and women staring at Japanese men in American uniforms.

• • •

As the men of the 442nd came off the front lines, President Roosevelt was reelected for a fourth term, carrying thirty-six states in defeating the Republican governor of New York, Thomas E. Dewey, by almost four million votes. The camps were never an issue in the campaign, but in his first press conference after the election, November 21, 1944, the president was asked about the imprisonment of American Japanese. His answer was rambling and he emphasized his feelings that if Japanese were scattered around the country, instead of being concentrated in California, there might be fewer resettlement problems. Then the man who ordered that the *Nikkei* be rounded up three years before shocked his own aides by saying, "It is felt by a great many lawyers that under the Constitution they can't be locked up in concentration camps."

Another reporter asked, "I was wondering if you felt the danger of espionage had sufficiently diminished so that the military restrictions that were passed could be lifted?"

"That I couldn't tell you," answered the president, "because I don't know."

He did know. That issue had been secretly decided almost a year before.

On Monday, December 18, 1944, six weeks after Roosevelt's reelection, the Supreme Court handed down its decisions on the cases initiated almost three years before in the names of Fred Korematsu and Mitsuye Endo. After all that time and talk, the

Supreme Court sided with the government and the army when it came to the mass detention. And yet, the day before the decisions came down, the War Department announced that Japanese and Japanese Americans were now free to live anywhere they wanted to in the United States, including in California and the rest of the West Coast.

In the Korematsu case, the Court voted 6 to 3 that his arrest was constitutional. Justice Hugo Black wrote the majority opinion, saying, "Korematsu was not excluded from the Military Area because of hostility to him or his race. . . . Properly constituted military authorities feared an invasion of our West Coast and felt constrained to take properly constituted security measures."

In dissent, Justice Robert Jackson wrote, "Korematsu . . . has been convicted of an act not commonly a crime. It consists merely of being present in the state whereof he is a citizen. . . . A citizen's presence in the locality was made a crime only if his parents were of Japanese birth." Then Jackson added this stinging line: "The Court for all time has validated the principle of racial discrimination. . . . The principle then lies about like a loaded weapon, ready for the hand of any authority that can bring forward a plausible claim of an urgent need."

A second dissenter, Justice Frank Murphy, called the decision a "legalization of racism" and wrote, "All residents of this nation are kin in some way by blood and culture to a foreign land. Yet they are primarily and necessarily a part of this new civilization of the United States. They must accordingly be treated at all times as the heirs of the American experiment and as entitled to all of the rights and freedoms granted by the Constitution."

Murphy went on to say:

> Such exclusion goes over the very brink of constitutional power and falls into the ugly abyss of racism. . . . Racial discrimination of this nature bears no reasonable relation

to military necessity and is utterly foreign to the ideals and traditions of the American people. The reasons [for exclusion] appear to be largely an accumulation of much of the misinformation, half-truths, and insinuations that for years have been directed against Japanese-Americans by people with racial and economic prejudices.

Mitsuye Endo's case was the only internment case where the Supreme Court ruled in favor of the plaintiff. The Court agreed that the government itself, according to the decision, had already conceded that she was a loyal American, given that she had been a California state employee with no connections to the Japanese government. The ruling in her case was both unanimous and narrow. The Court ruled that, regardless of whether the United States government had a right to exclude people of Japanese ancestry from the West Coast during World War II, it could not continue to detain a citizen that the government conceded was loyal to the United States.

All of the decisions were carefully written so as not to discuss the Constitution or question military decisions. By the time the decisions finally came down on December 18, 1944, Korematsu was a welder in Salt Lake City. Mitsuye Endo was working as a secretary in Chicago, and her brother, Hiro Endo, was one of the Nisei soldiers who rescued the Lost Battalion.

The Supreme Court decisions came at almost the same time as the War Relocation Authority announced that all of the relocation camps would be closed down within six months to a year. There were mixed reactions in the camps about the announcement. Many of the older Issei, particularly the bachelor farm workers, had grown used to the spare comforts of camp life. Younger people had their doubts, too.

From Minneapolis, Fusa Tsumagari had some of the same reservations as Louise Ogawa in Chicago, writing to friends,

"Those with property are wanting to go back, but wondering what the sentiment will be. Of course we know good friends like you would be glad to have us back, but others who do not know us or understand us may not be so glad. As for us not so fortunate to have property in California, we're content to stay here for a while, or maybe for the rest of our life."

As soon as the announcement was public, the anti-Japanese drumbeats of 1942 were heard again in the West. Elsie Robinson, a *San Francisco Examiner* columnist, wrote that she would "slit the throat" of any internee who attempted to return to California.

• • •

On the night of November 29, 1944, in Hood River, Oregon, a town of three thousand people, the honor roll of local men in service, which covered one outside wall of the local courthouse, was defaced by black paint to cover up sixteen names—all Japanese Americans. The names covered were: George Akiyama, Masaaki Asai, Taro Asai, Noboru Hamada, Kenjiro Hayakawa, Shigenobu Imai, Fred Mitsuo Kinoshita, George Kinoshita, Sagie Nishioka, Mamoru Noji, Henry K. Norimasu, Katsumi Sato, Harry Osamu, Eichi Wakamatsu, Johnny Y. Wakamatsu, and Bill Shyuichi Yamaki. One Nisei name was left on the board: Isso Namba. Locals thought the name was Finnish. Another son of the valley never made it onto the wall in the first place, because Frank Hachiya of the Military Intelligence Service had enlisted in Portland.

The defacement job was done by members of Post 22 of the American Legion.

Spectacularly located in a valley above the Columbia River Gorge and under Mount Hood, Hood River was home to 431 American Japanese, many of them farmers who had made Hood River apples and cherries famous around the country. It seemed an idyllic place; certainly it was to young people. In the week after Pearl Harbor, students of Oak Grove High School published this poem in the school newspaper:

> To those of Hood River—if you please
> They are our friends—these Japanese
> Not "Japs" or even Japanese
> They are Americans, our schoolmates these.

Those feelings were shared by Nisei schoolmates. George Akiyama, who was fifteen, wrote to Glen Oaks's principal, Vienna Annala, from the Fresno Assembly Center, "How is everybody back in the best community in the best place in the world? I am quite fine and so is everybody else, except the heat is getting to me . . . 130 degrees. . . . Although this may be a great sacrifice to all of us, it is so little we can do to help our country win this horrid war and we are all proud to do this one small cooperation."

Hood River County had a population of almost twelve thousand before the evacuation of the *Nikkei* in May of 1942. Those farmers and their families were the subjects of Exclusion Order 49. When the story of the painted-over names got around the country, Post 22 was suddenly as big a name brand—for hatred—as Hood River apples. The Legionnaires were condemned by newspapers across the country, with *PM* in New York urging Oregon officials to send in the National Guard to restore the names. The *New York Times* and papers in Salt Lake City and Des Moines, Iowa, compared the Legionnaires with Hitler. "The Tops in Blind Hatred," was a headline in *Collier's* magazine. Legionnaires themselves were divided—while many posts, particularly in the East and Midwest, condemned their fellow Legionnaires in Hood River, more than a dozen American Legion posts in other states took Japanese names off their own honor rolls.

Federal officials, beginning with Secretary of War Stimson, attacked Post 22 and the town. Outraged letters flooded newspapers around the country. White soldiers in Europe, some of them writing to local newspapers, said that they would be dead if not for the bravery of Nisei comrades. Three local soldiers, Kenneth and Don Butzin and Hale Lyon, men from Hood River, wrote from Europe saying they wanted their names removed from the courthouse wall unless the Japanese American names were put back up.

The self-styled superpatriots of Hood River—boasting that their county was a national leader in war bond sales—did not back down. On December 22, five days after Washington announced that Japanese and Japanese Americans could return to the West Coast, Post 22 paid for advertisements in the *Hood River County Sun*, ads that were also distributed as posters.

STATEMENT TO RETURNING JAPANESE

Under the War Department's recent ruling you will soon be permitted to return to this county.

FOR YOUR OWN BEST INTERESTS, WE URGE YOU NOT TO RETURN.

Public records show that there are about 25 or 30 families, out of some 600 Japanese, who have not already sold their property in Hood River County. We strongly urge these to dispose of their holdings. If you desire assistance from this Post in disposing of your land, we pledge ourselves to see that you get a square deal.

If you do return, we also pledge that to the best of our ability, we will uphold law and order, and will countenance no violence.

HOOD RIVER POST NO. 22
AMERICAN LEGION
DEPARTMENT OF OREGON

In another broadside, referring back to Pearl Harbor, Post 22 asserted, "Every adult Japanese in this valley knew what was brewing. NOT ONE TOLD!"

There were two small newspapers in the county. The *Sun's* editorial was headlined: "They Must Never Come Back." The competition, the *Hood River News*, never directly attacked Post 22 or its members, but it did print four editorials from out-of-state papers attacking the post and its members. It also printed twenty-five letters, all but two of them critical of the Legion post.

From January to March of 1945, the Hood River campaign was centered around six more full-page newspaper advertisements signed by Kent Shoemaker, a former commander of Post 22, who was the county clerk. The first one appeared on January 26 in both the *Sun* and the *News* under the headline, "So Sorry Please, Japs Are Not Wanted in Hood River." The ad, which included Post 22's resolutions, was signed, "Yours for a Hood River without a Jap."

That ad was an open letter to Reverend W. Sherman Burgoyne, the pastor of Asbury Methodist Church. It played off a letter to the editor printed in the *News*, in which Burgoyne wrote, "Every person in Hood River is disgraced." That week, Reverend Burgoyne came close to disgracing himself, writing to Post 22, "Personally I don't think any group of foreign language or habits should be allowed to congregate in a single place, no matter what race they may be. It keeps them from thinking and living 'American.'"

The next Shoemaker ads showed maps of Japanese-owned land and listed the names of 480 local residents he said were against letting any *Nikkei* return to the valley. Next came an ad quoting anti-Japanese copy from *Reader's Digest*, with 421 other names, under the line, "We, the undersigned residents and taxpayers of Hood River County, are one hundred percent behind Hood River Post No. 22, American Legion, in ALL their efforts to keep the Japs from returning to this county." The fourth and fifth of the six ads listed 384 more names including former Oregon governor Walter M. Pierce, a former state senator, George Wilbur, and an "educator" named T. S. Van Vleet who concluded, "A Jap is just an 'educated,' unbridled, sadistic modernized barbarian." That last Shoemaker ad was headlined, "No Japes Wanted in Hood River." "Japes" was defined as a combination of "Japs" and "apes."

The white men of Hood River were also traveling the state and appearing at mass meetings organized by the Oregon Property Owners' Protective League. On March 13, a meeting in the town of Gresham was advertised by posters reading, "How Will We Rid the Coast of Japs? Get the answer to this problem that vitally affects you and every Oregon resident at the patriotic MASS MEETING at Union High School—$100 in Door Prizes Given Away."

While the ads were running in Hood River, Sergeant Frank Hachiya, the local boy working as an interpreter in the Philippines, was killed in action. The *Honolulu Star-Bulletin* told that story under the headline, "Sergeant Hachiya, Spurned by Legion Post, Dies Hero's Death in P.I."

Anti-Japanese racism was not only in Hood River, of course. Lieutenant Colonel James Hanley, an officer from another small town, Mandan, North Dakota, was a commander of one of the three battalions in the 442nd, and he happened to read a short commentary in his hometown newspaper, the *Mandan Daily Pioneer*, saying, "There are some good Jap Americans but it [doesn't] say where they're buried." Hanley, a friend of the editor, Charles Pierce, wrote home:

Yes, Charlie, I know where there are some GOOD Japanese Americans—there are 5,000 in this unit. They are American soldiers and I know where they are buried. I

wish I could show you some of them, Charlie. I remember one Japanese-American. He was walking ahead of me
in a forest in France. A German shell took off the right side
of his face.

Hanley went on to describe other incidents of heroism and
self-sacrifice by Nisei, and then wrote:

I wish the boys of the "Lost Battalion" could tell you what
they think of Japanese Americans. . . . The marvel is, Charlie, that these boys fight at all—they are good soldiers in
spite of the racial prejudice shown by your paragraph. I
know it makes a good joke—but it is the kind of joke that
prejudice thrives upon. Our system is supposed to make
good Americans out of anyone—it certainly has done in
the case of these boys. You, the Hearst newspapers, and a
few others make one wonder what we are fighting for. I
hope it isn't racial prejudice.

But it was Hood River and its American Legionnaires that
became a national symbol of intolerance. Post 22 continued to
refuse to recognize the service of Japanese Americans for four
more months, even after the national commander of the more
than 12,245 American Legion posts in the country, Edward
Schieberling, who had himself urged that *Nikkei* not try to
return to their homes and property on the West Coast, reversed
himself and told Post leaders that their actions were hurting the
Legion and "the war effort."

Post 22 responded that Japanese could not be assimilated in
American society. Its members maintained that position into
April, finally restoring the names of the sixteen Nisei on April
29, 1945. By then, national grocery chains were reporting local
boycotts of Hood River's famous apples, and bankers in Portland

were refusing to lend money to some Hood River farmers. There were also reports, which proved to be untrue, that the post's charter might be revoked by officials of Oregon's state organization.

• • •

Stanley Hayami's first letter home from Europe was dated February 7, 1945, from "Somewhere in France." He wrote that France felt in some ways like the United States, though there were some differences: the houses looked older, and some were destroyed by bombs. He also noticed that the French, at least the ones he had seen so far, seemed very poor, wearing tattered clothes and scavenging for scraps.

> We were having "chow" near the railroad tracks, and being a wasteful people, we threw some of the food we didn't feel like eating on the ground. Pretty soon some old Frenchmen came by and picked up the scraps of bread and baloney. One of them saw me watching and so he pointed at the baloney and said "Woof." I guess he had a little pride and wanted me to think that he was picking it up to feed to his dog, but I don't think poor Frenchmen like him spend a great deal of their time looking for scraps just so they can feed it to their dogs.

His older brother, Frank, was also in France during the "champagne campaign" on the French Riviera. He wrote home to report the day when by chance he happened to see Stanley and reported that his brother was gaining weight and strength since leaving the camps. Frank was in his jeep just behind the lines when he saw Stanley. They spent a couple of hours talking that afternoon. He told his parents that Stanley was "looking very fine—and sure has gained much weight since I saw him back in Heart Mountain—nice and husky now. Big hands and big body. And still smiling his nice big smile." He added: "We're O.K. Everything's nice and peaceful here."

Stanley's next letter was sent on February 27, saying that he had seen Marseille and Paris—from the back of a truck moving troops around France. Now, back in Southern France, he added:

> Right now I'm up front here, living on top of a mountain. The Jerries are on the next mountain. It's nice and warm up here, get enough to eat, don't do much, and the Germans aren't giving us too much trouble (not now, anyway). . . . I would just about forget the war if it wasn't for the artillery lobbing shells over us and if I couldn't see the dead Jerries lying around below. (They were killed before I got here when they tried to attack.) I didn't feel so good when I first saw the dead Jerries, but no one pays much attention to them when we go working around them—they're just part of the landscape now. So the dead ones don't bother me anymore—they say it's the live ones I should worry about.

He wrote again on March 19, using his middling Japanese, with an update on friends he had seen in the 442nd.

> When Murata came last year the 442 was in a very big battle. Murata *wa boku ni uimasu "senso wa tottemo kuwai desu"* [Murata tells me "war is very scary"]. Remember David Ito? He got a bronze star medal the other day. Remember Yo and Mas Tsuruda that lived near us in Pomona? Well their brother is in my company and he won a silver star!
>
> How are you folks at home? Frank says you may go home to California about May. . . . You oughta have a lot of fun if you go back to Calif.

In late March of 1945, the 442nd was ordered back into combat again as part of the Fifth Army near Pisa, Italy, under the command of General Mark Clark, the same General Clark who had argued against Japanese internment in 1942. He had asked General Eisenhower if the 442nd could be brought back from France. "They are the best goddamned fighters in the U.S. Army," he told Ike. General Clark wanted the 442nd to lead the final attacks on the Gothic Line, a line along the Apennine mountains and ridges between Italy and Austria, the line Hitler called the last barrier between Allied forces and the German homeland. It was guarded by more than twenty-seven hundred German machine-gun nests and bunkers, constructed over a year by slave laborers. With Americans at the bottom of the ridges, the two sides had been deadlocked for the six months since the 442nd had withdrawn and been sent to guard the French-Italian border in comfort.

At 5:00 a.m. on April 5, 1945, the 100th/442nd charged into the no-man's-land between the two armies. The heroism of the next few days became a part of American legend. Private First Class Sadao S. Munemori, a twenty-two-year-old *Kibei* auto mechanic from Los Angeles and Manzanar, rushed forward under heavy enemy fire when his platoon leader was badly wounded, lobbing grenade after grenade into two German positions, silencing both. As he worked his way back to join his squad, an enemy grenade fell into a shell crater where two of his squad members had taken cover. He threw himself on top of the grenade, saving his two buddies at the cost of his own life. Private First Class Munemori was the first Nisei awarded the highest combat decoration the United States could give, the Medal of Honor.

Two weeks after that, the 442nd was attacking Colle Musatello, the last of the ridges marking the Gothic Line. Daniel Inouye, the Hawaiian who quit his medical studies to enlist and who won a battlefield commission as a lieutenant, had been shot in the chest in an earlier engagement, but the bullet was stopped by two silver dollars he kept for luck in a shirt pocket. On April 20, he was commanding a rifle platoon that charged up Musatello in the early morning hours. He was yards in front of his men, forty yards from the last German strongpoint on the ridge. He grabbed a grenade and as he wound up to throw it he felt a heavy pain in his side. When his men caught up with him, they saw that he was gushing blood from his side. Inouye kept advancing and then his legs gave out and he collapsed. The attack faltered. But Inouye got up and tried to throw his last grenade. He was stopped by a German rocket grenade that ripped off his right arm. He pulled the grenade from his dead hand and then threw it. Somehow he stood up and charged, firing a machine gun. He was hit again and began rolling down the hill. He was bleeding from his right side, with wounds in his stomach and in his right leg. "Get up that hill," he screamed to his men. And they did.

●　●　●

On April 22, only two days after the Nisei's heroic fight at Colle Musatello on the Gothic Line, three "kotonks" serving in the 522nd Artillery Battalion, Sus Ito, Yul Minaga, and George Oiye, came upon what looked at first to be lumps in the snow. They were bodies, some of the three hundred prisoners in one of 139 satellite concentration camps clustered around Dachau, the first of Hitler's concentration camps.

When Private Shiro Kashino, who joined the army from Minidoka, first saw the row of huts behind barbed wire at Dachau, he said, "This is exactly what they had built for us in Idaho."

One of the survivors, Solly Ganor, a sixteen-year-old inmate, was both amazed and terrified by his encounter with Japanese American soldiers, remembering later:

I thought, oh, now the Japanese are going to kill us. And I didn't care anymore. I said, "Just kill us, get it over with." The soldier tried to convince me that he was an American and wouldn't kill me. I said, "Oh, no, you are a Japanese and you're going to kill us." We went back and forth, and finally he landed on his knees, crying, with his hands over his face, and he said, "You are free. We are American Japanese. You are free."

The American soldier was named Clarence Matsumura, from the island of Maui in Hawaii. He remembered finding more survivors along the roadside. "Almost all of them were wearing black and white striped uniforms. I don't know how any of them could stand on their feet. They were nothing. They couldn't speak. Most of them were lying on the ground, many of them unconscious."

Matsumura began putting the survivors in barns, covering them with blankets, and giving them water and broth. Solly Ganor and the others could not swallow solid food. Some tried and some died, right there. Then the Americans started going into villages along the road, putting the German civilians out in the cold and putting the freed prisoners in their beds and on their couches and rugs.

Fifty years later, Ganor, who immigrated to Israel, received a telephone call from a hotel in Jerusalem, where a group of men, Nisei veterans, were staying on a reunion tour. He agreed to come to the hotel. "Solly," said an American guide, introducing the men, "this is Clarence Matsumura. We think he is the man who saved you."

Ganor remembered him. The two old men fell into each other's arms.

* * *

On April 23, Inouye's platoon, led now by Sergeant Gordon Taka-saki, was ordered to take a Tuscan village, San Terenzo, a well-fortified outpost of the Gothic Line. One of the men who had served earlier in the battle where Inouye had lost his arm was a new replacement, Private Stanley Hayami. He wrote home before the battle for San Terenzo, "Well, doggone, here I am in Italy now! After studying all that French, I gotta learn Italian! Fooey! Yes-terday was Easter and I went to the services. Reminded me of all the other Easters I've had. Guess I'll remember this one for a long time."

The Germans retreating north in Italy began surrendering in the hundreds, then the thousands. Army historians later reconstructed what happened in San Terenzo.

> Through heavy German mortar, machine gun and artil-lery fire, Sgt. Takasaki advanced exposing himself to heavy fire in his attempt to surround and disorganize the enemy. Wounded in the chest by machine gun fire, he continued to direct his men in battle. . . . His men cut the enemy escape road and brilliantly accomplished their mission. Sgt. Takasaki died in the last major campaign of the 442nd. Five other *Nisei* were killed in the engagement.

One of them was Stanley Hayami.

Stanley, whose brother Frank was wounded in the same engagement, was posthumously awarded a Bronze Star. The cita-tion reported that during the battle he had left his covered posi-tion and approached to help the men who had been wounded. Despite the shots directed at him from the hostile machine gun and sniper, he reached the first casualty, kneeled, and adminis-tered first aid. Still exposed to heavy enemy fire, he continued on to help another man. While aiding these men, he was mortally wounded.

Stanley was one of seven hundred Nisei killed in Europe. Sixty-seven more were missing in action. More than nine thousand were wounded.

That spring, the war in Europe was over. At Heart Mountain, the Hayami family celebrated V-E (Victory in Europe) Day on May 8, not knowing what had happened to their son Stanley. The telegram sent to Heart Mountain arrived the next day: "The Secretary of War desires me to express his deep regret that your son Pvt. Hayami Stanley K. was killed in Action in Italy 23 Apr 45. Confirming letter follows. J.A. Ulio the Adjutant General."

Talking later, Grace and her mother discovered that they both had the same dream on the same night in April. It was April 23, the day Stanley died. Both of them dreamed that Stanley had come to them asking for a glass of water.

Guy Robertson, WRA director of Heart Mountain, paid tribute to Hayami and five other young men from Heart Mountain who had given their lives in battle. The Boy Scouts Drum and Bugle Corps opened the ceremony with an overture. Wreaths were laid before the Gold Star Flag by Camp Fire Girls and Girl Scouts, while the Boy Scouts band played "Nearer My God to Thee."

GOING "HOME"

V-J DAY: AUGUST 15, 1945

Sergeant Ben Kuroki flew twenty-eight B-29 missions over Japan—that made his total fifty-eight bombing missions over Germany, Italy, and Japan—but his nerves were beginning to fray. He found himself thinking and dreaming of innocent women and children burning to death in the firestorms caused by the incendiaries his plane was dropping over the frail wooden and paper-screen houses of the Japanese capital.

Then the war was over.

On August 6, 1945, the *Enola Gay* dropped its bomb on Hiroshima; another B-29, the *Bockscar*, dropped one on Nagasaki. Two weeks later, Ben Kuroki's own war was ended by another American soldier, a drunken American, who stabbed him in the head while they were playing cards and arguing about which of them was "a better American." He lost a lot of blood; it took twenty-four stitches to close the wound. He was in a hospital on Tinian Island and could not go home with the rest of his crew.

The 442nd Regimental Combat Team, the Japanese American "Go for Broke" unit, earned more than eighteen thousand individual decorations, the highest number per capita of any unit in the army—including one Medal of Honor, fifty-three Distinguished Service Crosses, 588 Silver Stars, fifty-two hundred Bronze Star Medals, 9,486 Purple Hearts, and eight Presidential Unit Citations, the nation's top award for combat units. More than fifty years later, in June of 2000, President Bill Clinton awarded twenty additional Medals of Honor to members of the One Hundredth Battalion and 442nd Regimental Combat Team, the result of a reexamination of the files of dozens of Japanese American soldiers to see if any of them might have been denied awards because of possible prejudice by superior officers.

• • •

Months earlier, on December 15, 1944, Governor Earl Warren had received a letter from Major General Robert R. Lewis stating that "military necessity" should no longer be applied to the evacuation of California's Japanese and Japanese American population. "It is my hope," wrote Lewis, "that the return of those Japanese-Americans who choose to return may be accomplished without serious incidents. . . . I am confident that the fine Americans of your state will realize that among the American citizens of Japanese ancestry who are being permitted to return there are many families with sons or daughters now serving in our Armed Forces."

General Lewis and Governor Warren were more than a bit overconfident in assessing the attitudes of people in the three states of the West Coast. Four days after Lewis wrote to Warren, an army intelligence report stated: "There are still 100 Salinas boys in Japanese prison camps and the Salinas' mothers of those sons are somewhat bitter against the order permitting

Japanese to return [to California] and have stated that the Japanese knew what happened on Bataan and won't want to face us any more than we will be able to stand meeting them." Like fellow Legionnaires in Oregon, the commander of the Salinas American Legion Post No. 31 told a local newspaper, "We don't want Japanese here."

When Governor Warren was interviewed in 1971 as part of an oral history for the Bancroft Library at the University of California, he recalled how he was contacted by the secretary of the army early in 1945 and he said that he had immediately agreed to the return of the Japanese and Japanese Americans to their homes in his state.

"It was a Saturday morning and I was in Los Angeles," Warren said. "He told me that Monday at noon they were going to start letting the Japanese come back and asked me if I would help them do it. Well, I told him that I would. The war was all over and everything was—we had no need to fear anything."

Warren told Amelia R. Fry in his contribution to the Berkeley Oral History Project:

> I was on the telephone, I'll bet nine-tenths of the time between then and Monday noon when it was finally announced . . . telling [people] that it was going to be done, and telling them that when we advocated the relocation of the Japanese we did it because we thought it was in the interest of the war, and the war's over. The worst thing that could happen to the state of California would be to have us maintain a feeling of antagonism toward the Japanese who had lived in our state and who hadn't done anything wrong, and that I hoped they would cooperate with the federal government and with me in bringing them back to California so they could be happy here.

Warren then recalled a positive view of the return.

They came back and started right to school, you know. The kids all welcomed them and everything. We had maybe a half a dozen or so instances of hoodlums going by and throwing rocks into windows and so forth, but most of those were caught and prosecuted and were convicted of doing it and the thing was just washed out. I don't believe the Japanese were ever as happy in our state as they have been since.

Politicians are flexible folk. Warren and Los Angeles mayor Fletcher Bowron, who, among others, had called for the evacuation in 1942, realized that there was no way to stop the WRA and the army from going ahead with their resettlement programs. The governor and the mayor made a point of greeting returnees from the camps at Union Station in Los Angeles. That's where the newspaper photographers and reporters were.

• • •

By the beginning of 1945, after the White House released Public Proclamation 21, officially ending the evacuation, the population of the camps was down to almost 90,000. Without much publicity more than 25,000 American Japanese evacuees had already left, gone out to work, study, or fight during the first three years of the incarceration. In addition to the 4,300 students who went to colleges willing to accept them, most in the Midwest, more than four times as many Japanese American workers spread out to work in fields and factories and in offices and hospitals everywhere but on the West Coast. The majority of the permanently released Nisei—the farm workers were on temporary release—settled in seven states: Illinois (7,652); Colorado (3,185); Ohio (2,854); Idaho (2,084); Michigan (1,990); Minnesota (1,292); New York (1,131). A total of 25,778 Nisei, men and women, served in the U.S. Army between July 1, 1940, and June 30, 1945, winning 18,143 individual combat decorations in the ranks of the One Hundredth Battalion, the 442nd Combat Regiment, the 1399th Engineers Construction Battalion, the MIS in the Pacific, and a few smaller Japanese American units in Europe. An estimated 13,500 of those men were from the mainland and 12,250 were from Hawaii. More than 2,000 American Japanese and 800 Japanese from Peru and other South American countries had been sent to Japan on Swedish ships in exchange for American diplomats, missionaries, and other civilians held in Japanese camps from Manila to Tokyo.

Many had left the camps over the years, and since it was more than obvious by the beginning of 1945 that the United States was going to win the war in the Pacific, both the War Department and the War Relocation Authority were becoming more and more anxious to speed up the closing of the camps. The WRA barely checked anymore when evacuees wanted to leave, which is why it had no record at all of the whereabouts of at least twenty-three hundred supposed evacuees. Nearly all the camps were scheduled to be closed before the end of the year, some within months. The idea was to empty all the camps while keeping so-called disloyals at Tule Lake Segregation Center and in the Justice Department prisons in Bismarck, North Dakota; Santa Fe, New Mexico; and Crystal City, Texas. After the announcement of the closings, the WRA began shutting down camp schools and cutting back on water and electric supplies.

Predictably, those who willingly left the camps were the most Americanized of the evacuees. Most of those who came back "home" to the West Coast or went to midwestern or eastern states were, in general, single, educated Nisei, young men, and some very strong and ambitious young women. They were pharmacists, teachers, engineers, mechanics, farmers, hotel workers, domestics, and waitresses. Many of them went to welcoming cities stripped of Caucasian workers by the war. Almost 20,000 of the freed Nisei went to Chicago. Others headed for Denver, Salt Lake City, Cleveland, Minneapolis–St. Paul, and St. Louis. The state of Utah and the city of Cincinnati sent representatives to the camps to recruit workers. Some chose New Jersey, where the frozen food company Seabrook Farms had lost local workers to the military or defense plants. Seabrook and International Harvester were among the corporations that posted job openings in the camps. Most of those who left first were Christians. Quaker meetings and hundreds of Protestant churches and organizations helped find homes and jobs for their religious brethren. In addition, 250 Nisei from Topaz were working in munitions factories in Utah. Several dozen more were in Washington, D.C., working for the War Department.

When news of the camp closings spread, once again waves of confusion washed over those remaining in the camps. Jeanne Wakatsuki described some of the reactions at Manzanar: "By the end of 1944 about 6,000 people remained at Manzanar and those, for the most part, were the aging and the young. Whoever had prospects on the outside and the energy to go, was leaving, relocating, or entering military service."

The outlook for young Nisei was quite different from that of their elders. Children and young people more often than not had a different experience, a better experience. As the school in Manzanar was closing down, fifth graders in camp schools were asked by a camp magazine, *Whirlwinds*, what they liked and disliked about life there. They liked "the mountains, the creeks, the trees and birds, the bright stars, the snow in winter, the good drinking water, the free food, the free electricity and water." Their dislikes included "the desert, the wind storms, the hard winds, the cold winters, the fence around the camp, a one-room house."

The differences in the attitudes of the young and the old were picked up by the press. On August 31, 1945, three weeks after Hiroshima and Nagasaki were destroyed, a *Los Angeles Times* reporter, Tom Caton, reported from Manzanar under the headline, "Japs at Manzanar Hope for Change: Elders Planning to Leave Center Remain Doubtful and *Nisei* Admit Wishful Thinking." Caton quoted Jeanne Wakatsuki's mother, Riku, who looked forward to returning to Terminal Island. "It will be good to go back to fishing and canning. We should get along if we can get together in our little fishing villages again." That would never happen. The bungalows of the San Pedro fishing families were knocked down by bulldozers a week after the residents were evacuated.

By the end of August there were only 3,600 people in Manzanar, which once held 10,046 evacuees. While many of those still held there were afraid of what might happen if they stayed in California, many were determined to do just that. "I'm not going to worry about it," said Mrs. Alice Nitta, who was thirty years old, born in El Monte. Her husband was in the army in Germany. "Both my husband and I have lived all our lives in Los Angeles—he was born in Eagle Rock—and we consider it home. We're going back. . . . I think people will be pretty fair."

Jeanne Wakatsuki, who was ten years old at the time, later remembered, "To most of the *Nisei*, anything looked better than remaining in camps. For many of their parents, just the opposite was true." The American Japanese had no homes to return to. Wakatsuki wrote, "The very thought of going back to the West Coast filled us with dread. How will they look at us?" In addition to the traditionally racist organizations like the American Legion and the Native Sons of the Golden West, new groups had sprung up during the war, including No Japs Incorporated in San Diego, the Homefront Commandoes in Sacramento, and the Pacific Coast Japanese Problem in Los Angeles.

Of her father, Wakatsuki said:

Here he sat, a man without prospects, perhaps now without even a family in Japan to confirm his own history, fifty-eight years old, and his children scattered across the land: Woody in the army at Fort Douglas, Utah; Eleanor in Reno; her husband in Germany; Bill and Martha and Frances and Lillian in New Jersey. Ray now in the Coast Guard. . . . Papa already knew the car he'd put money on before Pearl Harbor had been repossessed. And, as he suspected, no record of his fishing boats remained. This put him right back where he'd been in 1904, arriving in a new land and starting over from economic zero.

The older generations had lost nearly all they had when interned, and for many reasons the oldest folks resisted leaving when camps closed. At Manzanar, some elderly residents refused to budge, and so they had to have their bags packed for them. Some had to be carried and shoved onto the buses.

• • •

Among the last residents of the camps were Issei and *Kibei*, many of whom had lost faith in the United States. Some had come to hate the country. Over the years the concentration camps had become a subject and target of propaganda from Tokyo and from Berlin as well. The *Shanghai Times*, a newspaper in occupied China, editorialized, "The Anglo-Americans in Japan and occupied China should be herded together and driven into interior regions where there are no modern facilities." The outcome of evacuation and almost three years of segregation and isolation was exactly the opposite of what the WRA had expected. Many Issei and *Kibei* insisted on speaking only Japanese. A few of the older evacuees killed themselves; many more tried.

There were also at least three thousand American Japanese still in prisons and separate, official "internment" camps—and more of them had become or were becoming anti-American in word if not deed. One of them, Henry Hideo in Santa Fe, wrote to a friend on August 10, four days before Japan surrendered to the United States, saying:

> I am interned in Santa Fe. Rights and freedoms are restricted, so I am having an awful time. The Caucasian officials here are big and seem strong. But they are good for nothing. They are useless. Also the censors here are all damn fools. . . . We are the people of the great Imperial Japan, from the beginning to the end, we are all faithful to our nation.

That part of the letter was censored and Hideo was put in solitary confinement.

At Tule Lake, two weeks later, Miye Ichiki wrote, "All I see and hear about these days is Atomic Bomb . . . and Japanese soldiers in American uniforms, and it makes me sick. I am glad to hear that a couple of United States soldiers I know have been killed in action." Ichiki went on to say, "It served them right for fighting for the United States. When I see any Japanese in the American uniform visiting this camp, I feel like killing them."

There were 5,461 Japanese Americans who had signed away their citizenship; almost all of them were at Tule Lake. Only 128 Nisei signed renunciation papers in the other nine camps. Most of the renunciations, however, were not because of pro–Imperial Japanese sentiment; they were made in the hysteria fueled by rumors and fear over what was going to happen as the war with Japan was ending. Would they all be sent to Japan? Would families be separated, depending on their ages or what papers members had signed? Where could they go and were they going to be attacked by white Americans if they left the camp?

What happened next at Tule Lake was predictable. As the camp calmed down, hundreds, then thousands of the renunciants begged to regain their American citizenship. The husband of a renunciant and the father of three children wrote this in a letter to Edward Ennis at the Justice Department:

> My wife picked up all the rumors and believed them. She thought if she renounced she would stay here. Otherwise she would be pushed out. We are from Hood River and that was a dangerous place. My wife was afraid to go there if we were made to leave. She felt that in some way she must fix things so the family could stay here together and her "fixing" was to renounce. . . .
>
> And, now, Mr. Ennis, isn't there some way that we can go out as an alien? She did not renounce out of disloyalty. She would never do anything against this country. She only wants us to be together. . . . Do help us if you can.

● ● ●

The timing of the events of 1944 and 1945 in the camps and in Washington were no coincidence. The Justice Department, representing the government, had done its political duty, making sure that Supreme Court decisions were not announced until after President Roosevelt was reelected on November 7, 1944. In fact, the Justice Department did more than its assigned duty. With help from Deputy Secretary of War McCloy, who ordered some evacuation records destroyed, the Justice Department withheld evidence indicating that race was the central factor in the army's decision to remove Japanese and Japanese Americans from the West Coast.

The president was determined that, once freed, the Japanese Americans and Issei, too, should not congregate in Little Tokyos again. He wanted them scattered around the country, figuring that a dozen or so here and there would not offend local people, white people. In his first postelection press conference, the president had said there was progress being made in scattering

Japanese Americans around the country. "After all," he continued, "they are American citizens and we all know American
citizens have certain privileges." The president believed that
"75,000 families scattered around the United States is not going
to upset anybody," and he went on to praise the Japanese Americans who had joined the war, saying, "We are actuated by the
very wonderful record that the Japanese in that battalion in Italy
have been making in the war. It is one of the outstanding battalions that we have."

The president's "scattering" ideas had some impact. Eighty-
eight percent of Japanese and Japanese Americans were in California before the war; that number dropped to 70 percent after
the war. Part of the reason was that companies and organizations
in other states provided better and more lucrative jobs, including white-collar positions, than young Nisei could get in the West
where many former evacuees were still being told, "We don't hire
Japs."

Whatever the president said then, many of the Issei distrusted
him and were afraid to leave the camps for parts unknown. After
Pearl Harbor, many had lost the lives they lived and the property they owned. Many were broken people who had no place to
go. One government estimate was that West Coast Japanese and
Japanese Americans lost 75 percent of their assets. The official
government figure, calculated in 1982 and reported in *The Wartime Handling of Evacuee Property*, was that evacuee losses
amounted to at least $250 million in real, commercial, and per-
sonal property, or approximately $3 billion 2013 dollars. In Los
Angeles and other California cities, their neighborhoods had been
taken over by other people, particularly by black people from
southern states, 150,000 of them, drawn west by the promise of
well-paying defense work in shipyards and aircraft factories.
When former residents came back to the area around the Los

Angeles city hall, what had been Little Tokyo was now called Bronzeville.

The relocation camps, miserable as they could be, had become the new homes of a majority of American Japanese, the only homes most of them had when the war ended. Many did not want to leave; they were convinced they had nothing to go back to in California or anyplace else. And they were afraid they would be beaten or killed wherever they went. If they agreed to leave, they were given a train ticket and $25. The camps ironically had become assisted-living homes for many of the elderly—and now they were being thrown out into the mercy of hostile streets. The most vocal and the most unfortunate of the camp residents were eight thousand "old bachelors," men without families or homes who had worked as migrant farm workers for decades. The camps were mean, but they were the best places some of those old and work-weary men had ever lived.

More than thirty years later, the official report of the Commission on Wartime Relocation and Internment of Civilians stated:

> They returned by the trainload to Los Angeles, San Francisco, and Seattle. Often elderly or infirm or burdened with heavy family responsibility, the last evacuees to leave piled into temporary shelters, hotels, converted Army barracks, and public housing. Very few could come back to their prewar holdings. Only about 25 percent of the prewar farm operators, for example, retained property. Many testified that their stored possessions had been lost or stolen. Sometimes taxes had not been paid.

The Nichiren Buddhist Church was a major repository in Los Angeles's Little Tokyo, storing the personal property of six hundred families. A postwar report stated, "[The building was] a hopeless mass of destruction. Furniture broken, mirrors smashed to smithereens . . . household goods scattered helter-skelter, trunks broken open, pictures thrown to the four winds. Most things of value, radios, typewriters, sewing machines, Persian rugs have been carried off."

One Nisei, John Saito, told the commission that his father had returned to Los Angeles in July of 1945, later finding work as a dishwasher in a skid row restaurant. John Saito followed his father soon after and they shared his hotel room. Saito recalled, "There was only one room, and only one bed. He worked the graveyard shift and I went to school during the day, therefore we managed to use the same bed at different hours of the day." The rest of the family was scattered; John's mother worked as a cook at a farm labor camp in Idaho, and his older brother was still overseas with the 442nd.

Versions of his story were common in the three West Coast states. Many of the groups that had called for evacuation in 1942 were still active and hostile in 1945, including the Seattle Chamber of Commerce and an organization called the Remember Pearl Harbor League. Many Christian leaders, including the evangelist Aimee Semple McPherson, continued to oppose the return. One of the more vicious anti-Japanese organizations with Christian connections, the Home Front Commandoes, distributed brochures titled "SLAP THE JAP: No Jap Is Fit to Associate with Human Beings."

Mutsuo Hashiguchi, the Washington state farmer who had sent an open letter to a newspaper saying he expected his family would be welcomed back, came home to find his house vandalized and debris thrown into his well. Neighbors told him truckloads of men came and looted the place on a day in the spring of 1942, the day he and his family left for the assembly center at Tanforan.

Another Washington resident, Mary Yogawa Saito, returned to Tacoma to claim her family's dry-cleaning business. "We sold our dry-cleaning business for a mere $600 with the stipulation we could reclaim our business for the same price when the war concluded," she recalled. "Arriving back in Tacoma, I discovered that our buyers had betrayed our agreement by selling the business and leaving the city. The new owners were hostile and uncommunicative. To make a long story short, with little money and very little faith in the American justice system, I tore up the contract in frustration."

There were also hundreds of violent incidents as the Japanese came home from the camps and from the war. There were anti-Japanese rallies in many towns, including Brawley, California; Gresham, Oregon; and Bellevue, Washington. In Placer County on the California side of Lake Tahoe, three men confessed to burning down the barn of an Issei named Sumio Doi, whose younger brother, Shig, was a sergeant in the 442nd Regiment. They were acquitted after their defense attorney proclaimed, "Remember, this is a white man's country."

Walt Hayami, Stanley Hayami's younger brother, recalled his family's return to San Gabriel.

"There was a family that went back before we did and one of the daughters in that family said it was quite hostile for Japanese Americans until the word came about Stanley." She had told the Hayami family, "The announcement of his death in combat was made in the high school assembly. After that, she said things changed quite a bit. So in that sense, some good came out of it."

Heisuke and Mitsuno Matsuda, given their $50 by the government, returned to Vashon Island on September 7, 1945. Mrs. Matsuda wrote to her daughter, Mary, still in nursing school in Iowa:

It is now one week since we got home. Mack has taken care of it fairly well, so Papa-san and I are rejoicing. He painted the house. It looks fine. Mrs. Peterson and Mrs. McDonald brought a lot of vegetables. They are delicious. . . . There are more Japanese people coming back to Vashon. They will come and stay at our place until they can find a place to live. It is wonderful, isn't it? The white people on Vashon, all of them, are very nice to us.

Still, the Matsudas had creditors and they had trouble with Deputy Hopkins, who had obviously pocketed profits from the farm he promised to oversee. Their biggest problem, because Issei could not own land, was that the property officially belonged to their son, Yoneichi, who was still in uniform in Europe. Then Heisuke was kicked by a horse and, with several broken ribs, could not leave the house and could not deal with the problems of not legally owning the farm—and harvesttime was coming. Sheriff Hopkins had offered to buy the farm, but the Matsudas refused to sell. Hearing that, Heisuke's doctor said he would contact the American Red Cross and ask them to contact the army and ask that they allow Yoneichi to come home early. The doctor did just that and it worked. Mrs. Matsuda wrote to Mary in Iowa, "You wouldn't believe what the doctor told us. The Red Cross worker who placed the call for Yoneichi's return was Mrs. Hopkins, the deputy sheriff's wife."

When Yoneichi Matsuda returned home in June of 1946, he retained a lawyer in Seattle and Deputy Hopkins, who had trouble providing records for anything, told the lawyer he was not doing well but offered to pay the Matsudas $2,000 for the trouble he caused them. "It isn't much," said the lawyer. "You could sue him and make him pay more."

"No," said Yoneichi. "I consider this blood money. . . . The money is not the issue. This has been a terrible time for my family and the deputy sheriff added to our misery. I just want him to think about the dishonest way he conducted himself."

Yoneichi had a better idea for what to do with the money: "You helped us save our farm when we really needed help. I'd like you to accept the money."

"You can't be serious," his lawyer said. "How will you pay your debts?"

"It's only money," was the answer. "We will earn more. The important thing is we still have our farm."

• • •

As the American Japanese returned to the West Coast, national media and the government, too, focused on the Hood River Valley. The mayor of Hood River, Joe Meyer, said, "Ninety percent are against the Japs. We trusted them so completely while they were here among us, while all the time they were plotting our defeat and downfall. They were just waiting to stab us in the back. . . . We must let the Japanese know they're not welcome here."

There were rumors that there would be trouble at the railroad station when the first former residents returned. That did not happen. A WRA employee, Clyde Linville, waited at the station and drove the first returnees to their homes. He did the same day after day. Still, upon returning many American Japanese were met with hostility. Most local stores refused to serve their former neighbors. Then Major General James Ulio, the army's adjutant general, traveled from Washington to the valley to say, "Here we are fighting a war for our lives and you're telling a citizen they can't buy groceries in your town?" He added that he had the authority to impose martial law—"at the point of a bayonet." The local supermarket, a Safeway, responded by offering returnees free carts of groceries.

Attitudes did change when white veterans returned to town and supported the Japanese families, often confronting their own parents. "What the hell do you think you're doing?" asked returning Army Air Corps engineer Ed Shoemaker to his father, Kent Shoemaker, the leader of the American Legion's anti-Japanese campaign. Joseph and June Haviland put a nine-line classified ad in the *Hood River News* saying, "Any Japanese-American soldier home on furlough will find friendship, good food, and a peaceful atmosphere in a comfortable home. . . . No phoning necessary. Welcome at any hour." Still, only 233 of the 431 American Japanese taken from the valley in May of 1942 returned to Hood River after the war.

One son of Hood River, Frank Hachiya, served in the war and had been killed in the Philippines by friendly fire while delivering maps of Japanese defenses. He had been buried outside the town of Palo on the Philippine island of Leyte. His body was returned to Hood River on September 11, 1948. Former Oregon governor Charles Sprague and Reverend Sherman Burgoyne were among the pallbearers when he was reburied in the town cemetery after a service at Asbury Methodist Church. He is honored each year at the town's Fourth of July ceremonies.

• • •

Most Nisei, the young people, were determined to return to normal lives after the war. Some, like Louise Ogawa of San Diego, chose to stay in the East and the Midwest. They sensed new lives coming; they felt more free and more American than they had ever been.

There were no Little Tokyos in Chicago or other middle-American cities, but the young people leaving for work or school were predictably inclined to go where other Japanese Americans, often relatives, had settled. A very wide generation gap had developed among American Japanese. Frank Aiso had been a strawberry farmer in Burbank, California, and had four sons in the army. He said, "I have been ill. My wife and I wish all of this had never happened, and it is hard for us to keep making changes.

But the sons, I know, will have no trouble." Their oldest son was Lieutenant Colonel John F. Aiso, the highest-ranking Japanese American in the U.S. Army, who became the director of the MIS language school. Aiso returned to Los Angeles after service in Tokyo on the staff of General MacArthur.

Kiyoko Nomura, a twenty-year-old from Santa Monica, who was the editor of the English-language edition of the *Manzanar Free Press*, also returned, saying, "People at first may be disapproving, but they'll get over it. I for one am going to try very hard to make everyone realize we who were born in this country, and that our parents, too, are good people."

By the summer, when Imperial Japan surrendered, there were just over forty thousand evacuees left in the other camps and fifteen thousand or so in Tule Lake. The majority of them were elderly. Many of them had been convinced against all evidence that Japan was winning the war and that the empire would reward them for their loyalty to the emperor. The rumor was that the victorious Japanese would give each family $10,000 plus $7,000 more for each child as recompense for their years in the camps. The end of that era finally came on March 20, 1946, when Tule Lake was closed. The last prisoners there were given $25 and a train ticket back to wherever they had been first picked up. There were more suicide attempts by old bachelors; one seventy-seven-year-old hanged himself the day before he was to leave with the last group. As in other camps, some had to be carried or pushed onto the trains. One old man ran back toward the camp as fast as he could, throwing his $25 on the tracks.

Most of the remaining Issei had aged before their time, seriously damaged by camp life. Ernest Besig, the ACLU attorney from San Francisco, wrote his impressions of those final days.

I learned that a Mrs. F . . . because of her worries and fears arising from her detention was committed by the [Tule

Lake] Center authorities to a mental institution for hammering one of her children to death and injuring another. A Mr. S, an internee, worried over his separation from his sons, tried to commit suicide by drinking gasoline. A Mrs. K, an internee, took pills in an attempt at suicide because she was being deported from the United States. Many mental cases were known to have been hospitalized at the Center because of their fear of pressure groups, continued detention, deportation, separation from their families, and the splitting of their families.

• • •

In the town of Westminster in Orange County, California, local officials locked the gates of the town cemetery to prevent the body of Staff Sergeant Kazuo Masuda, killed in Italy, from being buried there. He was one of four Masuda brothers who served in the 442nd. Their sister, Mary Masuda of Talbot, California, was one of the first Nisei to leave the camp at Gila River, Arizona, and return to the family farm. Within a few weeks midnight raiders came to her door and told her to get out. Frightened, she did.

Her brother was posthumously awarded the Distinguished Service Medal, the second-highest decoration in the United States Army. General Joseph "Vinegar Joe" Stilwell, a champion of Nisei soldiers and a senior officer ever willing to speak his mind, asked her to return to Talbot with him for a formal presentation of the medal—in the town. Said Stilwell on the steps of the little city hall:

> The *Nisei* bought an awful big hunk of America with their blood. . . . And I say we soldiers ought to form a pick-axe club to protect Japanese Americans who fought the war with us. Anytime we see a barfly commando picking on these kids or discriminating against them, we ought to bang him over the head with a pick-axe. I'm willing to be a

charter member. We cannot allow a single injustice [toward] the *Nisei* without defeating the purposes for which we fought.

The Masuda family was also supported by the *Santa Ana Register*. N. Christian Anderson III, the *Register*'s publisher, told an Orange County Forum luncheon how the often-fiery owner of the paper, R. C. Hoiles, came to the defense of Masuda's family after World War II. Hoiles spoke of how the Masudas had lived and farmed in Fountain Valley since the early 1900s, and how, despite their unjust internment in Arizona, Masuda and three of his brothers joined the U.S. military. He spoke of how one brother sacrificed his life for this country, dying in Italy. Hoiles railed against the treatment that Masuda's mother and sister encountered when met by hostile Orange County residents. He went on to strongly assert the family's right to live here and to reclaim their property. Ultimately the Masudas prevailed and got their farm back.

Other Japanese Americans, including veterans, continued to face humiliations. On his way home to Hawaii, where he would be hospitalized for rehabilitation for two years, Lieutenant Daniel Inouye, in full uniform, combat medals on his chest, one arm missing, went to a barbershop in San Francisco. The barber asked, "What are you?"

"I'm an American," Inouye replied.

"Don't give me that American stuff. You're a Jap and we don't cut Jap hair."

That story got all the way back to the White House. After reading it, President Harry S. Truman, who had taken office after President Roosevelt died on April 12, 1945, sent a letter to his widow, Eleanor Roosevelt, saying, "These disgraceful incidents almost make you believe that a lot of our Americans have a streak of Nazi in them."

Other veterans received varied responses upon their return. The tides of hatred in the West were not turning necessarily, but many Caucasians on the West Coast began the long process of looking to their better angels. Mitsuo Usui, one of the first Nisei to take advantage of the reopening of the West Coast, told this story about Los Angeles.

> Coming home, I was boarding a bus on Olympic Boulevard. A lady sitting in the front row of the bus saw me and said, "Damn Jap." Here I was a proud American soldier, just coming back with my new uniform and new paratrooper boots, with all my campaign medals and awards, proudly displayed on my chest, and this? The bus driver upon hearing this remark, stopped the bus and said, "Lady, apologize to this American soldier or get off my bus."

She got off the bus.

But the story did not end happily for Usui. He was on his way to Crenshaw Boulevard in Los Angeles to see the nursery his father had started in 1938 and then sold for $1,000 during the evacuation. His father asked him to go to Los Angeles and buy back the property.

"Still in my uniform," he said, "I hurriedly went to the nursery and asked if the owner would sell it back to us. The owner of the nursery now was not the same person to whom we sold."

The new owner said, "Yep, I'll sell you the nursery. Give me $13,000 for the land and $13,000 for the inventory."

"Impossible!" Usui exclaimed, and he went to the back of the property and kicked over a five-gallon can. The man followed, and Usui showed him some Japanese writings on the bottom of the can. "Can you see what's written here?" Usui said. "It says here this plant was planted from a seed on this date, was transplanted into a gallon-can on this date, and finally into this five-gallon can on this date. My mother planted all these plants in the five-gallon cans and all the trees in the back, and now you want to sell them back to us at these outrageous prices?"

All the new owner said in response was, "Well, that's the way the ball bounces."

Usui came home to tell his parents what had happened. His father just broke down and cried. Usui later said, "My father never recovered from this incident."

The Najima family, whose father was taken from their Petaluma, California, farm in the week after Pearl Harbor, had a happier ending to their story. The Najima brothers had figured out a way back in 1942 to try to save an expensive camera by using a fishhook to lower it into bottom of the family outhouse. As soon as they got back home, they raced to the outhouse and pulled up the string. The camera was none the worse for its smelly wear.

Many returning 442nd veterans received hard-won honors. Wilson Makabe from Loomis in Placer County, California, was in a wheelchair when he joined other 442nd survivors when the unit received a Presidential Unit Citation (its seventh) from President Truman on a rainy day in July of 1946. White House staffers had recommended that Truman not go to the ceremony outdoors on the Ellipse, but he said, "Hell, no, after what these boys went through, I can stand a little rain."

"You are to be congratulated for what you did for this great country," said the president. "You are now on your way home. You fought not only the enemy, but you fought prejudice and you have won. Keep up that fight, and we continue to win—to make this great Republic stand for what the Constitution says it stands for: the welfare of all the people all the time."

Makabe, whose father had been taken away by the FBI on the day of the Pearl Harbor attack, was one of the boys who had gone through a lot more than a rainy day. He was wounded in Italy and was in a full-body cast for more than a year. He spent more than two years in military hospitals and suffered through more than a dozen operations and the loss of a leg. He was allowed one free long-distance call when he reached the United States, arriving in Miami in December of 1944. He called one of his brothers, who told him the family house was burned down on the day it was announced that Japanese and Japanese Americans could return to California. After all he had gone through, he cried for the first time since he was a child. "I remember the pain and the hurt, the suffering in hospitals in Italy," he said. "That was nothing compared to this."

In his wheelchair, Makabe had been taken to the Orange Bowl football game in Miami on the last day of 1944. A retired army general named Hugh Harris, whose West Point roommate had commanded Makabe's battalion of the 442nd, came up to him in the stadium and said, "You know, it would be a privilege to be able to push you around and take you wherever you want to go."

Even with the house burned down and his family living in a two-room cabin, Makabe finally got home in 1947 and said, "We were very fortunate, compared to other farmers." They had another, separate property in town.

> We leased the place in Loomis for twenty-five dollars a month. And when we got back, we were happy and amazed to see that he [a neighbor] had kept the ranch in reasonable condition. And he did pay his rent, so we were one of the fortunate ones. Because I hear that some farmers came back to a disastrous situation. . . .
>
> We had bought, we had a 1939 Plymouth. It was blue. And my brothers, who were teenagers, said, "Hey, if we sell this, we're going to get nothing for it." So what they did was they put it in the garage and jacked it up. I think they took off the tires, and did everything to it, hoping that

when we got back it would be intact. And sure enough, when we got back, they put back the tires, they put the oil in, the water, started it, and believe it or not, it started. So we had a car.

He was walking, in great pain, when he finally got home to Loomis and that Plymouth. With only one leg—and that one was kept straight by iron bars—he still managed to drive. The first time he stopped at the local gas station, he struggled for several minutes to get out of the car to reach for the pump.

After the gas tank was filled, the owner, who had been a friend of his father, came out and said, "I'd like to talk to you."

"Hop in," Makabe said.

After he drove down the road a bit, the man said, "Y'know, I was one bastard. I had signs on my service station saying, 'No Jap trade wanted.' Now when I see you come back like that I feel so small."

The man began to cry.

EPILOGUE

F ew of the American Japanese mentioned in these pages were able to return to their prewar lives. Most of the older evacuees, the Issei, had to start over, more than three-quarters of them without money or property. Thousands of their children, the Nisei, decided not to return to the Pacific Coast, making their new lives in other parts of the country. The Pacific states, particularly California, had been greatly changed by millions of new residents who came west during the war to work in defense industries. With millions of veterans coming back to the United States ready to start their own families, there were housing shortages everywhere and the Japanese returning from the camps often found themselves in shoddy new government facilities, empty barracks, trailer parks, and quickly built apartments put up for the new migrants working in the defense plants. And nobody talked about what had happened to them from 1942 to 1945. Parents and grandparents were ashamed to talk about the camps and the young ones learned not to ask.

Edison Uno, a Nisei who was eighteen years old when he was released from detention after the war ended, devoted the rest of his life as a human rights activist trying to tell the story of the camps and organize Japanese Americans to demand government apologies and financial redress. Uno said of the silence, "We were like the victims of rape. We felt shamed. We could not bear to speak of the assault." That attitude began to change in the 1960s when Sansei, the third generation, many inspired by the black civil rights movement and growing anti–Vietnam War protests, began questioning their parents and grandparents about the camp years. A Sansei young woman I met, while researching the colony of Japanese Americans who remained in Arkansas after leaving the camps there, made an interesting, if defensive, point about the integration of Little Rock Central High School in 1957, telling me: "The black students didn't integrate that school. It had already been integrated by Japanese students in the 1940s."

There were, in fact, more than a few historical intersections between the Japanese American and African American experiences in the United States. The Little Rock confrontations were one of the first direct results of the U.S. Supreme Court's unanimous 1954 decision on school integration in the case of *Brown v. Board of Education*. That court, of course, was led by Chief Justice Earl Warren, who, as California's attorney general in 1942, was a principal force in the roundup and evacuation of Japanese and Japanese American residents of his state.

One of the first persons arrested on Terminal Island in Los Angeles was a merchant named Seiichi Nakahara who was recovering from an ulcer operation and died within twenty-four hours after his release from the hospital on January 20, 1942. His twenty-year-old daughter Yuri and the rest of his family were taken to the Santa Anita Assembly Center and then to the relocation camp in Jerome, Arkansas. In 1944, she was released from Jerome to help run a USO club for soldiers in Hattiesburg, Mississippi, where she met her future husband, William Kochiyama, a veteran of the 442nd Regimental Combat Team. Later, living in New York's Harlem, she became a radical civil rights activist. She befriended Malcolm X and joined his Organization of Afro-American Unity. She was famously photographed in 1965 cradling Malcolm's head as he lay dying after being shot in the Audubon Ballroom in the Washington Heights neighborhood of New York City.

Watching young black Americans marching through southern cities fighting for their rights and participating in anti-Vietnam protests in the 1960s caused many young Japanese Americans to begin questioning what happened to their own families in the 1940s: *Why didn't you fight back? Why did you let the government do this to you?* Some of those younger Japanese Americans decided they, too, would march and in 1969 they organized a pilgrimage to Manzanar to dramatize what had happened there almost thirty years before.

That was a beginning in turning shame and silence into a movement. Then came the books. Perhaps the most important of them was published in 1973 when Jeanne Wakatsuki Houston of Santa Cruz, California, finally began to tell her husband, James D. Houston, a Caucasian writer, what she remembered as a child taken to Manzanar when she was seven years old. After a couple of months of such conversations, the Houstons decided to tape-record her memories, then decided to prepare a short memoir to share with their immediate families and thirty-six nieces and nephews. They put together a small book, *Farewell to Manzanar*, a children's book they hoped might be used in classrooms to tell the stories of the great incarceration. There had been a number of books, some of them very good, about the evacuation before then, but they tended to be academic or legal studies published by university presses and small regional publishing houses. *Farewell to Manzanar*, however, struck a chord nationally. Nelson Algren, then a novelist at the height of his powers, reviewed the book, writing: "The Houstons have put together an account of the Japanese internment which never pleads for the readers' compassion, never sentimentalizes the victims and never tries to make the reader feel guilty. It casts a lucid, sinewy, and completely convincing light on both the prosecutors and persecuted." The book has sold more than a million copies and is considered one of the most successful children's books in publishing history. It is required reading in thousands of American school districts.

In 1976, Michi Nishiura Weglyn wrote and published a more comprehensive account, *Years of Infamy: The Untold Story of America's Concentration Camps*, which also had great impact. That same year, President Gerald Ford signed Proclamation 4417, "Confirming the Termination of the Executive Order Authorizing Japanese-American Internment During World War II." Said the president, "We now know what we should have known then, not only that evacuation was wrong, but Japanese Americans were and are loyal Americans."

Soon enough, there were more books, hundreds of them. Joanne Oppenheim, author of more than fifty books for young adults, edited extraordinary volumes on the letters of Clara Breed and the diary of Stanley Hayami. There were conferences and there was lobbying in Washington. The story was being heard for the first time by millions of Americans, particularly those who lived in the East and the Midwest and were often ignorant of the injustices of the West. One goal of Japanese American activists and their allies was to win redress for the financial losses of the families evacuated and held in

camps. One of the results of the new activism was the cre-
ation by Congress in 1980 of the Commission on Wartime
Relocation and Internment of Civilians. The 493-page report
of the commission, published in 1982, was titled *Personal Justice Denied*.

Perhaps the most significant sentences of the report were:
"In sum, Executive Order 9066 was not justified by military
necessity, and the decisions that followed from it—exclusion,
detention, the ending of detention, and the ending of exclusion—
were not founded on military considerations. The broad historical causes that shaped these decisions were race prejudice,
war hysteria, and a failure of political leadership."

Almost fifty years after the evacuation, the long campaign
for reparations by the JACL and other Japanese organizations
prompted Congress to pass and President Ronald Reagan to sign
the Civil Liberties Act of 1988, which included a formal apology for the evacuation and imprisonment. The act was sponsored
by Representative Norman Mineta and Senator Alan Simpson,
the two Boy Scouts who had met when local boys had come to
Heart Mountain to share pup tents. They were joined by fellow
supporters in Congress, including Representative Robert Matsui
of California, a former evacuee, and one of the 442nd Regimental Combat Team's heroes, Senator Daniel Inouye of Hawaii.
When President Reagan signed the bill, Matsui said, "It lifted
the specter of disloyalty that hung over us for 42 years because
we were incarcerated. We were made whole again as American
citizens." Mineta added, "Now, Congress and the President are
asking a second faith of those who had been wronged. We have
to make sure we don't break faith again."

The act provided $1.2 billion to enable payments of $20,000
to each of an estimated eighty thousand camp survivors. The
money was a pittance compared to the billions in 2014 dollars
American Japanese had lost, but, in the end, it was not about

money. It was about getting a formal apology from the government for stealing liberty and the pursuit of happiness. It was about unraveling the lies and deceptions of the 1940s. The first payments were made in 1990.

• • •

Wayne Collins, who had represented Fred Korematsu after he refused to report to the Tanforan Assembly Center in 1942, decided in August of 1945 to take on the cases, more than five thousand of them, of the Japanese Americans who were coerced or tricked into renouncing their citizenship. Many of them were children or confused parents; others were old people who had sought repatriation to Japan. Collins, a driven, angry, quixotic servant of the law, spent most of the rest of his life filing cases to allow those renunciants to regain their American citizenship. "During the war," according to Roger Daniels of the University of Cincinnati, an important historian of the evacuation, "a total of 5,766 Americans of Japanese ancestry formally renounced their citizenship, and a large number of non-citizen *Issei* applied for repatriation. After the war, as soon as transportation was available, the American government had begun shipping Japanese-Americans to Japan." In some cases, Collins actually went to ships to pull off his "clients"—they were never paying clients, although they were asked for donations later—as those vessels prepared to leave West Coast ports for Japan. A total of 4,724 persons were actually deported or repatriated from WRA camps. Of these, 1,659 were aliens; 1,949 were American citizens, mostly minors accompanying repatriating parents; and 1,116 were adult Nisei.

It was on November 13, 1945, that Collins filed two mass class equity suits (*Abo v. Clark* and *Furuya v. Clark*) and two mass class habeas corpus proceedings (*Abo v. Williams* and *Furuya v. Williams*) in the U.S. District Court of San Francisco.

These cases sought to determine nationality, prevent removal of American citizens to Japan, allow those there to return to the United States, and end the internment of the American Japanese community leaders still held in federal jails without charges. Federal judge Louis E. Goodman, in 1955, found the mass renunciations unconstitutional, stating: "It is shocking to the conscience that an American citizen be confined without authority and while so under duress and restraint for this government to accept from him a surrender of his constitutional heritage. . . . Not even the hysterics and exigencies of war excused the government for the egregious constitutional wrongs it had committed by imprisoning citizens not charged with a crime."

A federal appeals court upheld that decision but ruled that each renunciant's case had to be individually decided. That process took more than twenty years, with Collins, who obviously was something of a fanatic, often living for weeks in his little office to make sure he would not miss calls of desperate American Japanese. The last case he filed was heard and decided in 1968.

Collins also represented most of the more than twenty-three hundred Latin American Japanese, taken by force from their countries by the United States Army and incarcerated in the United States during the war. Most of them, held at Crystal City, Texas, were deported from the United States after the war as "undesirable aliens"—actually charged with entering the United States without proper documents. More than seven hundred were deported to Japan, but again on a case-by-case basis Collins did enable hundreds to remain and make their homes in the United States.

Collins died in 1974. Michi Weglyn's book, *Years of Infamy*, was dedicated to him and so was another, *Beyond Loyalty: The Story of a Kibei* by Minoru Kiyota, a man who saw some of the best and worst of America during and after the war. Kiyota was jailed at Tule Lake and was so angry about it that he, like many others, renounced his American citizenship. He was a bitter man, held until March of 1946 and released to accept a scholarship to the College of the Ozarks in Clarksville, Arkansas. Waiting for a train to go east from Oakland, California, he went into the station's coffee shop, which was filled with American servicemen on their way home from the Pacific.

He started to take a seat and the man behind the counter pointed to a sign: NO JAPS ALLOWED.

He got up to leave but was stopped by a hand on his shoulder. A young marine sergeant was behind him. "Be my guest, please," the marine said, taking Kiyota to a table with four other marines.

"Mister," said the sergeant to the counterman in a hard voice. "Give this man some ham and eggs and a cup of hot coffee and be quick about it!"

The marines asked Kiyota what he was doing. He said he had just been released from a detention camp.

"A what?" one said. "But you're an American citizen, right?"

They talked for a while. Kiyota told his story until it was time for his train. As he thanked the marines and walked out, he noticed one of them stood up and ripped the NO JAPS ALLOWED sign off the wall.

Kiyota went to Arkansas, then returned to Berkeley to earn a degree from the University of California in East Asian Studies. He was drafted and served in army intelligence during the Korean War. But after a year or so, someone in Tokyo discovered his "No-No" record and renunciation application at Tule Lake. His passport was seized; he was essentially a stateless person in a foreign country. Collins, it happened, was arguing before the Ninth Circuit Court in San Francisco that the Renunciation Act

of 1944 was unconstitutional. He won that case in 1955. Kiyota
got his passport back and spent thirty years teaching religious
studies at the University of Wisconsin. "I am," Professor Kiyota
wrote of Collins in 1997, "one of the many beneficiaries of the
man's dedication to the American ideal."

. . .

Few of the officials who had pushed for the incarceration of
American Japanese had their careers harmed by their actions.
General John DeWitt was named commandant of the Army and
Navy Staff College in Washington, D.C. In 1950, Karl Bendetsen
was nominated to be assistant secretary of the army. One of the
witnesses during his confirmation hearings was the former provost of the University of California at Berkeley, Monroe Deutsch.
Said Deutsch: "The appointment of a man whose utterances
reveal him as possessing racialist points of view analogous to
those of Hitler, would be most unfortunate."

Bendetsen was confirmed by the Senate. Telephone records
released by the army in the 1980s revealed that in January of 1943
Karl Bendetsen told another officer: "Maybe our ideas on the Oriental have been all cock-eyed. . . . Maybe he isn't inscrutable."
In later years, he downplayed his role in the Japanese evacuation
but did publicly oppose reparations for the American Japanese
held in the relocation camps.

Earl Warren's rise to the governorship was in large part thanks
to the popularity of the evacuation. He was appointed the four-
teenth chief justice of the United States by President Dwight
Eisenhower in 1953. When he sat down to write his memoirs,
he wrote only one sentence about his actions in the evacuation
of 1942 as attorney general and governor of California: "I have
since deeply regretted the removal order and my own testimony
advocating it, because it was not in keeping with our American
concept of freedom and the rights of citizens."

When Amelia R. Fry interviewed Warren in 1971 as part of an oral history for the Bancroft Library at the University of California, she brought up the subject of his involvement with the Japanese evacuation, and he broke down and burst into tears. The interview was stopped.

Clearly over time Warren had realized his role in the racism and panicked injustice driving the Japanese American incarceration. Some Americans could draw a connection between his remorse over the internment and the most famous and far-reaching decision of the Court during the so-called Warren years, the 1954 unanimous decision on public school integration in the case of *Brown v. Board of Education*; I am one of them. There is no doubt in my mind that Chief Justice Warren's historic action in 1954 was related to Attorney General Warren's disgraceful actions in 1942.

In memoirs, interviews, and oral histories, many of the officials who argued for or debated the American Japanese evacuation were publicly contrite, usually in a sentence or two, about what they did in 1942 and later. Secretary of War Stimson said, "To loyal citizens this forced evacuation was a personal injustice." Milton Eisenhower called it "an inhuman mistake." Justice William O. Douglas, who joined in the majority opinion in the Korematsu case, wrote that his opinion "was ever on my conscience." Tom Clark, the deputy attorney general who was later appointed to the Supreme Court, said, "Looking back on it today, it was, of course, a mistake."

Walter Lippmann was not apologetic. He insisted that his column advocating incarceration of the *Nikkei* was written to help protect them against white vigilante violence. Answering a 1968 letter from Palmer Hoyt, the editor of the *Denver Post*, Lippmann wrote: "I did indeed write the column you speak about and I felt at the time great anguish about doing it. My reason was that in the state of war hysteria after Pearl Harbor, Japanese, who are easily identifiable by mobs, might not be safe. . . . I felt then, and I still do, that the temper of the times made the measure justified."

· · ·

Courts, of course, are driven by the cases that are filed by lawyers and litigants. In 1982, eight years after Wayne Collins's death, a law professor and author, Peter Irons of the University of California at San Diego, was researching a book on the legal histories of Fred Korematsu and other Japanese Americans who challenged the 1942 evacuation orders. Irons discovered evidence that officials at the Justice Department had withheld or destroyed evidence before the Korematsu case reached the Supreme Court. He assembled a team of young Japanese American lawyers, all Sansei, or third generation, and together they prepared petitions that led to the dismissal of Korematsu's conviction forty years before by the Ninth Circuit Court of Appeals. The young lawyers continued their legal crusade and Gordon Hirabayashi's conviction was eventually vacated by the same court. The heart of Irons's team's argument was that the Supreme Court gave "special credence" to the solicitor general's representations and that it was unlikely the high court would have ruled the same way had the solicitor general exhibited "complete candor." The key witness in that case was Edward Ennis, the former assistant attorney general, who testified that the assistant secretary of war, John McCloy, had suppressed evidence in the three Nisei cases of 1942. Minoru Yasui, the third of the three dissenters, died before his case was resolved.

· · ·

On May 20, 2011, the United States Department of Justice, through acting solicitor general Neal Katyal, issued a statement, an extraordinary legal event, according to scholars: "By the time the cases of Gordon Hirabayashi and Fred Korematsu reached the Supreme Court, the Solicitor General [Charles Fahy] had learned of a key intelligence report that undermined the rationale behind the internment. The Ringle Report from the Office of Naval Intelligence found that only a small percentage of Japanese Americans posed a potential security threat, and that the most dangerous were already known or in custody. But the solicitor general did not inform the Court of the report, despite warnings that failing to alert the Court 'might approximate the suppression of evidence.' " Instead, he argued that it was "impossible to segregate loyal Japanese Americans from disloyal ones. Nor did he inform the Court that a key set of allegations used to justify the internment, that Japanese Americans were using radio transmitters to communicate with enemy submarines off the West Coast, had been discredited by the FBI and FCC [Federal Communications Commission]. And to make matters worse, he relied on gross generalizations about Japanese Americans, such as that they were disloyal and motivated by 'racial solidarity.' "

The 2011 statement continued: "The Supreme Court upheld Hirabayashi's and Korematsu's convictions. And it took nearly a half century for lower courts to vacate the decisions that sent the two men to jail."

The Justice Department statement, however, did not in any way negate the Supreme Court decisions of 1944. In fact, only the Court itself has the power to do that. So the 1944 dissent and warning of Justice Robert Jackson is as relevant today as it was then: the decisions amounted, in his words, to "a loaded gun" that the government could pick up at any time to serve real or imagined threats to national security. That is part of the reason that many Americans, I among them, believe or fear that in times of crisis, real or imagined, innocent members of any group could again be imprisoned without charges as a matter of "military necessity." The Japanese American experience clearly answered the question, "Could it happen here?" It did.

The questions now are about how it happened and whether it could happen again.

Not surprisingly, some of the Japanese Americans who spent time behind bars and barbed wire in the 1940s remained active in the civil rights and civil liberties causes and cases of other Americans as time went on. Within two weeks of the September 11, 2001, terrorist attacks on the World Trade Center in New York, hundreds of Japanese Americans in Los Angeles gathered to demonstrate against any mass arrests of American Muslims. Fred Korematsu filed amicus briefs in two Supreme Court cases challenging the detention without charges of Muslims at the American naval base at Guantánamo Bay, Cuba, stating: "Full vindication of the Japanese Americans will arrive only when we learn that, even in times of crisis, we must guard against prejudice and keep our commitment to law and justice."

After too many years, Japanese Americans and others who studied and protested the evacuations of the 1940s became heroes to many Americans who care about civil rights and liberties—and, eventually, to most Japanese Americans and to the many Caucasian civil libertarians who had shunned the few who originally fought or disobeyed the evacuation orders of 1942. One of the great ironies as history was revised was the awarding of the Roger N. Baldwin Medal of Liberty of the American Civil Liberties Union in 2001 to Fred Korematsu—the man Franklin Roosevelt's friend Baldwin had tried to deny ACLU representation. Both Korematsu and Gordon Hirabayashi were awarded the Presidential Medal of Freedom and both have streets named after them in San Jose, California. In addition, Korematsu was the first Asian American whose portrait was displayed in the "Struggle for Justice" section of the National Portrait Gallery in Washington, D.C. There is also a thirty-ton monument to him in the "Champions of Justice" Gallery in Oakland, California, along with Mahatma Gandhi, Nelson Mandela, and Dr. Martin Luther King Jr.

• • •

In March of 2006, in the Hood River Valley of Oregon, the county's history museum, with the approval of county commissioners, opened an exhibit entitled *A Circle of Freedom: Lost and Restored*. Among the exhibits were documents and photographs found in a barn by a World War II veteran named Bud Collins, who had become the historian of American Legion Post 22, the infamous post whose members had blacked out the names of local Japanese Americans serving in the military in Europe and the Pacific.

"I've been saving them for some reason," Collins told Linda Tamura, a local history professor, of the two apple crates of papers. "We all want to, you know, quit hashing it over, do away with it. But you can't turn your back on history. . . . These are the facts. This is history . . . it's too damn late to change it now."

The county administrator David Meriwether agreed. "This is a great nation, and we've done many wonderful things," he said. "This isn't one of them, and we always need to be mindful of how we treat and how we interact with each other." The museum director, Connie Nice, thought so, too, telling the *Hood River News*: "I'm hoping that people will just stop and think: Could we do that again? Are we doing that again, with Latinos or Mexicans or Muslims? . . . I'm not saying this little exhibit will change the world. But I want people to walk away and say, 'Maybe we didn't do that right' and I hope then that they're not going to repeat history."

BIOGRAPHICAL NOTES

Of the 120,313 Japanese, citizens and aliens, incarcerated by the War Relocation Authority, 54,127 returned to the three Pacific Coast states, California, Oregon, and Washington. A total of 52,978 relocated in other parts of the United States and Hawaii. Of the remainder, 4,724 were sent to Japan—most eventually returned to the United States in cases filed by Wayne Collins—and 3,121, including family members, were held in Justice Department internment. A total of 2,355 served in the U.S. military, and 1,322 ended up in state institutions. Over the course of the incarceration, 1,862 evacuees died in the camps.

Below is a short summary of the postwar lives of some of the men and women mentioned in this book.

John Aiso served during the American occupation of Japan after the war. He mustered out as a lieutenant colonel. He later became the first Japanese American judge named to the California Court of Appeals. A street in Los Angeles's Little Tokyo is named in his honor. He was killed there in a street mugging in 1987.

George Akimoto returned to Stockton and became famous as a poster artist for Hollywood films. He died in 2009.

Karl Bendetsen was appointed assistant secretary of the army in 1950 and then undersecretary two years later. He continued to pad and revise his résumé as the years went by, saying that he had also served in Hawaii and the Philippines and delivered secret messages from General Douglas MacArthur in Manila to General George Marshall in Washington. He also said that he was a pilot—stories that even his own family could not document. His son, a navy pilot, said he had never heard that his father was also a pilot. In 1954, Bendetsen retired from government to become chairman and chief executive of Champion International, the global paper company. In later years, he downplayed his role in the Japanese evacuation but did publicly oppose reparations for the American Japanese held in the relocation camps. He died in 1989.

Ernest Besig, the first director of the American Civil Liberties Union office in San Francisco, spent a long life taking on the government, representing Communists and the poet Allen Ginsberg. He died in 1998.

Francis Biddle resigned as attorney general after President Roosevelt's death and was later named by President Truman as the principal American judge at the Nuremberg trials of accused German war criminals. In his autobiography he expressed regret for not having argued more forcefully against the American Japanese evacuation. He died in 1968.

Fletcher Bowron served as mayor of Los Angeles until 1953. After being defeated in a gubernatorial primary, he was elected to the California Superior Court. He died in 1968.

Clara Breed became the city librarian of San Diego, retiring in 1970. The Smithsonian Institution incorporated the "Dear Miss Breed" letters into a lesson plan on the use of letters as primary historical documents. She died in 1994.

Ralph Carr, the governor of Colorado, an anti–New Deal Republican, ran for U.S. senator in November of 1942 and was defeated. Analysts said his stand on the evacuation and relocation was the principal reason for the end of his political career. In 1976, local Japanese Americans raised funds for a Carr statue in Sakura Square in Denver. He died in 1950.

John Franklin Carter wrote thirty books, both nonfiction and fiction. His syndicated column was titled We, the People. . . . He joined the presidential campaign of Harry S. Truman as a speechwriter. He died in 1967.

A. B. Chandler, called "Happy" Chandler, became the commissioner of Major League Baseball in 1945. He resigned in 1951 and died in 1991.

Tom C. Clark, after the war and after service as attorney general, was named an associate justice of the United States Supreme Court, where he served until 1967. He resigned the court in 1967, to avoid a conflict of interest when his son, Ramsey, was appointed attorney general by President Lyndon Johnson. On his retirement Justice Clark said: "I have made a lot of mistakes in my life. . . . One is my part in the evacuation of the Japanese from California in 1942. . . . I don't think that served any purpose at all." He continued, "We picked them up and put them in concentration camps. That's the truth of the matter. And as I look back on it—although at the time I argued the case—I am amazed the Supreme Court ever approved it." He died in 1977.

Ron Dellums, the Oakland boy who tried to stop soldiers from taking away his Japanese friend Rolland later served in Congress for twenty-eight years and was chairman of the Congressional Black Caucus. He was elected mayor of Oakland in 2005.

Lieutenant General John DeWitt was named commandant of the Army and Navy Staff College in Washington, D.C., and was awarded a Distinguished Service Medal by the army for his role in evacuating the American Japanese from the West Coast. He retired from the army in 1947 and was later raised to the rank of a four-star general. He died in 1962.

Milton Eisenhower became president of Kansas State University in mid-1943. In 1950, he was named president of Pennsylvania State University and six years later of Johns Hopkins University. He died in 1985.

Frank Emi, after being released from jail, became a civil servant, working for the post office and for the California Unemployment Division. After his retirement in 1980, he was active in the redress movement and died in 2010.

General Delos Emmons was commander of U.S. troops in Hawaii and successor to General John DeWitt as Fourth Army commander. He commanded army troops in Alaska before retiring. He died in 1965.

Mitsuye Endo, the only woman evacuee whose case reached the U.S. Supreme Court, moved to Chicago to work as a secretary after the Court ruled she had "proven loyalty" because of her work for the state of California. She married and had three children. She died in 2006.

Edward Ennis left the Justice Department after the war and worked for the American Civil Liberties Union for forty years, serving as chairman for most of that time. During his tenure as chairman, the ACLU became the first organization to call for the impeachment of President Richard Nixon in 1973. Ennis died in 1990.

Charles Fahy, the U.S. solicitor general during World War II, became a judge on the United States Court of Appeals. He died in 1978.

Dr. Fred Fujikawa, the Terminal Island physician, was released from the Jerome Relocation Center, where he was one of eight Nisei doctors to work at a tuberculosis sanitarium in Joplin, Missouri. A bill in the state legislature to prevent him from working with white patients was defeated. He died in 1992.

Major General Allen Gullion retired as provost general of the army in April 1944. He died in 1946.

Gordon Hirabayashi earned a PhD from the University of Washington and then taught at the American University in Cairo and the American University in Beirut before becoming chairman of the Sociology Department of the University of Alberta in Edmonton, Canada. There is some irony in that because Canada treated its West Coast Japanese at least as badly as the United States did, not allowing them to return to British Columbia on the Canadian Pacific Coast until 1947. Hirabayashi died in 2012.

Tetsuzo Hirasaki never fulfilled his dreams of college and worked for General Dynamics in Los Angeles. He died in 2006.

Bill Hosokawa, the editor of the Heart Mountain newspaper, was a reporter for the *Des Moines Register*, the editorial page editor of the *Denver Post*, and an author, whose best-known book is titled *Nisei: The Quiet Americans*.

Jeanne Wakatsuki Houston wrote two more books and a television screenplay of *Return to Manzanar* for the NBC network. She and her husband, James Houston, lived in San Jose, California, and raised three children.

Daniel Inouye, as noted, became the first congressman and later senator from the new state of Hawaii. His Distinguished Service Cross was upgraded to a Medal of Honor by President Bill Clinton after a review of records showed that the bravery of Nisei soldiers was routinely downgraded in official army reports. His second wife was Irene Hirano, who is president of the U.S.-Japan Council, a nonprofit group in Washington. He died in 2012, after fifty years in the Senate.

Estelle Ishigo and her husband, Arthur, a broken man who died in 1957, lived in trailer camp poverty for years. In 1972, an exhibit of her camp drawings was mounted by Japanese friends who had lost touch with her. The exhibit and a book of drawings were a success and led old friends from Heart Mountain to find her living alone in a Hollywood basement. She had lost both legs to gangrene. The friends from camp placed her in a nursing home and cared for her until she died in 1990. A film, *Days of Waiting*, on her life and art won the 1991 Academy Award for short documentaries.

Margaret Ishino worked for the Department of Labor in Washington, D.C., after the war and then returned to San Diego.

Harvey Itano, the Berkeley valedictorian sent to Tule Lake, was released to continue his medical studies at Washington University in St. Louis. A professor at the University of California in San Diego, his studies with Dr. Linus Pauling on sickle-cell anemia, a disease plaguing African Americans, marked the first time that a disease had been linked to a specific molecular defect. He later became the first Japanese American elected to the National Academy of Sciences. He died in 2010.

Saburo Kido, the Japanese American Citizens League president who was twice beaten badly in the camps, practiced civil rights law in Los Angeles. He died in 1988.

Charles Kikuchi, the diarist from San Francisco, was a psychiatric social worker for the Veterans Administration for twenty-four years. He died in 1977.

Marion Konishi, the valedictorian of the class of 1944 at the Granada camp, became a restaurateur, opening the first sushi restaurant in Chicago and running it for thirty-four years.

Joseph Kurihara, the embittered World War I veteran and Black Dragon leader, voluntarily accepted deportation to Japan, saying that he would work for democracy in his native land. Ironically, he worked there as an interpreter for U.S. occupation troops. He is considered by some a hero who first proposed redress for evacuees. He died in 1965.

Ben Kuroki, the air force gunner, became something of a celebrity after the war, speaking around the country on racial tolerance. He earned a journalism degree from the University of Nebraska and eventually owned two small newspapers in the state. He retired in 1984 and was awarded a Distinguished Service Medal in 2005 to add to his dozen other combat decorations.

Wilson Makabe, the crippled veteran from Loomis, California, and his family had to sell part of their property to settle a $1,200 tax arrears. The property was then offered back to them for $45,000.

Mike Masaoka became a lobbyist in Washington, advocating for American Japanese interests. He married the sister of Representative Norm Mineta. He died in 1991.

The Matsuda family. Heisuke and Mitsuno became American citizens in 1954. Yoneichi expanded the farm to fifty-eight acres and worked it with his father. He had won a Bronze Star for bravery in the war but never told his family. Mary moved to Seattle to complete her bachelor's degree at the University of Puget Sound, where she met her husband, Charles Gruenewald. They were married in 1951, then moved to Boston while he finished his master's degree in theology. He served as pastor of churches in Washington, Idaho, and Colorado. They had three children. She began to write a memoir at the age of seventy-six and it was published in 2005, on her eightieth birthday.

Robert Matsui served twenty-six years in Congress. He died in 2005 and was succeeded by his wife, Doris, who was elected in 2006.

John McCloy, called by *Harper's* magazine "the most influential private citizen in American history," the most honored of Wall Street lawyers, advised eight presidents from FDR to Ronald Reagan. His positions included high commissioner of the American occupation zones in Germany, chairman of Chase Manhattan National Bank, and chairman of the World Bank. However, in two days of testimony during the hearings of the Commission on Wartime Relocation and Internment of Civilians, he was outraged at a hostile greeting from Japanese Americans in the audience and from some commission members. He should not have been. His biographer Kai Bird wrote in 1992: "More than any other official, McCloy was responsible for the internment of the entire Japanese American community inside barbed wire camps for three years. His arguments had carried the day against the Justice Department's constitutional concerns." In his diary, Secretary of the Interior Harold Ickes wrote of McCloy: "I like McCloy a lot and I have seen him more than any other of the men in the Army but I am told he is more or less inclined to be a Fascist and this would not surprise me. I know of my own knowledge he is strong and capable." McCloy considered the commission's hearings "absolutely outrageous," but he came, convinced he would be seen as a patriot and an American hero. After the first day, he came back with his own lawyers to defend his actions between 1941 and 1945 as undersecretary of war.

Norm Mineta became mayor of San Jose, California, then a United States congressman, and finally served in the cabinets of two presidents, as secretary of commerce and secretary of transportation. A member of a Boy Scout troop, Troop 379 at Heart Mountain, he shared a tent with a local Scout from Troop 250 in Cody named Alan Simpson. Their friendship lasted in Washington, when Simpson was elected to the United States Senate from Wyoming and served eighteen years.

Curtis B. Munson returned to his businesses and investments after the war, traveling with his wife, Edith Cummings, a golfer who was the first woman athlete to appear on the cover of *Time* magazine. She was also the model for Jordan Baker in F. Scott Fitzgerald's *The Great Gatsby*.

Dillon Myer, a favorite of the Japanese American Citizens League and a champion of assimilation, became director of the Bureau of Indian Affairs. He died in 1982.

Isamu Noguchi continued sculpting after the war and also gained recognition designing public gardens, including one at Yale University and another at UNESCO headquarters in Paris. He was awarded the Medal of Freedom in 1987. He died in 1988.

Louise Ogawa returned to San Diego and worked as a clerk in city government. She married another San Diego evacuee, Richard Watanabe.

Paul Ohtaki, the newspaper reporter from Bainbridge Island, served as an army MIS translator in the Pacific Theater.

Governor Culbert Olson, after his defeat by Earl Warren in 1942, practiced law and became president of the United Secularists of America until he died in 1962.

Colonel Charles Pence, commander of the 442nd Regimental Combat Team, served thirty years in the army. After retiring he became a development officer for Augustana College in Moline, Illinois. He died in 2009.

Ezio Pinza rejoined the Metropolitan Opera and then was cast in the hugely popular Broadway musical *South Pacific*. He died in 1957.

Lieutenant Commander Kenneth Ringle commanded the USS *Wasatch*, an amphibious landing command ship in the Pacific during the war. He retired from the navy in 1953 as a rear admiral. In later years, he felt that his intelligence work in California and Hawaii retarded his career, preventing him from becoming an admiral. He died in 1963.

James Rowe served in several federal positions during the Truman presidency, then practiced law in Washington, D.C., after 1952. He died in 1984.

General Joseph Stilwell, a talented strategist who often had trouble getting along with allies, "Vinegar Joe," as he was called, commanded the Sixth Army in China. He lost that command because he made clear that he thought the commander of the America-backed Kuomintang, Chinese Nationalist leader Chiang Kai-shek, was simply a corrupt warlord fighting not the Japanese but his great rival the Communist Mao Tse-tung. In the end, Washington sided with Chiang and Stilwell was recalled. He died in 1946.

Theresa Takayoshi, who was half-Irish and had run an ice-cream parlor in Seattle, moved to Indianapolis from Minidoka with her husband and children after the war, then returned to Seattle twenty-five years later. Her husband worked as an accountant in Indianapolis. "During the years we were in Indiana, we met many, many nice people," she said. "They were all Caucasians and they all accepted us as one of them. And not one of them knew about the evacuation, not one. When I would tell them about it, they were aghast." The government paid the family $100 as redress for losing the ice-cream parlor. She died in 1984.

George Takei, a child at Rohwer, became a successful actor, best known as Lieutenant Sulu in the *Star Trek* television series. He has written and directed plays and has been active in California Democratic politics and Japanese American causes for forty years.

Katherine Tasaki became a librarian in Chula Vista, California. She married another San Diego evacuee, Ben Segawa, who served in the U.S. Air Force during the Korean War.

Fusa Tsumagari worked as a secretary for the publisher McGraw-Hill in Chicago, then married Tom Higashioka, an engineer, and moved to San Mateo, California. Her brother, Yukio, became a doctor and practiced in Wyoming.

Yoshiko Uchida wrote more than a dozen books for children. She told her own story in one of them, *Desert Exile: The Uprooting of a Japanese-American Family*. She died in 1992.

Edison Uno worked for the JACL and other Japanese American organizations and was one of the first activists to argue that Japanese Americans should receive redress or compensation for their lost property and lost earnings. He died in 1975.

Minoru Yasui practiced law in Denver and became the chairman of the city's Human Rights Commission. He died in 1986.

NOTES

ABBREVIATIONS

BOH: Berkeley Oral History

DENSHO: Denshō.org

DOH: Denshō Oral History

HAY: Stanley Kunio Hayami and Joanne Oppenheim, *Stanley Hayami, Nisei Son: His Diary, Letters, & Story from an American Concentration Camp to Battlefield, 1942–1945*

HOS: Bill Hosokawa, *Nisei: The Quiet Americans*

JAH: Brian Niiya, *Japanese American History: An A-to-Z Reference from 1868 to the Present*

PJ: United States, Commission on Wartime Relocation and Internment of Civilians, *Personal Justice Denied: Report of the Commission on Wartime Relocation and Internment of Civilians*

INTRODUCTION

xix **"The House I Live In":** Joanne Oppenheim, *Dear Miss Breed: True Stories of the Japanese American Incarceration During*

World War II and a Librarian Who Made a Difference (New York: Scholastic, Inc., 2006), p. 29. The song itself had an ironic history, a surprising backstory. The records and sheet music stated that it was written by Lewis Allan. But there was no Lewis Allan. The writer was actually Abel Meeropol, a teacher at DeWitt Clinton High School in New York City for twenty-seven years. He was a member of the American Communist Party. He and his wife were the couple who adopted the children of Julius and Ethel Rosenberg after the Rosenbergs were executed as traitors for passing secrets of the atomic bomb to the Soviet Union. Meeropol was known for writing the lyrics of "Strange Fruit," a song about the lynching of black Americans made famous by the singer Billie Holiday. Part of the story of "The House I Live In" was that it lived on as a patriotic anthem, sung by Frank Sinatra at the second inauguration of President Ronald Reagan in 1985 and the rededication of the Statue of Liberty in 1986.

CHAPTER 1

1   **Pearl Harbor:** John Modell, *The Kikuchi Diary: Chronicle from an American Concentration Camp* (Chicago: University of Illinois Press, 1973), p. 42.

1   **"I felt that the world I had known":** *A Time to Fear*, directed by Sue Williams, DVD (PBS, 2004).

1   **Soon after hearing:** Brian Niiya, DENSHO, "Saburo Kido." Web, accessed December 7, 2013, http://encyclopedia.densho.org/Saburo_Kido/.

2   *Rafu Shimpo*: The government forced *Rafu Shimpo* to cease publication on April 4, 1942.

2   **In Nebraska:** Shiho Imai, DENSHO, "Mike Masaoka." Web, accessed December 8, 2013.

3   **Less than twenty-four hours after:** Jay Feldman, *Manufacturing Hysteria: A History of Scapegoating, Surveillance, and Secrecy in Modern America* (New York: Pantheon Books, 2011), p. 164.

3   **A few hours later:** Stephen C. Fox, "General John DeWitt and the Proposed Internment of German and Italian Aliens During World War II," JSTOR.org, June 19, 2011.

5   **There were, however:** Carey McWilliams, *Prejudice: Japanese-Americans, Symbol of Racial Intolerance* (Boston: Little, Brown and Company, 1944), p. 66.

6   **When Yoshiko:** Yoshiko Uchida, *Desert Exile: The Uprooting of a Japanese-American Family* (Seattle: University of Washington Press, 1982), p. 46.

7   **To the north:** Mary Matsuda Gruenewald, *Looking Like the Enemy: My Story of Imprisonment in Japanese-American Internment Camps* (Troutdale, OR: NewSage Press, 2005), p. 23.

7   **In Petaluma, California:** Megan Asaka, *Irene Najima Interview Segment 13*, DOH, August 4, 2008. Web, accessed December 1, 2010.

8   **Another "dangerous" person:** Megan Asaka, DENSHO, *Grace F. Oshita Interview Segment 8*, DOH, June 4, 2008. Web, accessed November 30, 2010.

8   **In Hood River Valley:** Linda Tamura, *Nisei Soldiers Break Their Silence: Coming Home to Hood River* (Seattle: University of Washington Press, 2012), p. 36.

8   **Barry Saiki:** Roger Daniels, Sandra C. Taylor, and Harry H. L. Kitano, *Japanese Americans: From Relocation to Redress* (Salt Lake City: University of Utah Press, 1986), p. 15.

8   **The FBI roundup:** Feldman, *Hysteria*, p. 160.

10 **In Hood River Valley:** Tamura, *Nisei Soldiers Break Their Silence*, p. 28.

10 **The FBI arrest lists:** Brian Niiya, DENSHO, "Kenneth Ringle," March 19, 2013. Web, accessed June 13, 2013, http://encyclopedia.densho.org/Kenneth%20Ringle/.

11 **Another "A" list:** Michael L. Cooper, *Fighting for Honor: Japanese Americans and World War II* (New York: Clarion Books, 2000), p. 1.

12 **Lieutenant Commander Ringle, whose:** Roger Daniels, *Prisoners Without Trial: Japanese Americans in World War II* (New York: Hill and Wang, 1993), p. 23.

13 **"The entire 'Japanese problem' ":** K. D. Ringle, *Ringle Report on Japanese Internment*, Navy Department Library, January 26, 1942. Web, accessed June 13, 2013.

15 **One of FDR's private:** Brian Niiya, DENSHO, "Munson Report," March 19, 2013. Web, accessed June 13, 2013, http://encyclopedia.densho.org/Munson_Report/.

16 **For about two weeks:** Morton Grodzins, *Americans Betrayed: Politics and the Japanese Evacuation* (Chicago: University of Chicago Press, 1949), p. 380.

17 **There were some:** Yoon Pak, " 'Dear Teacher': Letters on the Eve of the Japanese American Imprisonment." NCSS Online Teachers' Library: U.S. History Collection, September 2001. Web, accessed September 2010.

19 **"I was at the bus stop":** Greg Robinson, *By Order of the President: FDR and the Internment of Japanese Americans* (Cambridge, MA: Harvard University Press, 2001), p. 116.

19 **The president of the:** McWilliams, *Prejudice*, p. 160.

20 **The leader of one:** Frank J. Taylor, "The People Nobody Wants," *Saturday Evening Post*, May 9, 1942.

21 **Assistant Attorney General:** Miriam Feingold, *Japanese American Oral History Project*, Calisphere, Berkeley, California, University of California, The Bankcroft Library, September 8, 1975. Web, accessed June 7, 2011.

23 **The second-ranked:** Joseph W. Stilwell, *The Stilwell Papers* (New York: William Sloane Associates, Inc., 1948), pp. 2–11.

26 **The FBI officials:** Tamura, *Nisei Soldiers Break Their Silence*, p. 38.

29 **"There is a monstrous fifth":** Ronald Bishop, *To Protect and Serve: The "Guard Dog" Function of Journalism in Coverage of the Japanese-American Internment* (Columbia, SC: Association for Education in Journalism and Mass Communication, 2000), p. 70.

30 **At the same time, General DeWitt:** Fox, "General John DeWitt."

31 **The confusion and fear:** Oppenheim, *Dear Miss Breed*, p. 22.

CHAPTER 2

33 **Then the governor gave:** Daniels, *Prisoners Without Trial*, p. 42.

34 **The president, in:** Richard Drinnon, *Keeper of Concentration Camps: Dillon S. Myer and American Racism* (Berkeley/Los Angeles: University of California Press, 1987), p. 259 et al.

35 **Stories like that:** Leo Katcher, *Earl Warren: A Political Biography* (New York: McGraw-Hill Book Company, 1967), p. 138.

36 **California's capital:** Wikipedia, "Florin, California," May 1, 2010. Web, accessed June 13, 2010. en.wikipedia.org/wiki/Florin,_ California.

36 **And as early as February:** McWilliams, *Prejudice*, p. 107.

37   **The papers were joined:** Katcher, *Earl Warren*, p. 145.

38   **To the south:** Aljean Harmetz, *Round Up the Usual Suspects: The Making of* Casablanca*: Bogart, Bergman, and World War II* (New York: Hyperion, 1992).

40   **"The necessity for mass":** Katcher, *Earl Warren*, p.147.

40   **General DeWitt:** *PJ*, p. 73.

44   **Despite what he had:** McWilliams, *Prejudice*, p. 116.

50   **Enraged by the:** Franklin D. Roosevelt Presidential Library and Museum, "Document 4: Memorandum to the President from Attorney General Francis Biddle, February 17, 1942."

55   **At the same time:** Katcher, *Earl Warren*, p. 145.

CHAPTER 3

59   **As the islanders were frantically:** John Allen, *Hikoji Takeuchi Interview Segment 5*, DOH, November 7, 2002. Web, accessed April 10, 2011.

61   **In the end, the DiMaggios:** Daniels, *Prisoners Without Trial*, p. 51. Joe DiMaggio enlisted in the army in February of 1943. He was assigned to Special Services and spent most of his time on the mainland and in Hawaii playing baseball for the Seventh Army Air Force team with several Yankee teammates. He returned to the Yankees in September of 1945. His brothers, Vincent and Dominic, both major league players, for the Pittsburgh Pirates and Boston Red Sox, also enlisted.

62   **In Monterey, an Issei:** McWilliams, *Prejudice*, p. 133.

63   **With West Coast:** Robinson, *By Order of the President*, p. 248.

69   **On March 24:** DENSHO, *Civilian Exclusion Order No. 1*, March 25, 1942. Web, accessed April 10, 2011.

70   **"You trying to sell":** Allen, *Hikoji Takeuchi Interview Segment 5*, DOH.

71   **Thirteen of the marchers:** *Bainbridge Island Review*, March 28, 1942, p. 1.

74   **The Matsudas:** Gruenewald, *Looking Like the Enemy*, p. 44.

75   **Frank Emi:** Frank Abe, *Frank Emi Interview Segment 1*, DOH, March 20, 1994. Web, accessed December 22, 2010.

75   **The Najimas of Petaluma:** Megan Asaka, *Irene Najima Interview Segment 13*, DOH, August 4, 2008. Web, accessed June 20, 2011. www.denshovh-nirene-01-segment13.com.

76 **In Sacramento, a state:** Stephen Magagnini, "Japanese Americans Celebrate Hero Who Saved Their Farms," *Sacramento Bee*, February 13, 2010. Web, accessed June 5, 2010.

76 **When the war ended:** "Bob Fletcher Dies at 101; Saved Farms of Interned Japanese Americans," *Los Angeles Times*, June 3, 2013. Web, accessed June 8, 2013.

76 **The same kind of thing:** Robert B. Cozzens, BOH, p. 45.

77 **Another eleven-year-old, Ben Tateishi:** Cooper, *Fighting for Honor*, p. 10.

78 **Yoshimi Matsura was about:** Tom Ikeda, *Yoshimi Matsura Interview Segment 12*, DOH, June 17, 2009. Web, accessed December 3, 2010.

78 **Hideo Hoshide and his girlfriend:** Tom Ikeda, *Hideo Hoshide Interview 1 Segment 36*, DOH, January 26, 2006. Web, accessed December 3, 2010.

82 **One Washington State strawberry:** Deborah Kent, *The Tragic History of the Japanese-American Internment Camps* (Berkeley Heights, NJ: Enslow Publishers, Inc., 2008), p. 47.

94 **Hirabayashi, a senior:** American Friends Service Committee, Gordon Hirabayashi's Statement Against the U.S. Internment of Japanese Americans, January 6, 2012.

CHAPTER 4

98 **The governor of Arizona:** McWilliams, *Prejudice*, p. 67.

101 **In Lone Pine, a:** Jessie A. Garrett and Ronald C. Larsons, *Camp and Community: Manzanar and the Owens Valley* (Fullerton: California State University, Japanese American Oral History Project, 1977).

102 **Estelle Ishigo:** Robinson, *By Order of the President*, p. 258.

106 **After they arrived:** Jeanne Wakatsuki Houston and James D. Houston, *Farewell to Manzanar* (Boston: Houghton Mifflin, 1973).

107 **The end of the trail:** *PJ*, p. 151.

108 **"There is going to be":** Matthew T. Estes and Donald H. Estes, "Hot Enough to Melt Iron: The San Diego Nikkei Experience 1942–1946," *Journal of San Diego History* 42, no. 3 (Summer 1996): 2. Web, accessed June 27, 2013.

113 **The peaceful endurance:** *JAH*, p. 143. See also Delphine Hirasuna, *The Art of Gaman: Arts and Crafts from the Japanese American*

Internment Camps 1942–1946 (Berkeley, CA: Ten Speed Press, 2005).

113 **Jeanne Wakatsuki:** Houston and Houston, *Farewell to Manzanar.*

113 **While the overwhelming:** Ibid.

120 **Returning to the camps:** Estes and Estes, "Hot Enough to Melt Iron."

CHAPTER 5

125 **"Soon barracks only":** Uchida, *Desert Exile*, p. 119.

127 **"I was the first Jap":** Larry Dane Brimner, *Voices from the Camps: Internment of Japanese Americans During World War II* (New York: Franklin Watts, 1994), p. 50.

128 **"The earth around Poston":** Estes and Estes, "Hot Enough to Melt Iron."

128 **Isamu Noguchi arrived:** Masayo Duus, *The Life of Isamu Noguchi: Journey Without Borders* (Princeton, NJ: Princeton University Press, 2004), p. 162.

129 **By mid-summer Isamu:** Ibid., p. 170.

130 **Fathers dug foxholes:** George Hirahara interview.

130 **Charles Hamasaki, who:** Brimner, *Voices from the Camps*, p. 50.

131 **Frank Emi, the:** Frank Abe, *Frank Emi Interview II Segment 5*, DOH, January 30, 1998. Web, accessed December 10, 2010.

131 **At the beginning:** Oppenheim, *Dear Miss Breed*, p. 140.

132 **Ever cheerful, Louise:** Estes and Estes, "Hot Enough to Melt Iron."

133 **On December 8, 1942:** Ralph G. Martin, *Boy from Nebraska: The Story of Ben Kuroki* (New York: Harper & Brothers, 1946), p. 73.

134 **As the first Christmas:** Oppenheim, *Dear Miss Breed*, p. 145.

135 **The Japanese American:** Ibid., p. 146.

136 **"Yesterday night I got":** HAY, p. 30.

139 **"Dec. 25, 1942":** Ibid.

141 **By the end of 1942:** Klancy Clark De Nevers, *The Colonel and the Pacifist: Karl Bendetsen, Perry Saito, and the Incarceration of Japanese Americans During World War II* (Salt Lake City: University of Utah Press, 2004), p. 177.

141 **At the same time, Governor:** Tamura, *Nisei Soldiers Break Their Silence*, p. 44.

CHAPTER 6

143 **At the beginning:** *JAH*, p. 60.

145 **Bill Hosokawa:** HOS, p. 414.

146 **The first instructor:** Joseph D. Harrington, *Yankee Samurai: The Secret Role of Nisei in America's Pacific Victory* (Detroit, MI: Pettigrew Enterprises, 1979), p. 9; James C. McNaughton, *Nisei Linguists: Japanese Americans in the Military Intelligence Service During World War II* (Washington, D.C.: Department of the Army 2006), p. 91.

146 **"No American":** Harrington, *Yankee Samurai*, pp. 9, 15.

146 **The work of:** McNaughton, *Nisei Linguists*, p. 159 et al.

147 **When camp was over:** Harrington, *Yankee Samurai*, p. 184.

147 **The MIS:** Ibid., Kindle location 3993 et al.

149 **Among the most:** Ibid., Kindle location 5712.

149 **One irony:** Ibid., Kindle location 2408.

150 **One of the *Kibei*:** Ibid., p. 159.

150 **Staff Sergeant Roy:** Ibid., p. 252.

150 **On the tiny:** McNaughton, *Nisei Linguists*, Kindle location 5955.

150 **After the war:** Lyn Crost, *Honor by Fire: Japanese Americans at War in Europe and the Pacific* (Novato, CA: Presidio Press, 1994), p. 31.

151 **Ben Kuroki:** Martin, *Boy from Nebraska*, p. 83 et al.

152 **The Americans had:** Ibid., p. 106 et al.

153 **There was:** McNaughton, *Nisei Linguists*, Kindle location 1648.

153 **The Pearl:** *JAH*, p. 224; Michi Nishiura Weglyn, *Years of Infamy: The Untold Story of America's Concentration Camps* (New York: Morrow Quill, 1976), p. 153.

154 **At the same time:** *JAH*, p. 269.

154 **Methodist bishop:** Daniels, Taylor, and Kitano, *Relocation to Redress*, p. 118.

155 **Following President:** Robert Asahina, *Just Americans: How Japanese Americans Won a War at Home and Abroad* (New York: Gotham Books, 2006), p. 51 et al.

155 **"Last Tuesday":** HAY, p. 59.

156 **the young men:** *JAH*, p. 61

158 **At Heart Mountain:** Ibid., p. 66.

159 **Question 28 was worse:** Question 28 asked: "Will you swear unqualified allegiance to the United States of America and faithfully defend the United States from any and all attack by foreign or domestic forces, and forswear any form of allegiance to the Japanese emperor, to any other foreign government power or organization?" The male citizens answered question 28 as follows: 15,011, "yes"; 340, "qualified yes"; 4,414, "no"; 375, "qualified no"; 128 made no reply. In other words, 73.7 percent answered affirmatively; 21.7 percent answered negatively. Of the female citizens, 15,671 answered "yes"; 376, "qualified yes"; 1,919, "no"; 210, "qualified no"; 226, "no reply"—85 percent affirmatively, 10.4 percent negatively. Of the male aliens, 20,197 answered "yes"; 137, "no" (96.4 percent affirmative, 0.7 percent negative). Of the female aliens, 14,712 (96.5 percent) answered "yes"; 263 (1.8 percent), "no." Considering the entire group, citizens and aliens alike, and before any changes were made in the replies given, 65,079 (87.4 percent) answered "yes"; 6,733 (9 percent) answered "no."

159 **James Hatsuki:** Daniels, Taylor, and Kitano, *Relocation to Redress*, p. 7.

160 **Two days later:** Katcher, *Earl Warren*, p. 148.

164 **Easter Sunday of 1943:** Tamura, *Nisei Soldiers Break Their Silence*, p. 104 et al.

165 **Still, no matter:** Everett M. Rogers and Nancy R. Bartlit, *Silent Voices of World War II: When Sons of the Land of Enchantment Met Sons of the Land of the Rising Sun* (Santa Fe, NM: Sunstone Press, 2005). p. 182.

166 **Earl Warren, now:** Katcher, *Earl Warren*, p. 148 et al.; Weglyn, *Years of Infamy*, p. 154.

166 **"There isn't any":** *PJ*, p. 220 et al.

168 **The same day:** Weglyn, *Years of Infamy*, p. 163 et al.

169 **Representative John Costello:** Ibid., p. 151.

169 **The press continued:** De Nevers, *The Colonel and the Pacifist*, p. 223.

169 **"Soft restraint":** "Says Japs Benefit: Representative Asserts Camps Get Scarce Foodstuffs," *New York Times*, January 10, 1943.

170 **One of them, Congressman:** Weglyn, *Years of Infamy*, p. 229.

170 **On December 6:** Robinson, *By Order of the President*, p. 250.

CHAPTER 7

172 **After his Easter:** HAY, p. 72.

172 **That same day:** Ibid.

173 **Senator Chandler:** Drinnon, *Keeper of Concentration Camps*, p. 64; HOS, p. 377.

174 **In a smaller:** HOS, p. 376.

175 **High school graduations:** Calisphere, http://content.cdlib.org /ark:/13030/ft3c6003sr/.

175 **And Stanley:** HAY, p. 89.

175 **On the seventeenth of:** Ibid., p. 86.

176 **In late August:** Ibid., p. 87 et al.

176 **Even Hayami's brother:** Ibid., p. 85.

177 **In September of 1943:** Estes and Estes, "Hot Enough to Melt Iron."

178 **A state assembly:** McWilliams, *Prejudice*, p. 259.

179 **Governor Warren then:** Ibid., p. 263.

179 **Dorothea Lange, already:** Linda Gordon and Gary Y. Okihiro, *Impounded: Dorothea Lange and the Censored Images of Japanese American Internment* (New York: W. W. Norton & Company, 2006), p. 5.

179 **Adams, the visual:** Ansel Adams, *Born Free and Equal: The Story of Loyal Japanese Americans, Manzanar Relocation Center, Inyo County, California* (New York: U.S. Camera Publishing, 1944), p. 13.

181 **During 1943, the:** McWilliams, *Prejudice*, p. 257.

181 **Within days, the WRA:** Robinson, *By Order of the President*, p. 248.

181 **At the beginning:** Weglyn, *Years of Infamy*, p. 156.

181 **WRA director Myer:** *PJ*, p. 208.

183 **At its peak, Tule Lake:** Jim Tanimoto, *A Frightening Incident in Tule Lake*, DOH, December 10, 2009.

183 **The extra contingents:** Weglyn, *Years of Infamy*, p. 161.

185 **Jim Tanimoto, classified as:** Tanimoto, *A Frightening Incident.*

186 **Most nights:** Drinnon, *Keeper of Concentration Camps*, p. 127 et al.

186 **California's former immigration:** Martin, *Boy from Nebraska.*

187 **On January 14:** *Fife* (Washington) *Free Press*, April 8, 2009, p. 1.

188 **At the same time:** Ronald Magden, *Robert Mizukami Interview Segment 12*, DOH, April 11, 2000. Web, accessed December 22, 2010.

189 **The Uchida family:** Uchida, *Desert Exile*, p. 141.

189 **Earlier in 1943:** *Most Honorable Son*, directed by Bill Kubota, DVD (PBS Home Video, 2007).

190 **Kuroki continued on:** Martin, *Boy from Nebraska*, p. 155 et al.; *Most Honorable Son*.

192 **Frank Emi:** Remarks before Association for Asian-American Studies, Washington State University, March 24, 1988.

193 **Then Kuroki:** *Most Honorable Son*.

194 **Two days later:** Martha Ferguson McKeown, "He Was an American at Birth—and in Death," *Portland Oregonian*, May 25, 1946. Ms. McKeown was a teacher in Hood River and Hachiya had been one of her students.

CHAPTER 8

195 **In the first week:** Anne O'Hare McCormick, "The Outlook from a Japanese Relocation Camp," *New York Times*, January 8, 1944.

196 **Secretary of War:** Greg Robinson, *A Tragedy of Democracy: Japanese Confinement in North America* (New York: Columbia University Press, 2009), p. 251; Smith, *Democracy on Trial*, p. 369.

197 **After the meeting:** Smith, *Democracy on Trial*, p. 370.

197 **"The more I think":** Ibid., p. 369.

197 **On May 24, 1944:** Drinnon, *Keeper of Concentration Camps*, pp. 43 et al., 280–81; Weglyn, *Years of Infamy*, p. 312.

201 **A grand jury:** *JAH*, p. 162; Frank Abe, *Frank Emi Interview Segment 20*, DOH, January 30, 1998. Web, accessed December 22, 2010.

202 **After their second:** *JAH*, p. 162; Drinnon, *Keeper of Concentration Camps*, p. 127.

202 **Before the trial:** *Ernest Besig Interview Segment 4*, DENSHO, October 1, 1992; Drinnon, *Keeper of Concentration Camps*, p. 128.

202 **In spite:** Drinnon, *Keeper of Concentration Camps*, p. 127.

202 **Besig, had been trying:** Ibid., p. 128.

204 **Whatever his skills:** John Christgau, "Collins versus the World: The Fight to Restore Citizenship to Japanese-American

Renunciants of World War II," *Pacific Historical Review* 54, no. 1 (February 1985).

204 **Back in Washington:** Smith, *Democracy on Trial*, p. 327.

205 **Though only 117:** Drinnon, *Keeper of Concentration Camps*, p. 126.

208 **George Nakamura:** Smith, *Democracy on Trial*, p. 284.

209 **The breakup:** Gruenewald, *Looking Like the Enemy*, p. 154 et al.

211 **Stanley Hayami:** HAY, p. 105.

211 **Yet, at the same time:** Ibid., pp. 115, 57.

212 **The class of 1944:** Manzanar yearbook, Japanese American National Museum, Los Angeles.

213 **"This will probably":** Oppenheim, *Dear Miss Breed*, p. 217.

216 **The talk:** Ibid., p. 214.

216 **Tom Kawaguchi:** Asahina, *Just Americans*, p. 51.

216 **Stanley Hayami:** HAY, p. 125.

218 **Back "home":** Ibid., p. 137.

218 **"Chicago is":** Oppenheim, *Dear Miss Breed*, p. 225.

219 **"I have heard":** Ibid., p. 234.

CHAPTER 9

220 **On May 28, 1942:** Estes and Estes, "Hot Enough to Melt Iron."

221 **Because of the One Hundredth's:** C. Douglas Sterner, *Go for Broke: The Nisei Warriors of World War II Who Conquered Germany, Japan, and American Bigotry* (Clearfield, UT: American Legacy Historical Press, 2008), p. 17; www.goforbroke.org/history/history _historical_veterans_100th.asp.

222 **One of the men chosen:** Ken Burns and Lynn Novick, *The War*, PBS, September 2007. Web, accessed July 14, 2011.

222 **Not surprisingly:** Calisphere, content.cdlib.org/ark:/13030/ft1h 4n99xm/.

223 **Commanding officers:** Asahina, *Just Americans*, p. 59.

223 **The mainlanders had lighter:** Sterner, *Go for Broke*, p. 20; Asahina, *Just Americans*, p. 60.

224 **At Shelby:** Asahina, *Just Americans*, p. 60.

224 **"Arriving":** Ibid., p. 62 et al.

225 **As the mainland:** Sterner, *Go for Broke*, p. 10.

225 **The 442nd left:** Ibid., p. 37.

225 **On June 6:** *JAH*, p. 277.

226 **"All three companies":** Asahina, *Just Americans*, p. 106.

226 **The 442nd Combat Regiment:** GoForBroke.org. During World War II, an infantry battalion constituted four companies: three rifle companies and a heavy weaponry company. Three battalions constituted a regiment and three regiments constituted a division. The 442nd Regimental Combat Team, meant to be a self-contained fighting force, a segregated one with white officers and Japanese American enlisted men, included the 552nd, 232nd Combat Engineer Company, 206th Army Ground Force Band, Anti-tank Company, Cannon Company, medical detachment, headquarters company, and two infantry battalions, one of them the One Hundredth Battalion.

226 **On July 11:** "George Saito," http://www.youtube.com/watch?=so 8paiTodq8, accessed November 2, 2010.

227 **In September of:** Asahina, *Just Americans*, p. 144.

227 **It was not:** Ibid.

227 **"Banzai!":** *Banzai* means literally "a thousand years of life." In Japan, it was used as a tribute to the emperor. The phrase *Tennuoheiko Banzai*, often used by Imperial Japanese soldiers in the Pacific, can be translated as "Long live the emperor."

227 **Next the Nisei:** Asahina, *Just Americans*, p. 158.

228 **After the Bruyères:** Ibid., p. 161; Sterner, *Go for Broke*, p. 174; Crost, *Honor by Fire*, p. 184.

231 **The article did:** Asahina, *Just Americans*, p. 193. Robert Asahina, in his formidable and impressively researched book *Just Americans: How Japanese Americans Won a War at Home and Abroad*, identified Lieutenant C. O. Barry as actually in the medical attachment of the 141st Regiment of the Thirty-Sixth Division.

231 **After the press:** Asahina, *Just Americans*, p. 189. The debate over whether General John Dahlquist should have bypassed Biffontaine and was using Nisei as "cannon fodder" has continued through the decades. At least one 442nd officer, a lieutenant colonel named Gordon Singles, met Dahlquist years later and refused to shake his hand. There was never any question about Dahlquist's personal courage. He went to the front line, within forty yards of a German machine-gun emplacement, and one of his staff, Lieutenant Welles Lewis, son of the writer Sinclair Lewis, was killed there, his blood splattering Dahlquist. Later in the last year of

the war, Dahlquist was formally and publicly reprimanded by General Eisenhower because he had shaken hands and had lunch with the Nazis' Field Marshal Hermann Goering, who was captured near Munich by his division.

232 **On Monday, December 18:** Peter Irons, *Justice at War: The Story of the Japanese American Internment Cases* (New York: Oxford University Press, 1983), p. 325 et al.

233 **In dissent, Justice:** Fred T. Korematsu Institute for Civil Rights and Education, "Ex Parte Mitsuye Endo," http://korematsuinsti tute.org/institute/aboutfred/internmentcases/ex-parte-mitsuye -endo/.

234 **From Minneapolis:** Oppenheim, *Dear Miss Breed*, p. 235.

235 **On the night:** *JAH*, p. 167; Tamura, *Nisei Soldiers Break Their Silence*, p. 143 et al.

236 **"To those of Hood River":** Tamura, *Nisei Soldiers Break Their Silence*, p. 41.

236 **Hood River County:** Ibid., p. 147 et al.

239 **Anti-Japanese racism:** Ibid., p. 170.

241 **Stanley Hayami's:** HAY, p. 148 et al.

243 **At 5:00 a.m.:** Sterner, *Go for Broke*, p. 110 et al.

243 **Two weeks after:** Ibid., p. 151.

244 **When Private Shiro Kashino:** Vince Matsudaira, *Kash: The Life and Legacy of Shiro Kashino*, KIRO-TV, Seattle, 2012.

244 **One of the survivors:** Solly Ganor, *Light One Candle: A Survivor's Tale from Lithuania to Jerusalem* (New York: Kodansha International, 1995), p. 292 et al.

246 **One of them:** HAY, p. 174 et al.

CHAPTER 10

248 **Sergeant Ben Kuroki:** Martin, *Boy from Nebraska*, p. 188.

249 **The 442nd:** Sterner, *Go for Broke*, p. 144; Crost, *Honor by Fire*, p. 312.

249 **Months earlier, on December 15:** Weglyn, *Years of Infamy*, p. 192.

249 **"There are still 100":** Asahina, *Just Americans*, p. 229.

250 **When Governor Warren:** *PJ*, p. 217.

251 **their resettlement programs:** Arthur A. Hansen, *REgenerations Oral History Project: Rebuilding Japanese-Americans Families, Communities, and Civil Rights in the Resettlement Era—*

Resettlement: A Neglected Link in Japanese America's Narrative Chain, Japanese American National Museum, 1997. Web, accessed February 22, 2012, p. xix.

251 **By the beginning:** Nigel Hamilton, *The Mantle of Command: FDR at War, 1941–1942* (New York: Houghton Mifflin Harcourt, 2014), p. 486; Robinson, p. 261.

252 **More than 2,000:** In 1996, in a class action lawsuit brought by Peruvians, the United States admitted wrongdoing and paid $5,000 to each surviving Latin American detainee.

254 **"I'm not going to worry":** For more information on Alice Nitta, see JapaneseRelocation.org.

254 **Jeanne Wakatsuki, who:** Houston and Houston, *Farewell to Manzanar*, p. 121.

255 **There were also:** Rogers and Bartlit, *Silent Voices of World War II*, p. 139.

256 **At Tule Lake:** Ibid., p. 315.

256 **There were 5,461:** Weglyn, *Years of Infamy*, p. 247.

256 **What happened next:** Ibid.

259 **The Nichiren:** www.archivetoday/SKEob; HOS, p. 436.

260 **One Nisei, John Saito:** *PJ*, p. 241.

260 **Mutsuo Hashiguchi:** James Arimo, *Mitsuko Hashiguchi Interview Segment 62*, DOH, July 28, 1998.

261 **Another Washington resident:** Robinson, *A Tragedy of Democracy*, p. 257.

261 **There were also hundreds:** Asahina, *Just Americans*, p. 230 et al.

261 **In Placer County:** Robinson, *A Tragedy of Democracy*, p. 260.

261 **Walt Hayami:** HAY, p. 180.

261 **Heisuke and Mitsuno:** Gruenewald, *Looking Like the Enemy*, p. 194.

262 **Still, the Matsudas:** Ibid., p. 197.

262 **When Yoneichi:** Ibid., p. 198.

263 **As the American:** Tamura, *Nisei Soldiers Break Their Silence*, p. 172.

263 **There were rumors:** Ibid., p. 165.

263 **Attitudes did change:** Ibid., p. 167.

264 **There were no:** HOS, p. 394.

265 **Kiyoko Nomura:** Michael Patrick Rowan, "All Along the Watchtowers: Photographs of Manzanar at Gunpoint, Framed in Barbed

Wire," research paper for City College of San Francisco Honors Program. Available online at voiceslikeyours.com/pdfs/MRowan_ Watchtowers.pdf.

265 **"I learned that":** Drinnon, *Keeper of Concentration Camps*, p. 128.

266 **In the town of Westminster:** Sterner, *Go for Broke*, p. 101.

267 **The Masuda family:** Crost, *Honor by Fire*, p. 153.

267 **On his way home:** Asahina, *Just Americans*, p. 229.

267 **That story got all:** Robinson, *A Tragedy of Democracy*, p. 276.

268 **"Coming home":** *PJ*, p. 259 et al.

269 **The Najima family:** Megan Asaka, DENSHO, *Irene Najima Interview Segment 13*, DOH, August 4, 2008. Web, accessed December 1, 2010.

269 **Makabe, whose father:** John Tateishi, *And Justice for All: An Oral History of the Japanese American Detention Camps* (New York: Random House, 1984), p. 250 et al.

EPILOGUE

273 **There were, in fact:** Robinson, *A Tragedy of Democracy*, p. 258.

276 **"In sum":** *PJ*, p. 459.

276 **Almost fifty years:** "Understanding the Civil Liberties Act of 1988," Anti-Defamation League, 2013, http://www.adl.org/assets /pdf/education-outreach/Understanding-the-Civil-Liberties-Act -of-1988.pdf.

277 **Wayne Collins, who had represented:** Robinson, *A Tragedy of Democracy*, p. 258.

278 **Collins also represented:** Daniels, Taylor, and Kitano, *Relocation to Redress*, p. 142.

278 **Collins died:** Irons, *Justice at War*, p. 368 et al.

278 **Minoru Kiyota:** Minoru Kiyota, *Beyond Loyalty: The Story of a Kibei* (Honolulu: University of Hawaii Press, 1997), p. 155.

281 **In memoirs, interviews:** *PJ*, p. 18.

282 **In 1982, eight years:** http://korematsuinstitute.org/institute/about fred/.

282 **On May 20, 2011:** The Supreme Court hearing had originally been scheduled for May 1, 1944, but was postponed when the solicitor general, Charles Fahy, said the government needed more

time to prepare its case. Almost exactly sixty-seven years later, on May 20, 2011, Acting Solicitor General Neal Katyal issued a statement titled "Confession of Error: The Solicitor General's Mistakes During the Japanese-American Internment Cases" (http://www.justice.gov/opa/blog/confession-error-solicitor-generals-mistakes-during-japanese-american-internment-cases). The report cited a review of Justice Department documents, indicating that in 1943 and 1944 Solicitor General Charles Fahy failed to tell the Court of relevant reports minimizing the danger posed by Japanese Americans living on the West Coast. His omissions and misstatements came in the cases of *Korematsu v. United States* and *Hirabayashi v. United States*.

BIOGRAPHICAL NOTES

287 **John Aiso:** *JAH*, p. 98.
288 **Francis Biddle:** Ibid., p. 113.
289 **Tom C. Clark:** *PJ*, p. 378.
289 **Lieutenant General John DeWitt:** *JAH*, p. 128.
289 **Milton Eisenhower:** Ibid., p. 130.
290 **Edward Ennis:** Ibid., p. 135.
290 **Dr. Fred Fujikawa:** Tateishi, *And Justice for All*, p. 208.
290 **Major General Allen Gullion:** *JAH*, p. 153.
290 **Gordon Hirabayashi:** Ibid., p. 163.
291 **Daniel Inouye:** Ibid., p. 174.
291 **Estelle Ishigo:** *Days of Waiting*, DVD (San Francisco: Mouchette Films, 1989).
291 **Harvey Itano:** Weglyn, *Years of Infamy*, p. 108.
291 **Saburo Kido:** *JAH*, p. 201.
291 **Joseph Kurihara:** Ibid., p. 212.
292 **Ben Kuroki:** *Most Honorable Son*.
292 **Mike Masaoka:** *JAH*, p. 226.
292 **The Matsuda family:** Gruenewald, *Looking Like the Enemy*, p. 219.
292 **John McCloy:** Kai Bird, *The Chairman: John J. McCloy, the Making of the American Establishment* (New York: Simon & Schuster, 1992), p. 16.
293 **Norm Mineta:** *JAH*, p. 232.

293 **A member of a Boy Scout troop:** Donna Kato, "Plan for Former Intern Camps Divides Wyo. County," Knight-Ridder News Service, February 19, 1992.

293 **Curtis B. Munson:** *JAH*, p. 241.

293 **Dillon Myer:** Drinnon, *Keeper of Concentration Camps*, p. 254.

293 **Louise Ogawa:** Oppenheim, *Dear Miss Breed*, p. 258.

294 **Lieutenant Commander Kenneth Ringle:** Kenneth Ringle Jr. interview.

294 **General Joseph Stilwell:** Stilwell, *The Stilwell Papers*, p. 351.

295 **George Takei:** *JAH*, p. 325.

295 **Fusa Tsumagari:** Oppenheim, *Dear Miss Breed*, p. 236.

295 **Yoshiko Uchida:** Uchida, *Desert Exile*, p. 146 et al.

295 **Minoru Yasui:** *JAH*, p. 360.

BIBLIOGRAPHY

Adams, Ansel. *Born Free and Equal: The Story of Loyal Japanese Americans, Manzanar Relocation Center, Inyo County, California.* New York: U.S. Camera Publishing, 1944.

Asahina, Robert. *Just Americans: How Japanese Americans Won a War at Home and Abroad.* New York: Gotham Books, 2006.

Austin, Allan W. *From Concentration Camp to Campus: Japanese American Students and World War II.* Chicago: University of Illinois Press, 2004.

Bell, Ted. "Interned and Shunned During War." *Sacramento Bee,* May 10, 1992. Web, accessed June 5, 2010.

Beyond Barbed Wire . . . a Part of History America Wants to Forget! Directed by Steve Rosen. DVD. VCI Entertainment, 2001.

Bird, Kai. *The Chairman: John J. McCloy, the Making of the American Establishment.* New York: Simon & Schuster, 1992.

Bishop, Ronald. *To Protect and Serve: The "Guard Dog" Function of Journalism in Coverage of the Japanese-American Internment.* Columbia, SC: Association for Education in Journalism and Mass Communication, 2000.

Brill, Helen Ely. "Oral History Interview #406." Philadelphia, PA: The American Friends Service Committee, August 17, 1991.

Brimner, Larry Dane. *Voices from the Camps: Internment of Japanese Americans During World War II.* New York: Franklin Watts, 1994.

Cooper, Michael L. *Fighting for Honor: Japanese Americans and World War II.* New York: Clarion Books, 2000.

———. *Remembering Manzanar: Life in a Japanese Relocation Camp.* New York: Clarion Books, 2002.

Crost, Lyn. *Honor by Fire: Japanese Americans at War in Europe and the Pacific.* Novato, CA: Presidio Press, 1994.

Daniels, Roger. *Prisoners Without Trial: Japanese Americans in World War II.* New York: Hill and Wang, 1993.

Daniels, Roger, Sandra C. Taylor, and Harry H. L. Kitano. *Japanese Americans: From Relocation to Redress.* Salt Lake City: University of Utah Press, 1986.

Days of Waiting. Directed by Steven Okazaki. DVD. Farallon Films, 1990.

De Nevers, Klancy Clark. *The Colonel and the Pacifist: Karl Bendetsen, Perry Saito, and the Incarceration of Japanese Americans During World War II.* Salt Lake City: University of Utah Press, 2004.

Donlan, Leni. *How Did THIS Happen Here?: Japanese Internment.* Chicago: Raintree, 2008.

Drinnon, Richard. *Keeper of Concentration Camps: Dillon S. Myer and American Racism.* Berkeley/Los Angeles: University of California Press, 1987.

Duus, Masayo. *The Life of Isamu Noguchi: Journey Without Borders.* Princeton, NJ: Princeton University Press, 2004.

Feingold, Miriam. "Tom C. Clark: Civilian Coordinator to the Western Defense Command." Japanese American Oral History Project. Calisphere, University of California. September 8, 1975. Web, accessed 2011.

Feldman, Jay. *Manufacturing Hysteria: A History of Scapegoating, Surveillance, and Secrecy in Modern America.* New York: Pantheon Books, 2011.

Fisher, Anna Reeploeg. *Exile of a Race.* Sidney, BC: Peninsula Printing, 1965.

"Florin, California." Wikipedia, the free encyclopedia. May 1, 2010. Web, accessed June 13, 2010.

Fox, Stephen C. "General John DeWitt and the Proposed Internment of German and Italian Aliens During World War II." JSTOR.org, June 19, 2011.

Franklin D. Roosevelt Presidential Library and Museum, www.fdr library.marist.edu. Web, accessed July 8, 2013.

Garrett, Jessie A., and Ronald C. Larsons. *Camp and Community: Manzanar and the Owens Valley.* Fullerton: California State University, Japanese American Oral History Project, 1977.

Girdner, Audrie, and Anne Loftis. *The Great Betrayal: The Evacuation of the Japanese-Americans During World War II.* London: Macmillan Company, 1969.

Going for Broke: They Believed in America, When America No Longer Believed in Them. Hosted by Senator Daniel K. Inouye. DVD. Questar, Inc., 2005.

Gordon, Linda, and Gary Y. Okihiro. *Impounded: Dorothea Lange and the Censored Images of Japanese American Internment.* New York: W. W. Norton & Company, 2006.

Grodzins, Mortin. *Americans Betrayed: Politics and the Japanese Evacuation.* Chicago: University of Chicago Press, 1949.

Gruenewald, Mary Matsuda. *Looking Like the Enemy: My Story of Imprisonment in Japanese-American Internment Camps.* Troutdale, OR: NewSage Press, 2005.

Handlin, Oscar. *The Uprooted: The Epic Story of the Great Migrations That Made the American People.* Boston: Little, Brown and Company, 1951.

Hansen, Arthur A. *REgenerations Oral History Project: Rebuilding Japanese-Americans Families, Communities, and Civil Rights in the Resettlement Era—Resettlement: A Neglected Link in Japanese America's Narrative Chain.* Japanese American National Museum, 1997. Web, accessed February 22, 2012.

Harmetz, Aljean. *Round Up the Usual Suspects: The Making of Casablanca: Bogart, Bergman, and World War II.* New York: Hyperion, 1992.

Harrington, Joseph D. *Yankee Samurai: The Secret Role of Nisei in America's Pacific Victory.* Detroit, MI: Pettigrew Enterprises,1979.

Harth, Erica. *Last Witnesses: Reflections on the Wartime Internment of Japanese Americans.* New York: Palgrave Macmillan, 2001.

Hayami, Stanley Kunio, and Joanne Oppenheim. *Stanley Hayami, Nisei Son: His Diary, Letters, & Story from an American Concentration Camp to Battlefield, 1942–1945.* New York: Brick Tower Press, 2008.

Hayashi, Brian Masaru. *Democratizing the Enemy: The Japanese American Internment.* Princeton, NJ: Princeton University Press, 2004.

Hebblethwaite, Cordelia. "Pain and Redemption of WWII Interned Japanese-Americans." BBC News Magazine, February 18, 2012. Web, accessed February 18, 2012.

Hess, Jerry N. "Oral History Interview with Tom C. Clark." Harry S. Truman Library and Museum, Washington, D.C., October 17, 1972.

Hirabayashi, Lane Ryo. *Japanese American Resettlement: Through the Lens.* Boulder: University Press of Colorado, 2009.

Hiro: A Story of Japanese Internment. Directed by Keiko Wright. DVD. Hiro Productions, 2011.

Hosokawa, Bill. *Nisei: The Quiet Americans.* New York: William Morrow, 1969.

Houston, Jeanne Wakatsuki, and James D. Houston. *Farewell to Manzanar.* Boston: Houghton Mifflin, 1973.

Howard, John. *Concentration Camp on the Home Front: Japanese Americans in the House of Jim Crow.* Chicago: University of Chicago Press, 2008.

Ichioka, Yugi. *Before Internment: Essays in Prewar Japanese American History.* Stanford, CA: Stanford University Press, 2006.

The Idaho Homefront: Of Camps and Combat. DVD. Boise: Idaho Public Television, 2007.

Inada, Lawson Fusao. *Only What We Could Carry: The Japanese American Internment Experience.* Berkeley, CA: Heyday Books, 2000.

Irons, Peter. *Justice at War: The Story of the Japanese American Internment Cases.* New York: Oxford University Press, 1983.

———. *A People's History of the Supreme Court: The Men and Women Whose Cases and Decisions Have Shaped Our Constitution.* New York: Penguin Books, 1999.

Jacoby, Harold Stanley. *Tule Lake: From Relocation to Segregation.* Grass Valley, CA: Comstock Bonanza Press, 1996.

"Japanese Put Under F.B.I. Inquiry Here: Records Seized Show Donations to Tokyo for Army and Navy." *Los Angeles Times,* November 13, 1941.

Katcher, Leo. *Earl Warren: A Political Biography*. New York: McGraw-Hill Book Company, 1967.

Kato, Donna. "Plan for Former Intern Camp Divides Wyo. County." Knight-Ridder News Service, February 19, 1992.

Kent, Deborah. *The Tragic History of the Japanese-American Internment Camps*. Berkeley Heights, NJ: Enslow Publishers, Inc., 2008.

Kiyota, Minoru. *Beyond Loyalty: The Story of a Kibei*. Honolulu: University of Hawaii Press, 1997.

Leal, Antonio. "Oral History Interview #406." American Friends Service Committee, August 17, 1991.

The Lost Village of Terminal Island. Directed by David Metzler. DVD. Our Stories, 2007.

Lukesh, Jean A. *Lucky Ears: The True Story of Ben Kuroki: World War II Hero*. Grand Island/Palmer, NE: Field Mouse Productions, 2010.

Malkin, Michelle. *In Defense of Internment: The Case for "Racial Profiling" in World War II and the War on Terror*. Washington, D.C.: Regnery Publishing, Inc., 2004.

Manzanar with Huell Howser. Written and produced by Huell Howser. DVD. Huell Howser Productions, 2004.

Martin, Ralph G. *Boy from Nebraska: The Story of Ben Kuroki*. New York: Harper & Brothers, 1946.

Masuda, Minoru. *Letters from the 442nd: The World War II Correspondence of a Japanese American Medic*. Seattle: University of Washington Press, 2008.

McCormick, Anne O'Hare. "The Outlook from a Japanese Relocation Camp." *New York Times*, January 8, 1944.

McNaughton, James C. *Nisei Linguists: Japanese Americans in the Military Intelligence Service During World War II*. Washington, D.C.: Department of the Army, 2006.

McWilliams, Carey. *Prejudice: Japanese-Americans, Symbol of Racial Intolerance*. Boston: Little, Brown and Company, 1944.

Minear, Richard H. *Dr. Seuss Goes to War: The World War II Editorial Cartoons of Theodor Seuss Geisel*. New York: New Press, 1999.

Modell, John. *The Kikuchi Diary: Chronicle from an American Concentration Camp*. Chicago: University of Illinois Press, 1973.

Most Honorable Son. Directed by Bill Kubota. DVD. PBS Home Video, 2007.

Muller, Eric L. *American Inquisition: The Hunt for Japanese American Disloyalty in World War II.* Chapel Hill: University of North Carolina Press, 2007.

———. "Representative King's Investigation and the Ghost of Hearings Past." The Faculty Lounge: Conversations About Law, Culture, and Academia. March 8, 2011. Web, accessed March 10, 2011.

Newton, Jim. *Justice for All: Earl Warren and the Nation He Made.* New York: Riverhead Books, 2006.

Niiya, Brian. *Japanese American History: An A-to-Z Reference from 1868 to the Present.* New York: Facts on File, 1993.

Okubo, Miné. *Citizen 13660.* New York: Columbia University Press, 1946.

Oppenheim, Joanne. *Dear Miss Breed: True Stories of the Japanese American Incarceration During World War II and a Librarian Who Made a Difference.* New York: Scholastic, Inc., 2006.

Pak, Yoon. " 'Dear Teacher': Letters on the Eve of the Japanese American Imprisonment." NCSS Online Teachers' Library: U.S. History Collection, September 2001. Web, accessed May 6, 2012.

Perl, Lila. *Behind Barbed Wire: The Story of Japanese-American Internment During World War II.* Tarrytown, NY: Benchmark Books, 2003.

Rabbit in the Moon: A Documentary/Memoir About the World War II Japanese American Internment Camps. Directed by Emiko Omori. DVD. The Furumoto Foundation, 2004.

Ringle, K. D. *Ringle Report on Japanese Internment.* Navy Department Library, January 26, 1942. Web, accessed June 13, 2013.

Robinson, Greg. *By Order of the President: FDR and the Internment of Japanese Americans.* Cambridge, MA: Harvard University Press, 2001.

———. *A Tragedy of Democracy: Japanese Confinement in North America.* New York: Columbia University Press, 2009.

Rogers, Everett M., and Nancy R. Bartlit. *Silent Voices of World War II: When Sons of the Land of Enchantment Met Sons of the Land of the Rising Sun.* Santa Fe, NM: Sunstone Press, 2005.

Sakurai, Gail. *Japanese American Internment Camps.* New York: Children's Press, 2002.

"Says Japanese Benefit: Representative Asserts Camps Get Scarce Foodstuffs." *New York Times*, January 10, 1943.

Smith, Page. *Democracy on Trial: The Japanese American Evacuation and Relocation in World War II.* New York: Simon & Schuster, 1995.

Starr, Kevin. *Embattled Dreams: California in War and Peace, 1940–1950.* New York: Oxford University Press, 2002.

Sterner, C. Douglas. *Go for Broke: The Nisei Warriors of World War II Who Conquered Germany, Japan, and American Bigotry.* Clearfield, UT: American Legacy Historical Press, 2008.

Stilwell, Joseph W. *The Stilwell Papers.* New York: William Sloane Associates, Inc., 1948.

Tamura, Linda. *Nisei Soldiers Break Their Silence: Coming Home to Hood River.* Seattle: University of Washington Press, 2012.

Tateishi, John. *And Justice for All: An Oral History of the Japanese American Detention Camps.* New York: Random House, 1984.

Taylor, Frank J. "The People Nobody Wants." *Saturday Evening Post,* May 9, 1942.

Time magazine, confidential internal office memorandum from the Los Angeles bureau to the New York bureau, November 15, 1941. Courtesy of John Godfrey Morris, director of photography.

A Time to Fear. Directed by Sue Williams. DVD. PBS, 2004.

"Transcript of Telephone Conversation: Allen W. Gullion and Mark W. Clark." National Archives, Record Group 389, February 4, 1942.

Uchida, Yoshiko. *Desert Exile: The Uprooting of a Japanese-American Family.* Seattle: University of Washington Press, 1982.

———. *Journey to Topaz.* Berkeley, CA: Heyday Books, 1971.

Unfinished Business: The Japanese-American Internment Cases. Directed by Steven Okazaki. DVD. Mouchette Films, 1984.

United States, Commission on Wartime Relocation and Internment of Civilians. *Personal Justice Denied: Report of the Commission on Wartime Relocation and Internment of Civilians.* Washington, D.C.: U.S. Government Printing Office, 1982.

Valor with Honor. DVD. San Jose, CA: Torasan Films, 2008.

The War. PBS. September 2007. Web, accessed July 14, 2011.

Weglyn, Michi Nishiura. *Years of Infamy: The Untold Story of America's Concentration Camps.* New York: Morrow Quill, 1976.

Wehrey, Jane. *Images of America: The Owens Valley.* Charleston, SC: Arcadia Publishing, 2013.

White, G. Edward. *Earl Warren: A Public Life*. New York: Oxford University Press, 1982.

Yamamoto, Eric K., Margaret Chon, Carol L. Izumi, Jerry Kang, and Frank H. Wu. *Race, Rights, and Reparation: Law and the Japanese American Internment*. New York: Aspen Publishers, 2001.

ACKNOWLEDGMENTS

I had wanted to write this book for a long time for the simplest of reasons: to answer the question, "How could this have happened here?" I had wandered the bare ruins of several of the "Relocation Centers" of World War II, hoping I might hear the voices of the Americans there. I couldn't, of course; there was only the howling wind. The winds became words late in the 1960s and 1970s when young Japanese Americans, inspired in part by the black civil rights movement and anti–Vietnam War protest, urged their families to tell their stories. They created Japanese American foundations and museums; writers and researchers collected and saved those words in thousands of interviews and oral histories describing a dark stain on American history. I am in debt to thousands of Americans who became historical archaeologists to dig up a story sure to be lost in the tales of World War II and the American ascendance in the second half of the twentieth century. So I am grateful to the witnesses and scholars of this extraordinary time in American history. I am especially grateful to two of my guides through this world: Lane Ryo Hirabayashi of the University of California, Los Angeles, and Robert Asahina, who pointed me in directions I never would have found on my own.

I am also in debt to two extraordinary young women: my assistant Sue Gifford and Emi Ikkanda, my editor, under John Sterling at Henry Holt and Company. Emi and I may not have always agreed on how to analyze this American history, but this would be less of a book without her passions and insights. Michael Shashoua helped with research in New Mexico. There are a million moving parts in this story and no one could take it on without the smarts of many other people. It was an adventure and I am grateful to so many people from the National Park Service and the Japanese American National Museum in Los Angeles who took this journey with me. They are a national treasure.

On a more personal basis, I am deeply grateful to hundreds friends and members of my family in Los Angeles, New York, Sag Harbor, and Paris. I worked on this book during the most difficult events of my life and could not have seen it through without their love and help. I am leaving out many more names than I am including here, but I must mention my children, Jeffrey, Fiona, and Cynthia Reeves, and Conor O'Neill, Colin O'Neill and his wife Deneen, and Mary Ann and Jack Garvey, Ann Beirne, Mary and Roger Mulvihill, my agent, Amanda Urban, not only for her usual professional excellence but for many other things, and her husband, Ken Auletta, Nancy Candage, Dr. Janet Pregler, Marcia and Paul Herman, Millie Harmon Meyers, Alice Mayhew, Leslie Stahl and Aaron Latham, Kay Eldredge and Jim Salter, Myrna and Paul Davis, Amanda Kyser and Robert Sam Anson, Gail Sheehy and Clay Felker, Bina and Walter Bernard, Ellen Chesler and Matt Mallow, Jean Vallely Graham, Meredith and Tom Brokaw, President Barack

Obama, Cynthia and Steven Brill, Liv Ullman, Susan Alberti, Fran and Roger Diamond, Susan and Alan Friedman, Heidi Shulman and Mickey Kantor, Nancy and Len Jacoby, Roger Gould, Ken Turan and Patty Williams, Ron Rogers and Lisa Specht, Alice and David Clement, Diane Wayne and Ira Reiner, Aileen Adams and Geoff Cowan, Susan and Donald Rice, Nancy and Miles Rubin, Linda Douglass and John Phillips, my colleagues at the Annenberg School of the University of Southern California, most of all Mary Murphy, Nancy and Richard Asthalter, Berna and Lee Huebner, Connie and Dominique Borde, Elizabeth Johnston, Pat Thompson and Jim Bitterman, Pat and Walter Wells, Judith Symonds, Sarah Stackpole and Ward Just, Ina and Robert Caro, Sarah and Mitch Rosenthal, Marlise and Alan Riding, Lynne and Russell Kelley, Pat Hynes, Ralph Schlosstein and Jane Hartley, Deb and Kevin McEneaney, Susan Lacy and Halstead Welles, Kathleen Brown and Van Gordon Sauter, Anne Graves, and, above all, Patricia Rivera.

RICHARD REEVES

INDEX